PASSION PLAY

**A Season
with the Purdue Boilermakers
and Coach Gene Keady**

Mark Montieth

Bonus Books, Inc., Chicago

92   91   90   89   88   5   4   3   2   1

Library of Congress Catalog Card Number: 88-71145

International Standard Book Number: 0-933893-73-6

Bonus Books, Inc.
160 East Illinois Street
Chicago, Illinois 60611

Typography: Point West, Inc.

Printed in the United States of America

Contents

Acknowledgements

This book would not have been possible without the cooperation and help of many people. Authors always say that, of course, but it was literally true in this instance.

Gene Keady didn't hesitate in giving his approval when I first brought up the idea of following his team through the 1987-88 season. From that moment on, he, his assistant coaches, the players and everyone else associated with the team could not have been more friendly or helpful.

I can't think of a better endorsement for a college basketball program in this era of jumbled priorities and twisted values than a head coach's willingness to throw open the doors to his program and allow an outsider to report on what he finds. Not many programs in the country could withstand such scrutiny without fear of probation, or at least embarrassment. Purdue's can, which makes it a winner every season, regardless of its record.

Along with a clear conscious, Keady also exhibited many other unique qualities for a veteran and successful coach: an unspoiled outlook, a genuine concern for his players, and relentless enthusiasm, decency and generosity. He was a pleasure to be around, through good times and tough times.

The assistant coaches, the blue collar guys—Bruce Weber, Kevin Stallings, Dave Wood and Tom Reiter—were equally helpful and generous, and added to the enjoyment of this effort immensely.

Then there's the players. College basketball is, when all the hype and money and fame and pressure are stripped away, a bunch of guys having a good time. Purdue's guys had a lot of fun (at least from December on), probably more than they were even aware of. Someday, five, 10 or 25 years from now, when the university calls them back for a reunion to honor one of the school's all-time great teams, they'll realize better how much fun they had.

And because they had fun, they were fun to be with. Each one of them was generous with his time, often willing to sit and talk when he no doubt had better things to do. Their candor was equally appreciated.

Also, I am indebted to Sports Information Director Jim Vruggink and his staff—assistants Mark Adams, Bob Goldring, Alan Karpick, Jan Winger and Karen Henricks; basketball secretary Lorraine Boland; Athletic Director George King and his staff, particularly Buford Byers, Bob King, Tanya Foster and Fay Flood; team trainers Dale Rudd and Denny Miller; team doctors Steve Badylak and Bill Combs; student managers Ed Howat, Shawn Lyon, Wayne Greene, Gary Harsh, Paul Walker, "Digger" Farwell, Mark Parkinson, Steve Pruzin, Alan Major, Shannen Priser and Gilbert Chew.

I also would like to thank many people at The *Journal-Gazette* in Fort Wayne, including Publisher Richard Inskeep, Editor Craig Klugman, Managing Editor Tim Harmon and Sports Editor Phil Bloom, along with my editor at Bonus Books, Michael Emmerich, for their patience and understanding throughout the project.

So many others deserve mention. I hope I get the chance to thank them in person.

1

Black Monday

Monday, October 19, 1987, dawned grey, dreary and unsettling across the United States. The stock market plunged 508 points, the worst crash since Black Tuesday in 1929, which kicked off the Great Depression. The political news was the same tired litany of discord, something about an Iranian president vowing to retaliate for a United States attack in the Persian Gulf. In the sports world, Billy Martin was hired as manager of the New York Yankees—for the fifth time.

The eerie mood fit snugly into West Lafayette, Indiana, where Purdue University's basketball team was in its first week of preparations for the upcoming season. Student tickets for the season's home games had gone on sale that morning, and a large portion of the 32,000-plus students on campus had gathered to stake their respective claims to the golden moments that seemed destined to await them inside Mackey Arena in the months ahead.

The previous season's team had been one of the best in the school's rich basketball history. It had won 25 of 30 games and mounted a fierce late-season drive that produced eight consecutive victories and a share of the Big Ten championship. But the momentum had coughed, sputtered and wheezed with a 31-point loss to Michigan in the final regular season game when a victory would have brought an outright championship, and then died abruptly with a 19-point loss to Florida in the second round of the NCAA tournament.

But all that seemed like a mere prologue to even better things to come. Four of the five starters, and eight of the top nine scorers, were returning from that team, bringing renewed hope and anticipation with them. And while the season was still a month away, a fever pitch was building. Every supposed basketball authority with a voice and an audience, it seemed, considered the Boilermakers among the nation's best teams. *Street and Smith's*, one of the oldest and most respected preseason college basketball magazines, had rated them number one. The Associated Press, in its poll of media members, had them second. *The Sporting News* picked them third.

Fueled by such visions of glory, a human ribbon nearly 700 yards long, chilled by a steady drizzle that seemed appropriate for the events of the day, snaked out of the entrance to the athletic ticket office. It followed along a looping, maze-like course through the plaza area between the ticket office and Mackey, then escaped into the parking lot via a long narrow tail.

Boredom, damp chill and $32 seemed like a reasonable price to pay for the chance to watch one of the elite teams in college basketball make amends, and, perhaps, history. But if the hardy students inching their way forward outside could have heard the conversation in progress in a basement lounge inside Mackey, they might have scrambled for warmer and drier places.

Purdue's coaching staff, head coach Gene Keady and assistants Bruce Weber, Kevin Stallings, Dave Wood and Tom Reiter, was in the midst of its daily morning meeting. The stated purpose of the gatherings was to plan the day's practice schedule, but it was much more than that. It also was a time to discuss recruiting, evaluate the present players, talk of upcoming opponents and swap stories. Ultimately, it was both a group therapy and a brainstorming session, an opportunity for the coaches to air whatever frustrations or ideas they had at the moment to a sympathetic and understanding audience.

And on this day, there were some heavy burdens to bear. While Wall Street wrung its hands over its sudden and dramatic downturn, Purdue's coaches felt buried in a crash of their own. The frustrations of the previous season, in which two ill-timed losses had stained an entire campaign of grand achievement, still lingered like a bad dream. The self-imposed pressure of the expectations for the upcoming season had already become entrenched. And worst of all, the cloud cover that had passed through six months earlier seemed to be rolling in again.

The bleakness had begun to settle even before classes began. On August 25, Troy Lewis, a 6-4 guard who had been the team's leading scorer the previous two seasons, fractured his right foot during a pickup game at Mackey. Lewis had driven for a layup and landed on the foot of teammate John Brugos, who was sitting on the black padding covering the basket support. A screw was inserted the next day. When practice opened on October 15, he still was hobbling about with the help of a cane, looking like an old man of 21 years.

A few days after Lewis' injury, two more seniors, Jeff Arnold and Dave Stack, went down. Arnold, 6-10 and 240 pounds, had been the team's top reserve the previous season, averaging 4.5 points a game and earning status as a crowd favorite because of his raw enthusiasm. Stack, a 6-7 forward, had played in just 12 games, but was expected to get his first shot at meaningful playing time. But the two had roomed together during the final summer school session and devoted themselves more to the local nightlife scene than to their studies. As a result, both had flunked all three of their courses. They still could practice with the team, but they would not be eligible for games until the start of the second semester in January.

Or, maybe, they would never make it back. Keady had received word that morning that Arnold was missing class again. Keady had laid down the rules when Arnold and Stack first became ineligible: they were not to miss any classes the first semester. One missed class would result in another missed Big Ten game. Two missed classes meant two more missed games. Three missed classes meant expulsion from the team, for good. And now Arnold was skipping class again.

"I'm going to kick him off the team!" Keady blurted out as the coaches gathered for their meeting.

Aside from the playing floor and the locker room, the lounge is the most common meeting ground for the team. It is plush by Mackey's spartan standards, decorated with woven grey carpeting, grey pinstriped wallpaper and color photographs of players from seasons past. The first half of the room, entering from the hallway, contains sofas, chairs and a portable color television set held up near the ceiling in the corner. The other half, divided by a wall and wooden sliding door, includes five round tables with black tops, a large-screen television, and a white message board—for use with a marking pen, not chalk—that runs the length of one side of the room. During the season, the coaches meet in it in the morning, the players watch video in it in the afternoon, and the underclassmen have study table in it at night.

And now it seemed as if Jeff Arnold's fate might be decided in it.

"He's an idiot, right?" Keady said. "He must be using 30 percent of his brain. I'm so pissed off I could cut him right now!"

The assistants, like the players, knew not to take Keady literally at moments like this. He was a coach whose bark was worse than his bite, and was loud enough to prevent him from having to clamp down very often. They had seen him go to bat for too many players over the years, seen him offer too many kids every possible chance to succeed, to believe he would change now. If a player's career did die, it was almost always because he had hung himself.

Arnold's case was a complicated one, full of points and counterpoints. He, like Stack, had been in and out of minor jams throughout the three previous seasons, missing a bus here and some classes there, and had often been on the edge of academic ineligibility. Yet he was an outgoing, free-spirited kid, a prototype California beach bum, who was popular among the team members. He was a projected starter, having worked hard over three injury-riddled seasons to build himself into a valuable contributor. Yet by flunking off the team before a season that held such great promise, and now by skipping class again, he had violated one of Keady's most favored credos: Don't let your teammates down. On the other hand, he was going to more classes than ever before, and he was making passable grades.

To cut him now, as Keady was tempted to do, would strip the team of a valuable player, for practice sessions if nothing else. And there were other factors to consider. It would be a dangerous move to drop a player, particularly an important one, during the fall recruiting period. Politically, it would make more sense to keep him on for the rest of the semester, or at least until the recruiting period ended on Nov. 19, and then let him go. Of course that could be viewed as using a player. But then hadn't Arnold been using the basketball program, to some degree? There was no simple answer.

"We'll give him one more week," Keady said, finally. "We'll make a decision next Monday."

At this infant stage of the season, the coaches would have been grateful if their worries ended with Lewis' foot and Arnold's and Stack's eligibility. These latest developments seemed to form a bridge, connecting the hopeful beginning of this season with the sour ending of the previous one. The team had gone overseas during the summer, playing various club and professional teams in Tahiti, New Zealand and Australia, and won nine of ten games. That had seemed to work as a salve for the wounds opened at the end of the previous season, but now new ones had opened.

On paper, it was virtually the same team that had accomplished so much the season before. Only two players had been subtracted, Doug Lee, a starting forward, and Tim Fisher, a backup guard. Four others, all freshmen, had been added. But somehow the group's chemistry had changed dramatically. What had been an eager, cohesive unit the season before had become one softened by success, haunted by frustration, and divided by ripples of anger and uncertainty.

The mounting off-court problems had eaten away at the team's framework. Lewis, an All-Big Ten guard the previous season and the team's best on-court leader, was sorely missed in practice. His absence in turn seemed to drain the enthusiasm of the other two eligible seniors, returning starters Everette Stephens and Todd Mitchell, which further aggravated the void of leadership. Some of the players, particularly the seniors, were openly bitter toward Arnold and Stack for flunking off the team. For a new season that held so much promise, the practices seemed strangely listless, particularly for a program founded on intensity.

Along with the five seniors, the team included two juniors, Melvin McCants and Kip Jones. McCants, a bulky 6-foot-9 center with a soft shooting touch, had been a starter since his first game as a freshman. Jones, a wiry 6-8 forward, was expected to assume the starting position vacated by Lee.

There were four sophomores: Tony Jones, the team's best athlete, who would be the first guard off the bench, and three frontcourt players, all about 6-9, Steve Scheffler, John Brugos and Ryan Berning, who had played little the previous season.

Two freshmen, both guards, also were on scholarship: Billy Reid, a slender 6-4 shooter who had played for his father in high school, and Dave Barrett, a stocky 6-0 Lafayette native who was pursuing basketball and baseball. Another freshman, Jimmy Oliver, a 6-5 promising athlete who had received one of the two Mr. Basketball awards in

Arkansas as a high school senior, also was on campus, but was academically ineligible and could not play in games or practice with the team.

To help fill the vacancies, Keady had added two freshman walk-ons: Eric Ewer, a 6-6 forward who had played on three consecutive high school state championship teams at Marion High School, and Kory Fernung, a 6-3 guard, who had led the state in scoring at Tri Central, a small, rural high school.

For the freshmen in particular, college basketball was already proving to be a rude awakening. All of them, including the walk-ons, had been big fish in their high school ponds. Now, they were minnows in much rougher waters. Barrett had received the harshest lesson on the first day of official practice. During a fullcourt scrimmage, Stephens swiped the ball from him just after he dribbled past the midcourt line. It had happened with such stunning speed that Barrett had hardly turned around by the time Stephens was dunking the ball at the other end. His new teammates hooted and hollered.

That evening, after dinner, the underclassmen returned to the lounge for study table. It was mandatory for everyone but the seniors and a few underclassmen who excelled in the classroom and was held four nights a week, two hours per night, with an assistant coach on hand to monitor. On this occasion, Lewis, who had stopped by the arena on his way home, couldn't resist taking another swipe at Barrett, this one verbal.

"Hey, guys, we've got to post some bail!" Lewis shouted as he entered the room. "Everette's in jail. The cops came and took him away."

Lewis paused, as heads turned his way.

"For theft!"

Everyone howled, everyone except Barrett, who was sitting at one of the tables with his back to Lewis and his nose in a book. Barrett didn't realize what Lewis was talking about at first. But as the direction of the joke became obvious, the frustration of his difficult first day on the job got the best of him. Tears welled up in his eyes and rolled down his cheeks.

Lewis didn't realize the effect his joke was having until Reid whispered at him. Lewis hadn't meant harm; it was simply the sort of mild hazing seniors typically dish out to the new kids, and he apologized for it later.

But if Barrett thought day one had been painful, he was only getting started. On the second day of practice, he was inadvertently elbowed by McCants in the mouth. He went down as if he had been shot, blood pouring out of his upper lip. He was later helped off the court, spitting blood all over Weber's shirt, and escorted to the team physician, Dr. Steve Badylak. It took six stitches to close the wound. Badylak speculated Barrett would have lost some teeth if he hadn't been wearing the molded rubber mouthpieces that had been issued earlier in the day.

In any case, it had been a difficult beginning for the new kid—and a symbolic one for the entire team. There was great hope. But there were wounds to heal, both physical and emotional. And the season was still a month away.

2

Fits and Starts

For the coaches, the first month after the start of official practice would be, in many ways, the most nerve-wracking portion of the season. Not only was there the business of launching a new team to attend to, they also were locked in battle against one of the most feared opponents of all: high school recruits.

Five years earlier, the National Collegiate Athletic Association had begun allowing high school prospects to sign with the colleges of their choice before the season began to alleviate the pressure from, and for, recruiters. By now, it had become standard procedure for the vast majority of the top-level players to sign in November, so it was vital for colleges to sign the majority of their recruits then. Toward the end of the basketball season, when the signing period resumed, the "flesh market" would resemble an old carcass that had been picked over by buzzards. Some talent still would be available, but not enough to provide sustenance to many of the elite teams.

For Purdue, this recruiting season was particularly crucial. Six scholarships were available, and the coaches thought it was essential to sign at least five players—players who no doubt would provide the foundation for the program's future strength.

Four years earlier, in the 1983-84 season, Keady had directed a patchwork team of lightly-recruited talent that had been picked to finish ninth in the Big Ten to the conference championship. That same year, he and his coaching staff, after being frustrated in previous efforts to sign the top high school players, broke through and landed Lewis, Mitchell and Stephens, all within a few days of each other, during the early signing period. Those three in turn became the nucleus of the team that won the next Big Ten title in '87, with considerable help from Lee and McCants, the other starters, and classmate Arnold, a late bloomer.

The next group of recruits, by sheer number alone, figured to be just as influential. Some of them would have to contribute as freshmen, either off the bench or as starters. By the time they were juniors and seniors, they would provide the program's next foundation, for better or worse.

But the pressure on those players to perform would come later. For now, the pressure was on the coaches to get the players they could win with. And that wasn't always easy at Purdue, where the university's high academic standards and conservative image sometimes clash with the wants and needs of a high school athlete.

Purdue's academic environment is more rigorous than at most public universities. There are no "gimme" majors to offer athletes who are unwilling or unable to handle a normal college curriculum. Unlike some schools, it has no general studies program, the free-form major that grew out of the 1960s in which students choose whatever courses they want to take, with no requirements. Even a physical education major, the traditional jock repository, includes a demanding load of anatomy and science courses. And everyone, regardless of major, has to take three semesters of foreign language, which many schools don't require.

Purdue's academic reputation is based on its engineering, science and agriculture programs. Earl Butz, the former Secretary of Agriculture, is an alumnus. So are moon walkers Neil Armstrong and Eugene Cernan, as well as 14 other astronauts. And so is popcorn magnate Orville Redenbacher.

But the supply of high school All-American basketball players who want to be farmers, engineers or astronauts is limited. And those athletes looking for a more basic major that will keep them eligible with a minimum of effort probably can find the going easier elsewhere.

Furthermore, the university's environment leans more toward substance than style, with a functional, no-frills setting that reflects its engineering roots. Mackey Arena, the 20-year-old home for the basketball team, is typical. Mackey is the Wrigley Field of basketball arenas, providing an intimate, rowdy atmosphere and a clear view for each of the 14,123 fans it holds. It also goes out of its way to avoid any hints of luxury. The fans sit on benches, rather than the cushioned, theater-style seats common in more modern arenas. The locker rooms are small and bare compared to those used by most major college teams. There are four scoreboards at floor level in convenient view for the players, but not an overhanging one. Many of the coaches' offices are cramped and ordinary. In short, the arena has everything it needs, but little more.

The university's bare-bone approach might be appropriate, even commendable, for a college athletic program, but it had proven to be a recruiting obstacle on occasion.

Purdue's recruiting challenge, then, was to find good players willing to give up some style—and perhaps some material goods as well—for the substance of a successful program and a quality education.

The coaches still had plenty of selling points to offer recruits, however. Purdue teams had won or shared more Big Ten championships, 17, going into the season than any other conference school. They had won more Big Ten games in Keady's seven seasons as head coach than any school but Indiana. All but two of the players who had completed their athletic eligibility under Keady had graduated. And only a few had transferred to other school, all in search of more playing time at a lower level. But the fact remained a fancy arena, a beautiful campus and a warm climate often made a bigger impression on high school athletes than tradition, success, academics and stability.

Most of the players who had signed with Purdue had done so for pragmatic reasons, such as distance from home, academic opportunity, and the quality of the basketball program. Lewis, the Indiana state scoring leader, co-Mr. Basketball and a third-team All-American out of Anderson, was probably the most highly-recruited player Keady had landed. He had also visited UCLA, Illinois, Duke and Kansas.

He came very close to signing with Kansas, where he was impressed with the campus, the community and the coach, Larry Brown. He was so won over by Brown's recruiting pitch at a local ice cream parlor, in fact, that he still insists he would have signed on the spot if Brown had pulled out the letter of intent that serves as contract between player and coach. Instead, Lewis flew home, where his parents' desire to have him stay close to them swayed him toward Purdue.

Mitchell had visited UCLA, Pittsburgh and Minnesota. But he didn't like the players he met at Pittsburgh, or the cold weather in Minneapolis. He was impressed with UCLA, but ultimately decided to stay within driving distance from his parents in Toledo.

Stephens, a late bloomer out of high school in Evanston, Illinois, had visited Kentucky, Iowa and Evansville. But he knew Kentucky and Iowa were recruiting other guards they wanted more than him, and Evansville was a smaller school that didn't have a nationally-recognized program.

Purdue got him largely because Weber had caught on to his potential before most other recruiters. Weber had driven to Evanston one fall afternoon to watch Stephens work out with his high school team. He already had been recruiting him, but the improvement he saw in Stephens that day excited him. He called Keady from the gymnasium and asked him to come up the next day to try to close the deal before other schools made the same discovery.

Stephens still laughs at the memory of Keady's unique sales pitch.

"I told him I had narrowed it to Purdue, Evansville, and Kentucky; Iowa was out of the picture because they had signed another guard," he said.

"And he started going off on me. He was driving, and I was in the passenger seat. He was yelling at me, saying stuff like 'Why do you want to go there? You want to go to Purdue. We treat you right. You'll get a good education!'

"He was yelling at me. Coach Weber was like, 'coach, coach, calm down.' But he was like, 'It's a good school, it's in the Big Ten, your parents can come see you!' He was rattling off all this stuff. 'So are you going to come here? We have the papers. You can sign right now.' I was going, 'I'm not sure.' And he's going, 'I don't understand how you can pick those kind of schools. You'll never play there. They recruit All-Americans all the time!'

"Later, I told him I'd let him know in a couple of days, and he let me out of the car. I was walking to my door and I was just so confused, man. I was nervous. All this was going through my mind. I was thinking, 'Gollee, should I go there?' I was just so confused after he got on me. I guess after I got out Coach Weber was saying, 'Coach, I think you might have been too hard.' And he was saying, 'Ah, shit, he can handle it. That's just a little bit of what I'm going to do when he gets here.'

"But I liked him just as he was and the way he presented the university and what to expect. He was real honest."

Stephens called Weber two days later, and, with a trace of fear in his voice, said he would attend Purdue.

But if honesty is the best policy in landing recruits, it isn't always the most successful one. Cheating is rampant, in varying degrees, among schools all over the country. Keady has suspected many times that he lost players because other schools had offered illegal enticements, although that was usually impossible to prove.

Over the years, alumni had approached Keady and offered to pitch in with illegal, but not uncommon, inducements to help attract players, but he had always readily declined. Once, while recruiting Russell Cross out of Chicago, he had come face-to-face with recruiting's dark side. After driving to Chicago one night to see Cross, a man presenting himself as Cross' representative told Keady he needed $30,000, for the supposed purpose of altering Cross' high school transcript to make him academically eligible. Keady said to forget it. As it turned out, Cross' transcript didn't need altering, and Keady got him anyway.

Some of Purdue's players had also had brushes with impropriety.

McCants was sent home from his visit to the University of Hawaii with two cases of pineapples—he gave one to his mother and one to his grandmother—and was promised a gold necklace for his girlfriend if he signed.

Kip Jones had returned from the Dapper Dan All-Star game the summer after his senior year in high school and asked Weber how much he would be getting paid. A player Jones had met at the all-star game who had signed with a Big East school had told Jones he would be making $200 a month. Jones assumed all the major colleges paid the top recruits something.

And Mitchell had been a party to one questionable, and ironic, episode on his visit at Minnesota. Before returning home, he was taken to a sporting goods store owned by the Gophers' coach at the time, Jim Dutcher. There, Mitchell was allowed to buy items at illogically-discounted prices, such as $2 for a sweatshirt and $5 for a new pair of shoes. Mitchell, who wasn't aware if it was legal or not (it only was if the same prices were available to everyone) loaded up. As he and the assistant coaches were carrying his bounty to the car, they saw none other than Indiana Coach Bob Knight across the street buying a newspaper. They quickly threw the goods in the trunk and took off, as if they had just robbed a bank.

"That was the last thing they wanted Coach Knight to see," Mitchell recalled.

Some other schools, while not breaking rules, take a Hollywood approach to the recruiting game. Reid had been particularly dazzled by his visit to Iowa the year before. There, he received an audio tape the team's radio play-by-play announcer had put together of an Iowa game with Reid's name dubbed in as the star player. He was shown the locker room, where a dressing stall had been prepared with his name and picture on it, just like the team members had. That night one of Iowa's players, Jeff Moe, took him to a local bar. They were allowed to cut in line, and Reid was introduced over the loudspeaker as a recruit. Everyone applauded.

"It was real impressive," Reid remembered. "When I came back the following Monday I was thinking I was going to go to Iowa."

Purdue's coaches go in for a more basic pitch. They might leave a fruit basket and a few basketball magazines showing off the Boilermakers' high preseason ranking for the parents in their hotel room at the Memorial Union on campus, but for the most part a recruit's visit is an orientation session. He usually joins the team members for dinner, meets with counselors in his field of academic interest and, if at all possible, watches a practice. If he's the sociable type, a few players take him to a campus party at night. If not, they take him to a movie or have him over to their apartment to watch television.

But regardless of a school's approach—basic or slick, legal or illegal—recruiting is a grueling, year-round war waged in high school gymnasiums and summer camps across the nation.

Purdue's coaches, like those at all Division I programs, attend the 30 or more summer camps and amateur tournaments across the country for a final look at the upcoming high school seniors and a sneak preview of the underclassmen. Keady and the two fulltime assistants, Weber and Stallings, are at one of them virtually every day for the entire month of July.

The struggle then escalates through the mail and over the telephone. Weber's phone bill during peak periods often runs as high as $1500 a month. Mailouts of photocopied newspaper articles about the team are sent to approximately 75 prospects on a year-round basis. And he arranges for letters to be sent, covering a wide range of topics, to interested recruits almost daily as the signing period approaches.

But the top recruits receive mail from dozens of schools at once, so the trick is to be noticed. Weber had recently begun sending the letters in variously styled envelopes, which featured different selling points. The hope was that if a player wasn't going to bother with opening his mail, he at least might notice what was on the envelope. Even the stationery itself was an issue. As a state-funded institution, Purdue has a policy regarding the type of stationery to be used for all university business. Weber had received a waiver and purchased more distinctive paper to impress the recruits.

The climactic recruiting battles are fought in the weeks leading up to the fall signing period, which lasts from the second Wednesday until the third Wednesday of November. In preparation for that, from September 17 through October 5, Purdue's coaches had paid home visits to the 18 players for which they had found mutual interest. On seven of those days they had met with two players, catching one in the afternoon and flying or driving to another city that night to see another. Thirteen of those players had then decided to advance the courtship by paying campus visits in return.

One of them, Keith Stewart, had already made a verbal commitment by the time practice began on the 15th. Stewart, a 6-0 point guard from Milwaukee with excellent quickness and a vertical jump advertised at 44 inches, was a good find. Reiter, a Wisconsin native who had coached high school basketball there, knew Stewart's high school coach. From that connection, the relationship had grown to fruition.

But filling the rest of the class would prove to be more difficult. The victory with Stewart was followed by a numbing loss. Eric Anderson, the most highly-rated of Purdue's recruits, had called a few days before his visit to say he had decided to sign with Indiana. It was a maddening turn of events for Purdue's coaches, who had been led to believe they were number one on Anderson's list. They thought they offered the perfect system, the perfect opportunity for playing time and the perfect location for him. Anderson, who lived near Chicago, said he agreed, but had based his decision on instinct.

A few days after Anderson said no, another top recruit said yes—and then changed his mind. Ron Curry, a 6-7 forward from Bloomington, Illinois who was generally rated among the top 50 high school players in the country, had given a verbal commitment in Keady's office, but later backed out and announced he would sign with Arizona instead, despite his parents' wishes that he sign with Purdue.

Now, on the 26th—the "next Monday" Keady had referred to as a deadline for deciding Arnold's fate—Purdue's coaches were awaiting word from another in-state recruit, Fort Wayne's Craig Riley. Riley, a 6-9 forward, was what college recruits were supposed to be, but often weren't: a student first and athlete second. He ranked first in his high school class, and was a late-blooming prospect who had attracted interest from several major programs. His final choices were Purdue and Kentucky.

But a hitch had developed over the weekend during his campus visit, one that affected both the team and the recruiting. Arnold and Stack had been arrested at a campus party hosted by members of the womens' volleyball team shortly before midnight Friday after a police officer responded to a noise complaint and asked everyone to leave. Arnold had waited for his girlfriend to get her coat, left, then returned after realizing he had forgotten his coat. He was then confronted by the officer, and when Stack joined the "debate" on Arnold's behalf, both were arrested for disorderly conduct.

Keady learned of the incident at 7:30 Saturday morning, and immediately called Weber. "You're not going to believe what happened!" he said. "Where's Riley?" The entire scenario had the makings of a horror story. The potential was there not only to lose two current players, but another one he hoped to get.

Riley, it turned out, had not been at the party. He in fact would spend an enjoyable Saturday evening with some of the team members, including Arnold, and not learn of the incident until later.

Riley and his parents had watched Saturday's practice, but couldn't have been very impressed. Lewis was still on the sidelines, and two other players had joined him: Mitchell, who had undergone arthroscopic surgery the day before for a slight cartilage tear in his

right knee—apparently suffered in an intrasquad scrimmage the previous Saturday—and Reid, who was suffering from tendinitis. Scheffler, although playing, also was hurt, having broken his nose in a
collision with Stephens the previous Tuesday, and was wearing an
awkward, heavy protective mask that limited his peripheral vision.

All of the players, aware of the previous evening's arrest, were
tense. They knew sparks were sure to fly, but didn't know when or
whom they would burn. The result was one of the all-time worst practices Keady could remember having at Purdue. He called it off half an
hour early and sent everyone home.

Monday, therefore, promised to be an eventful day. The charges
against Stack and Arnold had been dropped without pressure from
Purdue's athletic department, but that didn't solve the problem for
Keady. Two of his players, who had already used up their quota of second chances, had gotten in trouble yet again. The story of the arrests
was in the student newspaper, *The Purdue Exponent*, and would hit
the local paper, the *Journal and Courier*, the next day. In the midst of it
all, he was expecting to hear from Riley.

Keady calmly went over the practice schedule with the assistant
coaches that morning, then brought them up to date on Arnold and
Stack. He said he would address the issue at a team meeting that
afternoon before practice, then left for his office upstairs.

Ten seconds later, the phone rang. Weber answered. Keady's secretary, Lorraine Boland, was calling from upstairs, and she had Riley
on the line. It was the moment of truth. Weber rushed out the door to
catch Keady, who was walking up the arena steps to his office. Reiter,
meanwhile, grabbed the phone.

"Craig, this is Coach Reiter," he said. "We just finished our meeting, and we're looking for coach now. Oh, wait, here he is."

Keady took the receiver as the assistants stopped in their tracks.
Weber stood just outside the room, holding the door half open and
poking his head through the opening. He stared intently at the floor.
Something in Riley's voice when he answered the phone had given
him a gut feeling Riley had decided to go to Kentucky.

"Hi, Craig, what's the word?" Keady said.

Riley had a good one: yes.

"All right!" Keady shouted, sending a wave of relief through the
room. "Great!

"You made this coach happy, brother. It's a situation where we're really looking forward to working with you and helping you improve. What are you going to major in, engineering? That'll make your dad happy."

Keady thanked Riley, and hung up. "Whooo!" he shouted as he left the room. "That's two!"

Riley's announcement was a break for Arnold and Stack. If there was such a thing as a good time to get in trouble with Keady, this was it. Riley's announcement had softened the mood a bit, sending a ray of sunlight through the storm clouds that had been brewing overhead.

Keady was calm when he called the team together in the lounge. He began by introducing a new team member, Marvin Rea, a freshman from Gary. Rea had helped lead his high school team to the Final Four of the state tournament the previous season, and had won the Trester Award, a prestigious annual honor recognizing citizenship and academic excellence.

Rea, 5-8 and 135 pounds, hardly looked the part of a college basketball player. But he had impressed Weber and Stallings during an all-campus tryout for walk-ons at 6 a.m. on October 19, thus contributing another unusual element to that day. Although a poor outside shooter, Rea possessed impressive ballhandling and passing skills, and quickness. During a fullcourt one-on-one drill in the tryouts, he had quickly and continuously stripped the ball from his opponent, who eventually ran to the side of the court and threw up. At the very least, Weber figured, Rea could provide defensive pressure on Stephens during practice. As it was, Tony Jones was the only guard quick enough to challenge Stephens, and Jones would be practicing with the first team much of the time himself.

"We're glad to have you with us, Marvin, and we hope it works out for all of us," Keady said.

"Okay, what I wanted to do was bring you in and tell you some things that are going to happen and some things that aren't going to happen and put an end to The Stack and Arnold Show. When you're afraid to read the paper in the morning about your players, it's awfully embarrassing.

"Probably with these two, I've gone further than with any players in my 30 years of coaching, basically because of their families. Right or wrong, I did it. The final analysis will be told next April. The latest development on the disorderly conduct charge was removed. They're going to write letters to the officer, and that thing is ended.

"The problem is, enough's enough. I know some of you were at the party and were smart enough to walk away from it and be cool about it. But some people aren't as smart or tactful, or whatever the case may be, and it didn't work out that way for Dave and Jeff. It was another episode of a second-rate situation. Because I have compassion for my players, I like to give them a second chance. But I've given these guys enough chances for a lifetime."

Keady levied his penalties. They both would miss one more Big Ten game, to go with the three resulting from the academic ineligibility. And they would run stairs after practice, 50 trips to the top of the arena each day, until further notice.

"And if they don't think that's fair, then the door's there and they can get the hell out of here," Keady said. "I was concerned about them, but evidently they're not concerned about us, or they wouldn't have let it happen in the first place. An embarrassment to my players is enough. I know I'm going to be first-class and not embarrass you guys, and I expect the same treatment. Our whole goal this year was for everybody to be working towards a national championship, or at least trying to do well in March, right? Well, with these two it's not that way evidently. So that's the way it's going to be. You tri-captains, if you've got anything you want to say about it, I'd like to hear about it now."

The tri-captains had plenty to say. All three were angered by the incident, believing it should have been the last straw for their two classmates who had been tempting fate for the past three years. Mitchell had even stopped by the coaches' offices that morning to air his opinion.

Lewis, leaning his chair against the wall in the back of the room, went first. Then Stephens. Then Mitchell. Each one talked of the embarrassment he felt over the incident, and said he thought stiff disciplinary measures should be taken. Finally Stephens, buoyed by the growing momentum, spoke up again and sounded the bottom line to what all three were feeling.

"You all might be thinking this is bad, but I'm surprised the coaches didn't do more than that," he said. "Personally, I might have kicked you off the team."

Stallings and Wood spoke up as well, warning the two players against further trouble, then Keady concluded the meeting and sent the team out for practice.

"They'll never make it," Reiter whispered as he headed for the floor.

Obviously, the season wasn't off to the kind of start Keady was looking for. Two seniors, already ineligible, were now in hot water as well. Two other seniors were hobbled by injuries beyond the normal strains and bruises. As if to compound the aches and pains, Keady's wife, Pat, was in the hospital with a recurring kidney infection. And the practices continued to raise more question marks than exclamation points.

"We're not having any fun," Wood said, reflecting on the early practices. "There's no lack of hustle, but there's no enthusiasm, either. Nobody's talking. I told Tom yesterday, 'Something's wrong. I'm worried.' "

"Everybody's preoccupied right now with something," Reiter said.

For the coaches, most of the preoccupation continued to center around recruiting. In the next few days, Bill Robinson, a 6-11 center from Canton, Ohio, who visited the same weekend as Stewart, decided to attend Ohio State. Robinson based his decision on Ohio State's school of veterinary science school, which he explained to Keady in a neatly-written letter.

"Dear Coach Keady," it read. "I would sincerely like to thank you and the Purdue University coaching staff for all of the time and interest you have shown to me over the last year. Out of the three colleges I was choosing from, I liked your basketball program the most. However, I felt that I should go where I'll get the best education and I think Ohio State best fulfills my academic needs.

"Again, I would like to thank you and wish you and the Boilermakers the best of luck during this upcoming basketball season."

It was an unusual gesture from a recruit. And while Keady was sorry to hear of Robinson's decision, he had no complaint with it. Robinson had based his choice on academics, and was staying in his home state—two good reasons. But the refrain was hauntingly familiar.

"I liked your basketball program the most. However. . . "

A week later, another prospect, David Booth, an oustanding shooter from Peoria, Illinois, who was rated among the nation's top 50 high school players, had a Curry-like change of heart. Booth had made a verbal commitment in Keady's office before returning home. But a few hours later, he expressed second thoughts to Stallings on the telephone.

"Is everything all right?" Stallings asked, fully expecting an affirmative response.

"Well. . . ." Booth said.

"What's the problem?" Stallings asked.

"It's my mom," Booth said. "She's concerned about academics. She thinks you guys give grades."

It was the ultimate insult, if that indeed was Mrs. Booth's concern. Purdue had lost plenty of recruits who were scared off by its academic standards over the years. Now it was in danger of losing one because a player's mother thought the standards were too low.

Keady had always taken pride in the emphasis he placed on academics. In the late 1960s, while coaching at Hutchinson (Kansas) Junior College, he had even gone to the extreme of marching over to the dorm rooms of negligent players and literally dragging them out of bed in the morning to get them off to class. Of the 22 players who had completed their eligibility under him at Purdue, 20 had received degrees. James Bullock was playing professional basketball overseas, while Herb Robinson had just earned his badge with the police force in Lafayette, and was continuing to work toward his degree.

For the coaches, the incredible irony of if all was that Mrs. Booth wanted her son to go to DePaul, which had hardly distinguished itself as a bastion of academic/athletic coupling.

"Give grades?!" Keady shouted upon hearing of Booth's recant. "If we gave grades we wouldn't have two guys ineligible right now! That's unbelievable!"

It wasn't all that unusual for a recruit to make a verbal commitment during his campus visit and then back off later. McCants, for one, had committed at every school he visited: Michigan, Notre Dame, DePaul, Hawaii and Purdue. In his case, Purdue won out because it was far enough from his home in Chicago, but yet not too far, and wasn't a Catholic school, like his high school had been.

But for it to happen twice in two weeks *was* unusual. A few days later, with the coaches waiting anxiously next to the telephone in the lounge, Booth announced from Peoria that he would indeed attend DePaul. He later told Stallings he had wanted to attend Purdue, but was doing what would please the most people at home.

Booth's about-face didn't surprise the coaches, who knew the

longer he waited after backing off, the less their chances were of signing him. And it wouldn't be the last disappointment of the recruiting
season. Matt Nover, a 6-8 forward from Chesterton, a small community in northern Indiana, cancelled his recruiting visit after receiving
a last-minute invitation from Bob Knight to take a look at Indiana,
and wound up signing with Indiana. Nover had not been a high priority in Purdue's recruiting scheme, but his decision still rubbed a
sore spot for the coaches. By all logic, they should have had a good
chance to sign Nover. Purdue was only a couple of hours from Chesterton, and Nover's mother had attended Purdue's graduate school.
But over the years, Indiana had seemed able to pluck the vast majority of the in-state high school prospects it wanted, just as it had done
with Anderson. That was gradually changing as Purdue's success
grew, but Nover served up a reminder of the past frustration.

There was no time to pout, however. The recruits were continuing to parade through Mackey like entrants in a beauty contest, two at
a time. Derwin Webb, a 6-5 forward from Indianapolis and Woody
Austin, a 6-0 guard from Richmond, Indiana, visited next.

Webb, a good basketball player but a great athlete, wound up
choosing Louisville. Austin, however, presented a unique set of circumstances. He was an excellent athlete and proven scorer, having
averaged 23 points a game as a junior, but he stood just six feet tall—
two inches less than his listed height. More troubling was the fact he
didn't play point guard, which seemed to be his inevitable position at
any major college, and his ballhandling skills were suspect. And so
were his grades. He was a serious threat not to qualify academically,
which meant he would only be available for three years.

Because of those drawbacks, Purdue was virtually the only major
college program recruiting him. That in itself made the coaches nervous. They also weren't sure how Austin would fit in with their overall recruiting puzzle. They had already signed Stewart, a definite
point guard. And they were confident of signing Loren Clyburn, a 6-4
guard from Detroit, who they thought could play either guard position. Three guards in one class might be too many.

There was another hitch, too. Austin was the subject of various
rumors regarding past personal problems. Keady had received a few
vague, anonymous letters referring to them, but had received no negative reports from Austin's high school coach, George Griffith.

It would turn out that Austin had been in some trouble. He was
caught stealing a few purses from the school gymnasium the summer

after his sophomore year, and arrested for underage drinking in May of his junior year.

But Austin had seemed to put his life in order once he was made to realize the opportunities basketball could bring him. Griffith had tried to get that point across to him, and had also arranged to have Austin sit down with television commentator Billy Packer and former Indiana University guard Steve Alford when they were in Richmond for speaking engagements.

Keady hadn't been told the details of Austin's background, and he wasn't going to turn away a player based on gossip. He had met Austin, and seen nothing in him personally to warrant concern.

He also saw a player worth considering. In his mind, Austin fit the category of "athlete," someone who could succeed because of his raw talent and instinct. Keady also was feeling some pressure from Griffith, who was putting on a hard sell on behalf of his player.

It was ironic. After fighting so many recruiting battles at Purdue, winning some and losing some, Keady was having a player handed to him—but all of a sudden there were question marks attached.

Keady traditionally had avoided "overrecruiting" players at any one position, which allowed the kids he did sign a fair shot at playing time without fear of getting lost in the shuffle. That practice had been one of the major reasons his teams enjoyed such a low rate of transfer.

But such a system depended on the players staying healthy and eligible, something Keady knew all too well didn't always happen. Besides, his previous teams had lacked depth. And this season, with the injuries to Lewis and Mitchell and the ineligibility of Stack and Arnold, seemed proof enough that you can never have enough talent. Perhaps it was time to revise that policy.

The assistant coaches, however, wanted Keady to wait until the spring, to see if Austin would pass his entrance exam and improve his grade point average enough to become eligible. They were reluctant to bring in another player who would have to sit out his first year, particularly one whose size and style of play made him a questionable prospect to begin with.

By the time the team's third and final pre-season intrasquad game arrived, on November 10, the recruiting struggles were reaching their climax. The signing period would begin the next day, and many of the recruits around the country would be announcing their decisions on this night.

Two nationally-recruited center prospects, 7-0 Keith Tower, from Pennsylvania, and 6-11 Dave Siock, from New York, were to make their announcements that night. Both had also visited Purdue, and seemed genuinely interested, particularly Tower. Weber and Stallings had been wooing them, and their mothers, with letters and/or phone calls almost daily.

Tower's mother had unwittingly touched off a miniature crisis with an innocent-sounding comment in an interview with the *Exponent*. "He thinks very highly of them," she said of her son's opinion of Purdue's coaches and players. "He likes the basketball program. He is interested in [studying] communication, and that is the weakest link [for signing with Purdue]."

The quote had appeared near the end of a story on the back page of the paper, but it set off a flurry of phone calls and letters. Weber called the academic adviser for the athletic department, Tanya Foster, as soon as he saw the story upon arriving in his office. Foster had already received several phone calls from other professors and administrators, who were concerned about Tower's impression of the communications department. Statistics of the school's high job placement rate and defenses of its comparative lack of facilities were rushed to Tower to attempt to soothe his concern.

With announcements forthcoming, the shadows of Tower and Siock loomed large over the intrasquad game. It was played at Anderson High School, where Lewis had played.

The schools' gymnasium, known as "The Wigwam" (the school's nickname was the Indians) is one of the most historic high school gyms in the world. It seats nearly 9,000 people, and is sold out for virtually every Anderson game. Tickets are such a hot commodity in town they are often objects of dispute in wills and divorce settlements.

The place is special to the Lewis family, too. Troy's father, Bob, hit the first basket in the first game ever played in it in the early sixties, a hook shot from the baseline. And Troy had set the school's single-game scoring record of 50 points in it.

Lewis, a genuine local celebrity, was honored in a brief ceremony before the game, and briefly took the microphone to thank the fans.

"I have a lot of great memories from this place, and it's nice to be back," he said. "I'll try to put on a little show for you tonight."

But Lewis' foot, while improving, wasn't in show-stopping shape, yet. Besides, the coaches weren't looking for a solo act. He started poorly, missing several shots early in the game, and wound up hitting 10 of 26 field goals on his way to 25 points.

There were some encouraging individual performances, however. Mitchell, playing in his first game since his surgery, had 21 points, and showed no outward effects of the injury. Scheffler, finally shedding his mask, finished with 15 points and 15 rebounds. McCants led all scorers with 31 points.

And Brugos, who had come in for a severe tongue-lashing from Keady in the second scrimmage for delivering what was interpreted as a cheap shot, and following that with a bold display of sarcasm when Keady reprimanded him for it, played inspired and finished with 16 points and seven rebounds—a significant development considering the developments of the past few weeks.

Brugos was the square peg in Keady's round hole of a team. Whereas Keady's success was based on a disciplined, hard-nosed approach by players who could take a verbal licking from the coach and keep on ticking, Brugos was just the opposite. He was a free-spirited, sensitive, only mildly-dedicated athlete who tried the coaches' patience often with his lackluster practice habits.

But he was an intriguing player, in many ways. He had taken an I.Q. test the previous summer, and graded out just short of the genius level. He was carrying a double major in biology and art, and earning nearly an "A" average with minimum effort in the classroom.

But as in the classroom, most of his succcess in basketball was a result of his natural ability. He was nearly 6-10, and blessed with long arms, large, flexible hands and excellent hand-eye coordination. He was one of the team's best outside shooters, a good passer, and a dangerous shot-blocker when he was in the mood, but he didn't seem to be in the mood very often. He had done virtually nothing to stay in shape after the team returned from its overseas trip—his mother dubbed it his "wasted summer"—and reported to preseason conditioning underweight and weaker than he had been as a freshman. Since then, he had been a constant source of frustration for the coaches in practice, showing only fleeting intensity or interest.

This performance, although coming in a scrimmage, offered a ray of hope.

Keady, however, saw many more negatives than positives.

One of them, although not the major one, was Reid, who had scored 25 and 24 points in the first two scrimmages, but hit just three of 13 shots, including one of six three-point attempts.

Reid had been a pleasant surprise to the coaches the first few weeks of practice, but his performance had dropped off considerably in recent workouts. And he was showing every ounce of the frustration he was feeling. Many times, after missing a shot or making an error, he would jump up, stomp both feet on the ground and let out a yell before running back on defense. One day when Steve Reid, who had played at Purdue three years earlier, stopped by to watch his younger brother practice, he and Stallings came up with a nickname for the frazzled freshman: Norman—as in Norman Bates, the lead character in the movie *Psycho*.

But Keady was far more concerned with the overall performance in the scrimmage. Lewis' early crowd-pleasing attempts had gotten the game off to a ragged start, and it didn't improve much from there. The execution was poor, and the foul shooting even worse. The Blacks—Keady's starters and top reserves wear black shirts in practice, and the reserves wear white—had hit just 12 of 24 free throws in the first intrasquad game and returned to hit 11 of 22 this time. Kip Jones, who had hit 49 percent of his free throws as a junior, was still struggling, having hit just five of 22 foul shots in the three scrimmages.

"Some of you have to decide if you're going to play basketball at the Division I level or put on a circus, because that's what we had tonight," Keady told the players afterwards in the locker room. "We're going to practice free throws tomorrow night at the last of practice, and we're going to shoot two each. We're going to shoot 32 free throws, and if we don't hit 80 percent, we're going to practice free throws at 6:30 Thursday morning. That's where you're headed, guys. We're going to filter out the circus people and get some people that understand Division I basketball.

"I don't want to ruin this for Troy, because he's something special to me. But I'm going to tell you, guys, we've got a circus on our hands now."

While Keady talked to the players, Stallings ran to the phone to check on the other circus, recruiting. He had tried to reach Tower and Siock before the game, and again at halftime, but kept getting busy signals. This time, he got through.

Tower was going to Notre Dame. And Siock had chosen Syracuse.

Stallings passed the bad news along to the other assistant coaches, but not to Keady. The team was stopping to eat at a local restaurant on the way home, and would be joined by a few supporters. Stallings figured he should at least let the boss enjoy his dinner first.

Afterwards, as the bus pulled out of the restaurant parking lot and headed for home, he leaned over Keady's seat in the front and told him the bad news. Stallings started to explain the reasons he had been given for the decisions, but Keady cut him off, leaned back in his seat, closed his eyes, and didn't say another word about it the rest of the trip home.

Two more were lost. But there were still two to go. Clyburn and Chuckie White, a 6-6 forward, were coming in that weekend, and had shown a great deal of interest. Clyburn's coach, Perry Watson, rarely allowed his players to sign in the early period because he thought it drained their interest in their final high school season. But he had made an exception for Purdue out of respect for Keady. White, a junior college player from El Camino, California, was being recruited by several western programs, but none with as much recent success as Purdue.

After returning to Mackey, Weber immediately called Watson, just to check in. Oregon, Watson said, was trying to squeeze into the picture, but wasn't a threat.

Weber then called White's mother, who would not be flying out with her son, to explain the details of the scholarship that was being offered and to answer her questions.

Weber also had another major concern. His wife, Megan, was due to deliver their second child any day. Weber had put in a request, only half-jokingly, for her to wait until after recruiting ended to have it.

It was midnight in West Lafayette now, but not too late in California to take a phone call. Weber contemplated calling White's junior college coach, Paul Landreaux, to check in with him as well.

"I hope my wife didn't have the baby today," he said. He then picked up the phone and dialed.

Stallings, meanwhile, was on his way out the door.

"God, I hope this ends sometime!" he shouted.

"You might as well forget about that," Weber said.

The phone at the other end rang, and was answered.

"Hello, Paul? This is Bruce Weber from Purdue. Did I get you up? . . . "

Every year, Keady has his seniors make up a list of 10 team goals for the season. Most of them are to relate to team performance, but he expects others to involve academics and intangibles. This season, Lewis and Mitchell (Stephens missed the meeting) had come up with the most ambitious list yet:

1. Final Four!
2. Win 26 games
3. Win Big Apple NIT and Hurricane Classic
4. Win all home games
5. Win the Big Ten
6. Hold opponents to 65 points a game
7. Team GPA—4.4
8. Give two percent extra effort
9. Be competitive in all situations
10. Lose yourself to the TEAM!

The goals were printed in gold on black poster board, and hung in various places in Mackey. The motto for the year, as determined by Keady, was added at the bottom:

Purpose, Performance and Pride.

Keady has a motto for every season, an indication of his down-home, traditional coaching style. More often than not, it is an alliterative indication of his ideals for the game. In his first season, in the fall of 1980, he went with Defense, Desire, Discipline. Since then, the first letters of the mottos had changed more than the theories behind them:

Confident, Consistent, Congenial.

Attitude, Altitude, Academics.

Intelligence, Integrity, Intensity.

Hustle, Humble, Hungry.

The previous season it had been Improve, Have Fun, Compete.

While more cynical observers might scoff at the idea, the mottos represented Keady's sincere, fundamental and hopeful approach to the game. And it was an approach that usually seemed to rub off on the players, sooner or later. Weber recalled watching in wonderment over the years as some of the same players who had entered the program with a carefree, casual attitude stood up before postgame press conferences and enthusiastically credited Keady's "3 A's" or "3 I's" for the team's victory.

It had taken time for Keady's values to take root, however. His first team at Purdue, which he inherited from Lee Rose, who left after coaching the Boilermakers to the Final Four in 1980, finished 21-11 and placed third in the postseason NIT. His second team finished 18-14 and second in the NIT.

By his third season, players more suited to Keady's style and personality were becoming entrenched in the program. That team finished 21-9 and qualified for the NCAA tournament.

The 1984 season brought a breakthrough, and something of a miracle. Not one member of the team's starting lineup had been recruited by another Big Ten team, or any team of that quality. Ricky Hall was a 6-1 nonshooting defensive specialist whose only other choice was to play in the Mid-American Conference if Purdue had not reluctantly taken him. Steve Reid, Billy's older brother, was a 5-9 shooting guard, at least six inches shorter than most players at his position in the Big Ten. Jim Rowinski had come to Purdue as a 6-4 walk-on, but grown to 6-8 and pumped himself up in the weight room. Greg Eifert's second-best offer was from Dayton. Mark Atkinson had to go to junior college out of high school, and still was lightly recruited when Purdue took him two years later.

But that group finished 22-7 overall, and tied Illinois for the Big Ten championship with a 15-3 record. Rowinski was named the conference's Most Valuable Player, Hall was named its top defensive player, and Keady won conference and national Coach of the Year honors.

The rebuilding 1984–85 team, with a freshman class that included the seniors from this season's team, slipped a bit to 20-9. Subsequent teams improved to 22-10, and then to 25-5 and another conference co-championship in 1986–87.

Continuing the upward mobility would be a tall order this time around. At the end of the previous season, Keady had laid down a bold challenge to his players for the next campaign: reach the NCAA tournament's Final Four. It was one of the few uncharted territories left for his teams, which had produced two Big Ten co-championships and five straight NCAA tournament appearances, but had never moved past the second of the NCAA tournament's six rounds.

But even Keady thought the seniors' goal of winning 26 regular season games was stretching the boundaries of reason. In college basketball, winning 20 games is considered the hallmark of a successful season. Winning 25 elevates a team to an elite category. NBC television commentator Al McGuire, who had chosen Purdue the nation's number one team in the preseason, had seen the goals and considered 25 wins an unreasonable quest for any Big Ten team because of the rugged conference schedule.

Winning the Big Apple NIT, the invitational tournament that would open the regular season, however, was certainly a reasonable objective, as was winning the Hurricane Classic in West Palm Beach, Florida after Christmas.

Winning all the home games would be a first, but only a minor improvement. Purdue had lost just one game at home the previous year, and two the year before that. Winning the Big Ten had been the number one goal the previous season; now it had dropped to number five on the list, almost an afterthought.

Holding opponents to 65 points a game would be extremely difficult given the uptempo offense that had been installed over the summer. A team grade point average of 4.4 amounted to a C+ on Purdue's 6.0 scale, so that was a likelihood. The final three goals—hustle, competitiveness and selflessness—would be a matter of opinion, and vary from game to game.

Far and away, the focus of the season would be on the Final Four, to be played in Kansas City. Keady, as with everything, was blunt about his ambitions, and he didn't go along with the notion that talking about goals would jinx the effort.

He also had made some drastic changes in his game plan to achieve the goals. The late-season losses to Michigan and Florida the previous year, along with requests from Stephens, Lewis and Mitchell, had motivated him to overhaul his more conservative game plan and speed up the attack. With major input from the assistants, he introduced an organized fast break dubbed Early Break—E.B. for short—that was a prelude to the halfcourt offense, as well as a system of color-coded fullcourt presses. "Red" was man-to-man, all-out denial. "Yellow" was a 1-2-1-1 zone. "Gold" was a 2-2-1 zone. "Green" was token man-to-man pressure, intended to slow the opponent's tempo. The basic halfcourt man-to-man defense, "Blue," also had variations within it. Keady hoped the new system would make his team less predictable and more aggressive.

But all the changes and injuries were slowing the players' preseason progress. And on many days the spirit seemed to be lacking as well. Ironically, Arnold and Stack had become two of the most enthusiastic players in practice. Arnold, always one of the more vocal players anyway, had taken charge of the White team, dubbing it "The Misfits," and was playing with reckless abandon. That was a mixed blessing for Keady, who appreciated Arnold's positive response to his setback, but was now even more aggravated by his ineligibility.

The White team was dominating many of the practices. Its players—Arnold, Stack and the reserves— had something to prove. The Blacks, meanwhile, were burdened by the injuries to Lewis and Mitchell, lingering resentment toward Arnold and Stack, and a certain amount of complacency. For the seniors, preseason workouts weren't as exciting the fourth time around.

But with an exhibition game against the Czechoslovakian National team now just two days off, and the season opener, a first-round game in the National Invitation Tournament seven days after that, Keady wasn't comfortable with what he was seeing. The practices had not being going well, and the scrimmages hadn't offered much more hope. With recruiting grinding to a halt, it was time to crack the whip a little harder.

The format of Keady's practice sessions never varies. Each player is expected to be on the floor at least a few minutes before the scheduled start, unless he has a class conflict. The first order of business is to grab two tennis balls out of a box at the end of the floor and jog three laps, squeezing the tennis balls along the way to strengthen the wrists. He then shoots 25 free throws, and reports the results to a student manager so it can be charted. Each player also has an individual "pre-practice" routine to follow, consisting of prescribed drills designed to improve a specific aspect of his game, such as shooting, agility, or ballhandling.

That's followed by two sets of drills led by the coaches lasting about 20 minutes, and then a squad meeting. A chalkboard is set up at the corner of the floor, from where Keady discusses the "Emphasis of the Day." It changes for every practice. Sometimes it is specific, such as "Play good position defense without fouling." Sometimes it is more general, such as "Have an attitude towards improvement." During the season, the meeting might include a general discussion of an upcoming opponent. Keady also gives a brief State of the Union address, discussing the teams strengths or weaknesses of the moment.

The players then stretch for 10 minutes, spreading out on the floor in four rows, divided by class, with one or more of the seniors up front facing the group and calling the commands. It is a time to get loose, both physically and emotionally. Conversation flows freely between players and coaches.

After five minutes of ballhandling drills, and perhaps jumping rope, they get down to serious business. The drills are blocked off into segments ranging from five to 15 minutes, usually, such as 15 minutes of halfcourt five-on-five, 10 minutes of fullcourt press, five minutes of free throws, and 10 minutes of matchup zone.

Many of the drills, even free throws, are competitive, Black shirts against Whites, with the losers lining up at the end of the floor for a sprint—down and back in 10 seconds, 2 1/2 lengths in 30 seconds or a double suicide in 1 minute, 10 seconds. If one person in the group doesn't finish in the prescribed time, everyone runs again. Suicides are a traditional form of basketball conditioning, often known by other names such as Death Valleys, Killers, Baselines, or Gutbusters.

Starting from the end line, the players run to the foul line extended and back, to halfcourt and back, to the other foul line and back and to the opposite end line and back. In a double suicide, they run that course twice, without stopping in between.

Keady's strategy behind punishing the losers with sprints is twofold: It gets the players in shape, and it hones their competitive edge.

It is typical of Keady's open-door policy toward coaching that the practice schedules are a matter of public record. Each day's is typed up and copied and left in a stack at the end or side of the court, for the players to look over beforehand.

The "Emphasis of the Day" for Wednesday's practice reflected Keady's general concerns about the team: "This is a new year. Forget what has happened in the past. Dedicate yourself to a positive new year with open enthusiasm. Remember the three P's and never let your teammates down. We have the opportunity for a lot of fun and great experiences."

The fun would have to wait, however. As he had promised the night before in Anderson, Keady ended practice with a free throw contest. The players lined up along the baseline. Keady called them out to the foul line, one at a time, to shoot two apiece. With Berning sick with the flu, there were 15 players on hand, so they would have to hit 24 of 30 shots to avoid coming back at 6:30 the next morning for another hour of foul shooting.

Arnold, Mitchell and Stephens got them off to a six-for-six start, but it didn't last. Kip Jones missed both his attempts, and they wound up hitting 20 of 30.

"OK, see you at 6:30," Keady said, closing practice.

They returned early the next morning, wearing street clothes, gym shoes and yawns, to shoot some more. Keady tried to make it as enjoyable as possible under the circumstances by having them shoot 100 free throws each, and then holding the same contest run at the end of each shooting practice on the day of road games. The players divide into halves at each end of the floor, and shoot one free throw at a time. When they miss, they sit down on the sideline. The last player left wins, but not without listening to the heckles of his teammates, who shout anything they can think of to distract him. Few things are too personal, or too silly, to escape mention.

Brugos won this time, and everyone left in as good a mood as could be expected at such an early hour. But Keady's worries about his team didn't fade in the days leading up to the game against the Czechs. Although it wouldn't count on his team's won-loss record, Keady hoped the game would provide a barometer for its progress, and perhaps drive home some of the points he had been trying to make in practice.

"Two things need to happen to us," he told the coaches on Friday morning. "We need to keep coaching 'em and working hard, but the Czechs need to kick our ass to wake us up. Then maybe they'll start believing us.

"Todd and Troy are still pissed off about Arnold and Stack. They're not into this season yet. They need to shake it and start a new philosophy toward this year and get with it. And they need to get in shape."

Keady tried once again to snap the players to attention when the team met that afternoon before eating its pre-game meal.

"We're a little bit shook up about this team because we're starting our season sooner than normal," Keady said. "And we're trying to get you ready to play sooner than normal.

"But let me tell you something, guys, that may help you. In all coaching situations, it doesn't matter if it's baseball, basketball, tinker toys or whatever, you've got coaches in one group and you've got players in one group. And you've got a barrier between them. If we're going to Kansas City [for the Final Four], we've got to bridge this gap. It needs to be just a wall. Right now it's an ocean. It's like we're in Texas and you're in Hawaii. We've got to do something about that, guys."

Just the chance to play against another team before the home fans—12,515 showed up for the game, which wasn't part of the season ticket package—was enough to lift everyone's spirits that night. They had been practicing less than a month, a short amount of time to prepare for the first public showing, but it had been a grueling month. They all were anxious to see where they stood as a team.

One of Keady's coaching trademarks is the huddle. The players gather around him, and everyone raises a hand above his head and holds it toward the center of the circle, forming a crooked pyramid. Keady says, "Together!" The players respond, "We attack!" and they break.

Keady began the practice in the 1984 season that brought the Big Ten title, and has continued it ever since. Through the course of its season, the team probably huddles more often than some football teams do. It huddles at the end of virtually every practice, whether it has been good or bad. On the days it lifts weights, it huddles at the end of that, too. On game days, it huddles in the locker room before it takes the floor for pre-game warmups, huddles again before returning to the floor for the final warmup before the opening tipoff, huddles again at halftime and then again after the game, win or lose.

The players also huddle on their own, after they stretch before joining the coaches in the locker room before the game, and again at the edge of the court before taking the floor for pregame and halftime warmups.

This time, before the players took the floor for their final warm up, Stephens said a prayer. Keady often stresses religion as one of the three things his players should put ahead of basketball—the others being their families and studies— but he doesn't talk about it other than that. This team prayer would be the only one of the season.

"Dear Lord," Stephens said, "help us this season as we work to achive our goals. Because if we get to Lawrence, Kansas, it's going to be a lot of fun. Amen."

Stephens' geography was slightly off. He meant to say Kansas City, site of the Final Four, but everyone understood. Stephens explained later he had been thinking of a girl he knew from high school who attended the University of Kansas, which is located in Lawrence.

In case anyone was confused, though, there was another reminder of the team's intended destination above the doorway leading out of the locker room. It was a sign, black with gold lettering that read: "FINAL FOUR!" The players slapped it on their way out to the floor before the game and at halftime. That, too, was a Keady tradition. The season before, they slapped a sign stating "Think positive!" This year, the goal was more specific, and much more elusive.

The game proceeded like a sluggish boxing match, both teams landing some blows but nobody taking command. The Czechs, whose team was made up of older players with considerable international experience, took a 35-33 lead into the final minute of the half, before Purdue exploded with a quick flurry to end the half with a 39-35 lead.

The first half finish had made up for a multitude of sins, most notably continued problems at the foul line, where they had hit just 6 of 13 free throws. McCants had missed all four of his attempts.

But the highlight of the half had been a great effort from Mitchell, who dove head-first from behind a Czech player to knock his dribble loose on a fastbreak. The sound of Mitchell's flesh screeching on the hardwood was music to the ears of the coaches, who had been frustrated by his erratic effort in practice. The fact Mitchell had undergone minor knee surgery three weeks earlier made it all the more impressive.

The coaches always met before joining the players in the locker room at halftime to review the first half, plan strategy for the second half, and, on those occasions when things had not gone well, blow off steam while the players had some time to themselves. On the road, they would gather in any convenient spot, either a room close to the locker room or in a hallway away from fans. At home, they always met in a room across the hall from the locker room, which served as the coaches' locker room during the day and as the site for the press conference after games.

Aside from the free throw percentage, the coaches were reasonably pleased. They decided not to make an issue of the foul shots this time, fearing all the attention that had been devoted to the issue in the past few weeks was making the players uptight.

Keady congratulated the players on their hustle when he joined them in the locker room, then pointed out some flaws in the fullcourt press, which he diagrammed on the chalkboard.

"Hey, Melvin, we had a great trap one time and you were sitting back there picking your nose instead of rotating," he said. "You know which one I mean? You should have had an interception."

Stephens, sitting behind McCants, couldn't resist.

"Did you get that booger out, Mel?" he said quietly, but loud enough to get a laugh from McCants.

The cheerful mood continued into the second half, as Purdue gradually wore the Czechs down on its way to a 100-80 win. Within it, there were several personal triumphs.

The floor-burned Mitchell finished with 21 points and six rebounds in 30 minutes, both game highs. Reid swished his first shot attempt, from just in front of the three-point line on the left baseline. Scheffler, who had scored just 24 points the entire season as a freshman, scored eight in 18 minutes. Lewis moved well on his foot and hit eight of 12 shots on his way to 18 points. Tony Jones, who had struggled with his shooting as a freshman, dropped a three-pointer at the buzzer to put the team into triple figures. And Stephens' mother, Mattie, a vibrant woman from whom Everette had obviously inherited his radiant smile, got up from her front-row seat and danced with The Famous Chicken, the nationally-renowned mascot who had been hired to entertain the fans, during a timeout.

The locker room was jubilant. Exhibition or not, the game had helped erase some doubts.

"Good start, guys!" Keady shouted as the players huddled around him. "We've got a lot of things to do to improve, but we did some things tonight that we've been trying to do in practice, and that's very encouraging.

"Together!"

"We attack!"

A few moments later, Keady walked across the hall to address the media. "Well, if we can play like that in April, we'll be satisfied," he said.

The game also turned out to be an effective recruiting tool. Clyburn and White, who sat behind the team bench, had just seen the glamorous side of college basketball, full of emotion and pageantry. The next afternoon, White made a verbal commitment. Later that evening, Clyburn did, too. They would stand by their word, taking letters of intent home with them to be signed by their mothers, and returning them the next week.

Keady also had decided to go ahead and sign Austin, bringing the number of signees to five. It was a gamble, considering Austin's academic fine line, but he didn't want to risk waiting until spring and losing Austin to another team. With all the problems this preseason had presented, the idea of having an "extra" player at a position, and one who showed potential, was appealing.

As usual, not much of the recruiting season had made sense.

Riley, who had been on campus the night two players were arrested, and then seen a horrible practice the next day, said yes.

Curry and Booth said yes, then said no—one despite his parents' protests, one apparently because of them.

The player the coaches had spent the most time recruiting the past four years, Anderson, didn't even visit.

The two players the coaches had worked hardest to get the past few weeks, Tower and Siock, said no.

Four players the coaches had spent relatively little time recruiting, Stewart, Austin, Clyburn and White, all said yes.

But for Weber, already a grizzled veteran of the recruiting scene at 31 years old, the excitement wasn't quite over.

Weber, who had come to Purdue with Keady in 1980, is a genuine workaholic, the type of person who feels more stress from relaxing than from working. He rarely sleeps more than five hours a night. Along with his coaching and recruiting duties, he is the team's travel secretary, making all the hotel reservations for road trips.

He spends so much time at Mackey that his two-year-old daughter, Hannah, can't imagine him being anywhere else when he isn't at home. Whenever he returns home after a long recruiting trip, even if he has been gone a week or longer, she figures he has been at Mackey the entire time.

Hannah, in fact, played Mackey Arena instead of House. She pretended to be Lorraine, the secretary, and she took calls for Gene and said hello to Todd when he came in. The screened-in porch at her house was the locker room, and the staircase was the bleachers. Some nights, she sat on the stairs/bleachers and made Dad pretend to shoot baskets down below while she cheered him on.

But Hannah was about to get another playmate. After taking White and Clyburn to dinner Saturday night, Weber returned home at 11:30. Megan greeted him with the news she was ready to have the baby. Weber quickly arranged for a babysitter for Hannah, then took his wife to the hospital. She gave birth to a girl, Christine, within an hour.

Weber was up all night at the hospital, then returned home at 6 a.m. to get Hannah, who knew nothing of all that had happened overnight. He dropped her off at the Reiters, then took White to breakfast and to the airport for the flight home to California. He stopped by the hospital to see his wife and new daughter, then picked up Hannah and took her to the park for awhile, and then took her home.

It was about 9 a.m. by then. He pulled into his garage, parked the car, punched the remote control button to close the door—and fell asleep at the wheel.

He was the tired, but proud, father of seven—two girls named Hannah and Christine, and five boys named Stewart, Riley, Austin, Clyburn and White.

3

A Helluva Mess

The first few days of practice after the win over the Czechs were difficult, for the coaches as well as the players. It was as if the recruiting season had leveled them all with one big roundhouse punch.

Keady virtually ran Sunday's practice by himself, while the assistants recuperated. But things quickly heated up as Friday's opener against Arkansas-Little Rock in the NIT first round approached. The encouraging performance against the Czechs had done little to get rid of the signs of lethargy that had marked the earlier practices. The coaches thought the players were griping too much, they thought the eligible seniors weren't showing enough leadership, and they thought too many of the players weren't responding positively to criticism.

That seemed especially true when the criticism came from one of the assistants. Keady always seemed to be able to ignite a spark with a few choice words, but the assistants thought their pleas often fell on deaf ears.

Reiter, a former English major at Wisconsin who was now working on his second graduate degree, and a well-read student of classic literature, put the issue into perspective with an earthy analogy.

"Coach, have you ever had a dog who was always running around pissing and shitting in everyone else's yard?" he asked Keady at the coaches' meeting Tuesday morning. "And when the kids call him or mom calls him, he ignores them, but when dad comes home and yells for him, he comes running? That's the way it is with you. These guys listen to you a lot more than they do us."

Keady, who had lived on a farm in Kansas for part of his childhood, saw it another way.

"I've never seen a herd of cattle that didn't have at least one cow in it that goes off running through the fences and never stays with the rest of the herd," he said. "That's just the animal nature."

Keady's challenge, then, would be to corral his talent and get everyone headed in the same direction. It was one of the things he did best as a coach, even if it did put a massive strain on his vocal chords.

The practices on Monday, Tuesday and Wednesday were long, about three hours each, and intense. Thursday's was easier, in preparation for the game. They were taking their number two national ranking and testing it against Little Rock, a quick, athletic team that didn't have the look of a pushover.

"We've set some big goals this year," Keady said as the team huddled before the game. "And unless you get this one, those babies will be very difficult to get. So let's dominate the first five minutes and go from there.

"Together!"

"We attack!"

They didn't dominate the first five minutes, falling behind 10-5, but they did go on from there. A nine-point run broke them free from a tie at 25 midway through the half. The lead was 11 at halftime, quickly grew to 15 within the first three minutes of the second half, and was never in danger after that. The final score was 102-88. It hadn't been easy, but they all had seen much worse.

The victory moved them to the second round of the NIT. One more win, against Iowa State the following Tuesday, and they would be playing in Madison Square Garden in New York City—with a possible chance for a rematch against Florida, the source of so much anguish at the end of the previous season.

Mitchell scored 22 points in 31 minutes. Lewis finished with 18 points, a career-high 11 rebounds and eight assists. Perhaps best of all, the bench play that had been such a question mark the previous year was excellent. Berning, showing none of the nervousness that had plagued him the year before, hit all four of his field goal attempts, including a three-pointer, for nine points in 15 minutes. Scheffler had eight points and six rebounds in 14 minutes. Tony Jones had six points in 21 minutes.

But while Keady was generally pleased with the victory, he saw further signs of the same problems that had been creeping up in practice. The plague of missed free throws had continued, as they hit just 16 of 32. The defense had not been particularly stouthearted, either, and there was too much whining about referees' calls and being pulled from the game.

The team's improved bench play had inspired Keady to shift to a pattern of rotating subs for this season. Players would be pulled at certain intervals, beginning five minutes after the start of the game, almost regardless of how they were playing. The idea was to keep fresh bodies on the court and give the reserves more experience—all in a consistent and predictable manner.

In the interest of motivating his players to give 100 percent, Keady also has a longstanding policy that allows them to take themselves out of a game by tugging on their jersey. The deal is they can then put themselves back in when they're ready. Mitchell, however, had found a way to beat the system against Little Rock. When he saw Berning getting up off the bench to come in for him, he quickly tugged on his jersey so that he could retain the right of re-entry.

He got away with it at the time, but Keady, tipped off by the assistants later, called Mitchell's bluff in a meeting before the next day's practice. The players howled in delight over the red-handed catch.

The coaches, however, were growing frustrated with Mitchell. He wasn't lazy. In fact, he had probably worked the hardest of all the team members after the overseas trip the previous summer. He stayed on campus and devoted himself to weightlifting, increasing his bench press by 40 pounds, and worked on his ballhandling and shooting skills as well.

But he seemed to pick and choose his spots in practice, working hard in some drills and relaxing in others. That inconsistency was amplified by his mannerisms and appearance. He went about his work stoically, saying little and showing little emotion. Even during a routine activity such as stretching, he often seemed blasé. He wore his socks low, so that the only thing sticking up out of his hightop shoes was the tape used to wrap his ankles; it gave him a beach bum look that didn't fit in with Keady's hell-or-highwater approach.

Brugos viewed the three eligible seniors as fitting into distinct categories: Lewis was the leader, who took charge when necessary. Stephens was the follower, who always seemed eager to please. And

Mitchell was the individual, who preferred to go his own way. Although the lines were blurred—Mitchell also showed leadership, and he generally tried to do what the coaches asked—it was basically an accurate assessment.

Mitchell had learned independence at an early age from his father, who owns a successful commercial construction company in Toledo. Charles Mitchell, a University of Toledo graduate, founded the company about the time Todd was born and built it up gradually while his wife, Gladys, kept the books. The company nearly went bankrupt during the recession in the 1970's, but perseverence and a bank loan kept it afloat, and it bounced back strongly.

Mitchell got plenty of opportunities to exercise his independence as a kid, thanks in part to his father's financial security. He learned how to swim when he was four years old. He later dabbled in motocross, archery, golf and water skiing. When he was 12, he spent a month at a summer camp near San Francisco, hiking in Yosemite and trying his hand at whitewater canoeing.

He was still hanging on to his independent streak in college, which sometimes made him appear stubborn, even difficult, in the eyes of the coaches.

Keady considered him the most crucial link to this season's team, and told him so two days after the team returned home from the loss to Florida. Mitchell, although just 6-6, was a quick, explosive jumper who had always been most effective offensively close to the basket, where he could take advantage of his natural athletic ability. He wanted, however, to play away from the basket, where he could match up against smaller players and shoot from the outside more often, which also would help him prepare for a possible professional career. This season, with Kip Jones sliding into the starting lineup, he got his wish.

But it was an uneasy alliance. The coaches still thought he was most effective inside. Mitchell, who had worked hard to improve his shooting and ballhandling over the summer, wanted to prove he could score and penetrate.

Mitchell's independence also showed in his response to criticism. If one of the assistant coaches got on him for what he thought was an unjustified reason, he ignored him—at least for as long as he could get away with it. The assistant coaches thought he sometimes purposely made them call his name twice before responding.

Keady addressed the issue in practice Sunday, when he called the players to the chalkboard before practice.

"When somebody tells you something, guys, look them in the eye," he told them. "Some of you are getting a reputation. You can say that's bullshit, but if the coaches feel that way, then I want it corrected. So when a coach tells you something, listen. It's got nothing to do with being a big shot, it's trying to help you prepare for life. If you go in and work for Proctor and Gamble or whoever, and you have people under you, what do you want them to do when you talk to them? You want them to make eye contact and listen to you.

"I'm not interested in hurting your feelings. I'm interested in you becoming so thick-skinned you can handle anything that comes your way in society—whether you're a salesman or whatever—and in basketball."

Skins became hides in practice that day, as Keady interrupted drills to run sprints whenever he wasn't pleased with the effort or execution, which was often. He ended the workout by punching the ball over the backboard and sending the players in to the weight room.

Keady is an innovator among basketball coaches for making weightlifting a routine part of his program. For many years, sports folklore held that basketball players would ruin their shooting touch if they lifted weights, but it is gradually becoming more commonplace. Most coaches now have some sort of weightlifting program for their players, although it often is lightly supervised and only runs through the offseason.

Keady had added it to his practice routine when he took over at Purdue. In the off season, the players lift three times a week. Once the season starts, they lift twice a week, always under the supervision of a strength coach. Although many of the freshmen are at first reluctant, particularly the guards, everyone seems to embrace it over time. Many of the players, in fact, become more diligent about lifting weights than they do about playing basketball in the summer months. They notice the benefits on the court, and they don't mind the muscles, either.

The players also enjoy the weightlifting workouts because they offer a more relaxed atmosphere. Keady usually joins them, sitting on a countertop and joking with them while they move from station to station. No matter how mad he might have been in practice, he is always upbeat with them in the weight room.

By the time the players finished this workout, they were in high spirits again. They huddled enthusiastically and started to head for the door, but Keady stopped them. He then ordered them back onto the floor for 15 more minutes of practice, in search of a happier ending.

Keady had been pleased with the success his players showed with the new uptempo style against Little Rock. They got several easy points on fastbreak baskets, and gave up just one layup despite pressing throughout most of the game. But the second-round opponent, Iowa State, was expected to provide a tougher test of the new system. The Cyclones ran as if the court slanted downhill both ways. They weren't a well-disciplined team, and they had just one player of preseason acclaim, forward Jeff Grayer. But they had excellent athletes.

The previous week, one of Keady's "Emphases of the Days" had been simple: "Run!" His key to the game against Iowa State, written on the chalkboard in the locker room, was only slightly more detailed: "Be ready to play at a fast tempo; run, run, run. Not wild. There's a difference."

But the game ended up wild—eerie, too. Because it was played just two days before Thanksgiving, most of the students had left campus. A steady rainshower also helped keep the crowd down, as only 7,957 fans showed up at Mackey, barely more than half the capacity.

Mitchell had the flu, and took a Tylenol before taking the floor for the final pregame warmup. But if he didn't already have a headache, the game surely would have given him one. Both teams were running and pressing fullcourt at a breakneck pace, posing no threats to the 45-second shot clock. With Lewis hitting five of six three-pointers, Purdue gasped to a 51-50 halftime lead.

It jumped to a 66-61 advantage in the second half before Iowa State ran off seven points within a minute to take a 70-68 lead. From there, the game was up for grabs. Keady stripped off his sport coat and pumped his fist, igniting the crowd. Purdue took the lead at 84-82. Iowa State came back to go up 89-84. Lewis hit a three-pointer, Kip Jones scored inside and Stephens drove for a layup to put Purdue back on top, 93-90 with 3:52 left.

But then the bottom fell out. An Iowa State reserve, Mike Born, drove around Lewis for a layup. Lewis missed a three-pointer and Scheffler, going for the rebound, fouled Lafester Rhodes, who hit both shots to give Iowa State a 94-93 lead. Keady was up again, stoking the fans' fire for the final push. But Iowa State grabbed two offensive rebounds on its next possession and scored again. Stephens missed on the baseline. The rebound was knocked out of bounds to Purdue, but Mitchell missed on the inbounds pass. Stephens then fouled Terry Woods, who hit two more free throws to give Iowa State a 99-93 lead with one minute left.

The players on the bench were stunned. Homecourt losses were rare. Now they were on the verge of losing one in the second game of the season, to an unheralded team.

"We're getting beat on our homecourt," Brugos said from the end of the bench, shaking his head in disbelief.

Reid then turned to Arnold, sitting behind him.

"You better get ready next semester," he said. "We need you, buddy."

Keady called timeout to set up desperate measures. But Lewis missed another three-pointer and Iowa State rebounded. The game was over. The Cyclones went on to win 104-96. Purdue had hit just one of nine shots in the final 3½ minutes.

The only sound in Purdue's locker room, as the players silently took a seat in front of their lockers, was the gleeful shouts of the Iowa State players running by outside the door. Keady paced the room, head down, for a few moments, then addressed the players.

"There's not much you can say about a team that outplayed you," he said, quietly. "They outplayed us in about every category. They deserve to go to New York. There's not any joy in losing, guys."

His voice grew louder as his anger surfaced. All his preseason fears had suddenly been realized in one 40-minute nightmare.

"We fight too many obstacles! Hell, we're fighting guys wanting to be leaders, we're fighting guys who don't want to practice hard, we're fighting guys who want to do this...I can't fight you all to get you to do anything.

"You better get your asses cut in or I'm getting rid of you. I'm fighting guys who want all the publicity, I'm fighting guys who don't understand the game. It gets goddamn old. Why should I have to sell seniors? We've got guys who let us down in the summer, that's bullshit enough. I'll tell you what, guys, you're going to have a helluva time beating anybody. I'm not saying something I'm going to be sorry about tomorrow, either. I've seen it coming, and it's the best goddamn thing that could happen to you. You don't understand the mental toughness of the game to play at the big boys' level. Doug Lee was a helluva fighter last year, and we don't have anybody like that. That's a tough lesson to learn, guys. You can go around and rip Coach Keady because he's hard-nosed and won't let you shoot and all that bullshit, but I'm going to tell you guys, it's going to be a long year until you learn how to have the three goals I wrote on the board last week: mental toughness, physical strength and togetherness. Right now you don't have any of them. For two weeks we've been trying to sell you on doing it. For two weeks you've been fighting my ass.

"Guys, I don't know what it's going to take to convince you. If this is not enough, then I don't understand. I'll tell you right now, Illinois State is going to be tougher than this. And Wichita State is going to be tougher than Illinois State.

"Let's go, huddle up. We'll see you at 3 o'clock tomorrow.

"Together."

"We attack."

Keady's first reaction after a loss, every loss, is to blame himself, to search for things he might have been able to do differently to prepare the team better. He had really struggled with that feeling early in his coaching career, and had since come to the realization that players, even occasionally referees, can contribute to a loss as well. But his instinct was always to look within himself for explanations, and it was no different now.

"I've been trying to convince our guys that mental toughness, physical strength and togetherness is what we've got to get better at, and it's not been very easy to sell them," he told the reporters afterwards. "And that's my fault. Because I haven't sold them.

"It's a situation where maybe it will wake us up and maybe it will be worse than we thought. It was a great eye-opener for some of our guys who have been interviewed a lot and been thinking they're pretty hot stuff."

For one of his teams to score 96 points and lose was mindboggling to Keady. He had made defense the focus of the week's practices, and then watched his team give up 104 points. All of his starters had scored in double figures, led by Lewis, who finished with 28 points, eight rebounds and nine assists. But Iowa State had outshot them, outrebounded them and outhustled them.

After the game, the assistant coaches gathered in the office Weber and Stallings shared, while Keady returned to his office with Pat. He was still seething, cursing all that had gone wrong the past few weeks—the past several months, for that matter—as he relived the game. Sitting at his desk, he kicked his wastebasket, breaking the miniature backboard that was attached to it. A few minutes later he stopped to talk with his assistants on the way out.

"There were a couple of stretches where we ran them to death, but we don't have guys who hurt badly enough when they get beat on defense," Wood said.

"Oh, they don't care," Keady said. "They don't care if they ever stop anybody."

"And rebounding," Wood said. "There's a mentality to it."

"It's mental toughness, coach, and we don't have it," Keady said. "I'm going to tell you right now, coaches. We're going to struggle the whole year. It's going to be a helluva mess."

4

The Late Show

Keady isn't quite sure how he developed such a pure, blinding hatred for losing. He's thought about it often, and can only come up with the fact he tasted defeat so frequently early in his athletic career, on his junior high and high school teams, that it became ingrained. No doubt his classic Irish temperament and his tendency toward high blood pressure enter into the formula as well.

His is a controlled fury. Beyond kicking or throwing something behind closed doors, he always manages to keep his emotions in check. But losing brings such a deep, personal invasion of his pride that it nearly dominates his existence. The morning after a defeat, he wakes up with the immediate sensation that something horrible has happened; then, after the cobwebs clear, he remembers: a loss. The feeling generally lasts until the next victory comes along to wash it away.

The players know that the first few practices after a loss—particularly one at home—are sure to be more intense. And if the loss happened to come by a wide margin, or to a clearly inferior team, the first of those practices might take place only a few hours after the game, in the form of a special midnight edition.

The players say the very thought of encountering the coach after losses is a motivational factor in itself. The practices are intense enough when they're winning to tempt fate too often. And their record in close games seems to bear out the system. In the last five years, Purdue teams had compiled a 28-10 record in games decided by five points or less, or in overtime. If fear was a motivation, it apparently hadn't overwhelmed their poise.

The loss to Iowa State would put them to the test again. On one hand, it wasn't difficult to justify. The season was young, they were breaking in a new system, two of their starters had been battling injuries, another projected one was sitting behind the bench in street clothes and they had run into a hot team they had underestimated.

But the coaches saw the loss from another perspective. It had come at home, to a team that wasn't supposed to be that good, and it had revealed all the problems they had been talking, shouting and worrying about for the past month. The defense and shot selection had been lacking, particularly in the final minutes. Worse than that, the coaches thought, the spirit was missing. Nobody was slapping hands or patting backs on the court, and a few players—Lewis in particular—had muttered gripes when they were taken out of the game. All in all, they were relatively minor problems, the kind that often don't even merit attention. But Purdue's coaches didn't consider them trivial.

Losses also tend to make Keady question his system. In the process of blaming himself, he looks for answers, and the most obvious one usually is that something was wrong with the game plan, or even the overall system. In retrospect, it seemed apparent Purdue had played into Iowa State's hands by trying to run. Could it be that the switch to an uptempo style had been a mistake? Should they go back to the more patterned, disciplined game plan of previous seasons? When teams play uptempo, Keady thought, the players are in control at the end of a close game. When teams play a slower, more disciplined style, the coaches are in control. Keady wasn't comfortable not having the reins.

"Okay, let's look at it from a theory standpoint," Stallings said as the coaches met before practice the day after the loss, on Wednesday. "Are we going to have more talent than most teams we play this year?"

"No!" Keady blurted.

Two weeks earlier, he had voted Purdue number one in the United Press International poll. Now, he would drop it completely out of the Top 20. The other voters weren't quite as distressed, however. Purdue wound up 11th.

"If you honestly believe that, then we shouldn't run," Stallings said. "If you honestly believe it."

"Who have we got that's better than Ohio State's players, or Indiana's, or Iowa's, or Illinois?" Keady asked.

"I don't think Ohio State's got a single player as good as we do," Stallings said.

"Oh, bullshit!" Keady said, shaking in anger. "That's like last night. I walk on that court and Iowa State's got players! God damnit, we underrated them! We didn't emphasize their athletes enough. We don't have athletes!"

"We don't have athletes, Kevin," Weber said. "I said before, we're trying to run, and we only have one guy (Stephens) who's right for that style of play."

They debated the issue further, then Keady settled the matter.

"We're going to work on the same things we've been working on, but we're going to pick up our man sooner and see what happens," he said. "Then if we go to Illinois State and get beat, we'll come back here and play like we used to. We'll see what happens. We're not going to change up overnight.

"Maybe we're going to have to lose a couple of games, I don't know. But I don't think that's our big problem, anyway. I think it's compassion, pulling for each other, emotion. Those kind of things are what's killing us."

The "Emphasis of the Day," for that afternoon's practice, then, had nothing to do with rebounding or defense or running. It was three-fold: Compassion. Togetherness. Pulling for the other guy.

But this time Keady didn't settle for a brief chat on the practice floor before stretching. He walked out to the floor, where the players were shooting around, and called them into the lounge. He then let go with a 15-minute lecture.

He talked about his concern over the team's lack of emotion, his fear that the team was headed for a collapse. He said he wondered if the seniors were more interested in preparing for professional careers than this season, and he scolded Lewis for his reaction to being pulled from the game.

"This is a hardcore world, gentlemen," he continued. "You're not playing Division II basketball where they have 500 people come to the game and they don't care if you win or not. This is high-pressure basketball and if we don't get your ass in gear, we're not going to get where we want to get in March. It's that simple. And if you can't stand the pressure, Harry Truman, then you better get your ass out of the kitchen.

"I hope you understand that when I criticize somebody, guys, when I get after your ass, if you're not tough enough to fight through that and accept it as a reason for making you better, you're not going to make it in the competitive world. There's a reason behind it. It's not a punishment or it's not a thing to make you feel like you're not a good individual. You've got to fight through the criticism and say, 'I'm not too big for anything if we're going to win big.' It's that simple.

"Those kind of things are really scaring me a little bit. Because I'll tell you guys, when I went home last night, I was ready to quit this program. I had had it. Why should I work my ass off 365 days out of the year for a bunch of guys who are individualists. I can cash in my retirement and go play golf in Florida rather than put up with this bullshit. I don't get paid enough for that. I don't make much money myself. You might think this is all a bed of roses, but those assistants there aren't making as much as a hell of a lot of assistants in the country. And if you say, 'Well that's your tough luck,' that's bullshit. Because we care about you. And you're not going to have coaches treat you any better than we coaches do. You might have coaches treat you as well, but not any better. And I'm not talking about financial re-imbursement, either.

"And the next time, Troy, you wave off one of my coaches, you're through for the game. You understand that? That's bullshit. You're not going to do that to one of my assistants. They love you. They get after your ass because they love you, and they respect me enough to make sure you know what we're trying to do.

"We like all of you. We wouldn't have you here if we didn't like you. That's what I talked about the other day, the barrier between players and coaches. You think we like you or don't like you. That's a bullshit program attitude. Coaches that think, 'Boy, if I don't treat my players good they won't like me,' those guys are at the convention watching the tournaments and never being able to play in them. Be-cause you've got your coaches that are just happy to be in it, you've got your mediocre coaches and then you've got your coaches who make their players do the right thing. Until you understand that, and become sold on it, then you're not going to become a very good team.

"I walk out there awhile ago and we've got guys shooting jackass shots, 45-footers. When you walk on this court from now on I want you working on shots that will help you in a game. Get tired while you're working on your jump shots. Not thinking, 'Boy, we're going to practice for 2½ hours, I'm going to be tired.' Shit, you've got to work your ass off and be ready to play if we practice three hours. And you ought to be ready to practice a half an hour before we start, full blast.

"I know you knew I wasn't going to be very happy, but I'm sure you didn't think I was going to be unhappy about that. We don't have any togetherness right now, and until we get it, we're going to be mediocre. Because we have not proven we have any leaders, we have not proven we can stop anybody on defense and we haven't proven we have a bench. So that's what we've got to work on. You guys that haven't played much yet, John Brugos, David Barrett and Bill Reid, you better have your asses ready. Because if this continues, you might be starters in a week. Because we don't play favorites around here, we play guys that work hard and understand the game."

With that, Keady dismissed the players for practice. Now that the problems of the preseason had more clearly identified themselves, he was going to attack them head-on. It was his style not to let a problem, whether real or rumored, fester for long. And while he had been harping on many of the problems he had just talked about for several weeks, he had decided it was time for major surgery. Either the team would snap out of its coma, or reject the treatment—and risk death.

What followed, in the next five days leading up to the game at Illinois State, was part hell week and part love-in. Compassion became the watchword. If a player made a good play and nobody congratulated him, the coaches stopped practice and ordered them to. When a player drew a foul in a scrimmage, his teammates were told to huddle with him at the foul line and put their arms around each other while a coach set up the next play. The coaches knew it was forced, but were hoping it would become a habit.

One more problem came up during the week, however. Arnold—who the coaches thought was playing the best of his career, with enthusiasm and savvy—had told Wood and Reiter he thought the team had a problem between the blacks and whites. The coaches took it to mean he was indicating a racial problem, that the black players—who were, as a group, more talented and more mature than the white players on the team—had formed a clique and weren't communicating with the whites.

Arnold would say later he had meant a problem existed between shirt colors, not skin colors. "The Misfits," under his enthusiastic leadership, were often outplaying the Blacks in scrimmages, and loving every minute of it. But that only served to deepen the resentment of the other seniors.

The coaches knew that none of the blacks or whites on the team were bigoted, but they saw it as another indication of the team's lack of togetherness. Mitchell, Lewis and Stephens, all seniors, were the best of friends, and naturally stuck together. Stephens would make it a point to talk with the underclassmen on occasion, but Lewis and Mitchell generally kept to themselves.

"I don't know if we need to make a big deal of it, but that's part of our problem," Wood said.

"They have a feeling of superiority about the game itself, that the white guys aren't as good," Stallings said. "And they're not. But you can just sense that they feel that way."

"I don't think it's a black-white problem, I think it's a basketball problem," Keady said.

The team took a day off for Thanksgiving, but had to be back for two practices Friday, one at 11 a.m. and one at 4 p.m. Most of the players lived too far from West Lafayette to make a one-day trip home feasible, so they stayed on campus. Stephens spent the afternoon shooting, by himself, at the arena.

After Friday morning's practice, a workmanlike $2\frac{1}{2}$ hour session devoted mostly to drills, Keady, who was fighting a sore throat, sat down off to the side of the court, sipped from a Coke and sighed.

"It's hard to believe one guy can make as much difference as Doug Lee did," he said, referring to Lee's leadership. "He's the only starter we lose, and we're like a completely different team. And he wasn't *that* good."

"Not on defense, but he worked at it hard," Stallings said.

"Boy, it was a long day yesterday," Keady said. "A good day, because I got some rest, but a long day.

"I watched the Florida film the other day and all I can say is we must have done a lousy job teaching them. It was like we hadn't learned anything. And it's carried over. Hell, we've lost three of our last five games (dating back to the previous season), do you realize that? We must be doing something wrong. Hell, I can't coach, I can't play golf and I can't talk."

"I agree that you can't play golf, but I think you can coach," Stallings said, grinning.

"How many losing seasons have you had now?" Wood asked.

"Three," Keady said. "My first three years in high school. But one of those years we went to the state, so that doesn't count. We were 7-10, and then went to the state."

"Well, that's pretty good," Wood said. "So how many winning seasons in a row is that?"

"Hell, I don't know," Keady said.

"Well how many years have you been coaching?" Wood asked. "Count 'em up."

"We're not going to have a winning season this year if we don't get some things straightened out," Keady said.

"You could always retire," Wood said, smiling.

"No, you can't retire until you're 70," Stallings said.

"Right," Keady said. "Nineteen more years. I won't last that long for two reasons. They won't let me stay that long, and I'll get senile."

Right then, Dale Rudd, the trainer, came by with still more bad news. Arnold had wrenched his back while blocking out during a rebounding drill, and would have to miss that afternoon's practice— and probably more after that.

"Christ," Keady said, leaning back in his chair. "If it's not one thing, it's another. So now we can probably expect more behavior out of him."

"I'll tell you this. He's been working his ass off in practice," Stallings said.

"He should have gone-to-classed his ass off last summer," Keady said.

Keady opened that afternoon's practice with a new drill. He lined the players up at the end of the floor, from where they usually began sprints, and told them to count off by twos. That done, he told them to turn to the player at each side and give him a high five. That was all.

The workout that followed, without Arnold, was one of the best of the season. Brugos in particular was responding to Keady's plea for more effort and enthusiasm. The rest of the players were going with the program as well, either voluntarily or by necessity.

After Berning made a nice play, Keady stopped practice and asked for a round of applause. When the Black shirts huddled for a free throw during a scrimmage, Keady yelled, "C'mon, guys, touch each other!" They put their arms around each other. There was a five-minute controlled scrimmage, which the Black shirts won—that in itself was new and encouraging. Afterwards, they lifted weights. Keady's mood had brightened considerably now. He joked with the players and told stories about his childhood, about cutting the heads off of chickens with a hatchet when he lived on a farm as a kid, and about his gang of friends that also included five Mexican kids, two blacks and a redhead who looked exactly like Alfalfa, from the "Our Gang" comedy series.

"It was a great life, boy," he said.

This one was looking up, too. For the moment.

With all that had gone wrong already, and with the improvement shown in the recent practices, the coaches were beginning to think more optimistically as the team prepared to leave Mackey Sunday afternoon for the next night's game at Illinois State.

But problems continued. Stephens was a few minutes late for the scheduled 1:45 p.m. bus departure from Mackey Sunday afternoon. He hadn't been able to start his car, an older-model Nissan that was always giving him fits, and he had had to call for a jump. Still, he was only a few minutes late boarding the bus. At another, more pleasant, time in the season, Keady probably wouldn't have said anything about it. But this wasn't one of those times.

Keady said nothing as Stephens boarded the bus, but stopped Stephens at midcourt as the players were warming up for practice that night in Normal, Illinois to ask him about it. Stephens told him about the dead battery.

"I don't care if an atom bomb goes off, you shouldn't be late," Keady said.

One of Keady's standard practice routines the day before road games is a defensive drill in which the players practice taking a charge. They pair off. One starts to dribble along the sideline, the other gives him a short head start, then runs in front of him and plants his feet. The dribbler knocks him over—not viciously, but not softly, either—and then helps him up. They do it twice on one side, then switch places and do it twice more on the other side.

First-time visitors are often amazed to see *basketball* players knocking their teammates down the day before a game, but the players had grown to like it—or at least not mind it. The idea is to create a loose, but intense frame of mind for the game.

But the combination of the 2½ hour bus trip and current state of emergency had the players feeling uptight this time. They were quiet, somber and sloppy as they opened with a four-on-four fullcourt drill.

Scheffler mistimed a rebound.

"C'mon Scheffler, get a rebound," Stallings shouted from the other end of the floor. "You're not even close!"

A minute later, Scheffler let a pass slip out of his hands and out of bounds.

"Scheffler, get in the game," Stallings shouted. "We're off the bus now! Think!"

The workout continued along tentative and shaky lines.

"It's like the Roman Empire, guys," Keady shouted at one point. "There's complacency. Nobody's hungry."

Gradually, things picked up. Scheffler, playing for the White shirts, blocked out McCants nicely to get a rebound, then beat him inside at the other end for a basket. The Black shirts began to click, dominating the Whites—which was what the coaches wanted to see the night before a game.

"See, it's fun when you play like this," Wood shouted.

The mood was indeed brighter. The practice ended in good spirits. Lewis granted an interview with a local television station on his way out to the bus.

"How'd the interview go, Troy?" Keady asked as Lewis boarded.

"Fine," Lewis said. "I told them we'd beat them by 50 points. I said Illinois State wasn't worth shit."

Just kidding, of course.

But there still was the more serious matter of Stephens' tardiness. The coaches wondered if he had been at his girlfriend's apartment, where he often was, and if that had been the reason for his late arrival. Whatever the reason, Keady was angry. After the Iowa State loss, he had decided to rotate his three seniors in the captain's role, and Stephens was up first. This wasn't the kind of leadership he was looking for.

"That typifies the whole team," Keady said, discussing the matter with the assistant coaches later that night. "That's the way the whole thing's gone for six weeks. Everything is back-asswards."

Keady decided to leave Stephens on the bench for the start of the game. Tony Jones would start in his place. After that evening's video session, Keady addressed the team once again.

"We've got severe problems, men," he said. "I don't know what it will take to correct them, and maybe we can't correct them. But I guarantee you we're going to try. But there's some things going on that I don't like.

"It's just like today, I decide to pick a captain for the next three games because I think it will give us some leadership, but Everette shows up late for the bus. So for that, I'm not going to start him tomorrow night. Now it hurts me to do that to someone I respect so much, but that's bullshit. We can't have that.

"I don't know what's going on, but we've got to get it straightened out. Basketball has got to be number one in your life behind your studies and religion—if you've got that. But basketball has to be a top priority.

"If you've got a girlfriend nagging you, you better tell them to get lost. Because ten years from now you won't even remember their names. You're just a whisper for them to hold onto because you're a basketball player.

"I don't know if that's the case, but a few of you seem to have something bugging you. Maybe some people out there are telling you you're being exploited because you're not getting anything here. We're not going to give you any money besides your scholarship. That's tough shit if you don't like it. If people are telling you you're being exploited because you're making all kinds of money for the university and the NCAA tournament, that's bullshit. You're not being exploited. If anybody's being exploited, it's the coaches because you don't care if we win or not. You're not going to get anything illegal. So if you're thinking about that, get it out of your head.

"And if you have people back home in Decatur or Anderson or wherever telling you you don't need to worry about anything but your scoring, that's bullshit, too. This is a different world, with a different level of talent. You've got to do it our way here. You can't just worry about your points."

Stallings then talked about leadership, telling the seniors they had been good about offering criticism and advice to the underclassmen in practice, but not to each other.

Then Keady stood up and took on the latest possible problem, the perception of racial strife.

"There's something else that someone mentioned to me the other day and I hope to God this isn't true," Keady said. "Some people think the black guys on this team think they're superior to the rest of the guys. And that's bullshit. I'm not going to let color interfere with anything on this team. I don't see color. I see people and I see basketball players. When I started at Hutchinson [a junior college in Kansas where Keady had coached] I had two black players. When I left I had 13. And there were times I heard people make comments where I told them, 'If you don't go apologize to him, I'll knock your ass off.' I've never let color be a problem before, and I'm not going to start now. So if that's a hangup with you, get it out of your head now."

As the players returned to their rooms, Stallings asked for, and received, permission to go talk with some of them. His first stop was Scheffler's room. After playing well in the season opener, Scheffler had been held scoreless in a 15-minute appearance against Iowa State, and seemed to be struggling in practice again.

"Coach, how do you get confidence?" Scheffler asked Stallings.

That was his greatest challenge. He had come to Purdue the season before a rough draft of a college basketball player, a large, muscular—he benched pressed nearly 250 pounds—aggressive athlete, but lacking the game's refinements. He had been a bundle of nerves as a freshman, nearly hyperventilating when he made his infrequent game appearances; he played just 73 minutes all season. Although he had shown dramatic improvement over the summer, he still was unsure of himself on the court.

"Steve, you're the strongest player in the Big Ten; that's a good start," Stallings said.

Scheffler had another concern, too. A small-town, humble, polite, innocent and slightly eccentric kid, he had been the target of a great deal of kidding since the start of his freshman season. The fact he had dyslexia, a disorder which affected his reading ability and memory retention, made him stand out even more.

The year before, Lewis had tagged him with the nickname

George, after a character from a Saturday morning cartoon. Actually, George was smart; his partner, Lenny, was the slow one, always asking, "Which way did he go, George?" "What do we do now, George?" But Lewis, the team's most lively kidder, associated the name George with being slow, and had started calling Scheffler that. Not because Scheffler was dumb—he carried a B average—but because he was naive. He had even told the audience about it at the team's preseason banquet earlier this season. Several of the other players had picked up on the joke, shouting "George! George!" whenever they thought Scheffler blundered, on the court or off.

Scheffler was coming in for less kidding this season. But, he told Stallings, he still didn't feel a part of the group, and admitted he resented a few of the players for the way they treated him.

Stallings then stopped by the room where Lewis, Stephens, Mitchell and Tony Jones, four of the team's blacks, had gathered. He could hear them talking in serious tones as he approached the room, but they fell silent when he opened the door and walked in.

"Did I put a damper on your conversation?" he asked.

"Yeah, you sort of did," Mitchell said, looking him in the eye.

"Is there anything you're saying you can't say in front of the coaches?" Stallings asked.

"Is there anything the coaches are saying in their meetings they can't say to us?" Mitchell responded.

Tony Jones soon left for his room, but Stallings stayed and talked with the seniors. Mitchell told him they all felt they had reached the low point of their careers at Purdue. Not only had they been blasted for their lack of performance and leadership the past several weeks, now they were being questioned about having girlfriends and being racists—and one of them had been benched for being a few minutes late for the bus.

Stallings explained to them that the coaches knew racism wasn't a problem, and that they should ignore some of the things that had been said. But leadership and team togetherness, the coaches felt, was a problem.

"Have any of you guys ever gone to Steve Scheffler or Dave Barrett and just asked them how classes are going, or if they were having fun or if they had any questions about anything?" Stallings asked. "No, you haven't."

"Nobody did that with us when we were freshman," Mitchell said.

"But that doesn't mean you guys can't do it," Stallings said.

Stallings told them about his experience as a first-year player on Purdue's team in the 1979-80 season. A junior college transfer, he had joined the team as a sophomore, but didn't feel comfortable with the seniors, particularly the All-American center, Joe Barry Carroll. Then on one road trip, Stallings said, Carroll asked to room with him and the two sat up half the night getting acquainted.

Until then, Stallings had thought Carroll was a snob. After getting to know him, he realized Carroll was simply a quiet person who preferred to keep to himself.

"You are what others perceive you to be, even if that's not what you really are," Stallings said. He told Mitchell that if he loafed through stretching, that three rows of underclassmen behind him would loaf, too. He told Lewis that he was the funniest guy on the team, but it wasn't so funny if his jokes were hurting someone else's feelings.

The players talked for an hour longer with Stallings, until 1 a.m. They talked about Keady's hard-nosed style, and how it sometimes made them angry, but admitted it was effective, and sometimes necessary. Mitchell recalled working on a crew for the construction company his father owned in Toledo, and how his father would laugh every time he bumped his head on the scaffolding. He had hated that, but realized over time he had become tougher because of it.

Perhaps it would be the same way with this team. It certainly had been taking its lumps.

By game time the next evening, Keady was beginning to feel as if he were trapped in a hopeless maze, with trouble lurking around every corner.

Lewis had been late boarding the bus for shooting practice that morning. He claimed the clock in his room was five minutes late. Keady later checked it out and found that to be true. But now he had a dilemma. He already had benched Stephens for being a few minutes late for the bus out of West Lafayette, and it would be hard to justify treating Lewis any differently. But the whole matter was getting out of hand. Lewis, like Stephens, had never been a discipline problem. Keady, in fact, considered both of them two of the finest people he had ever coached.

Keady told the assistants at lunch he was going to start Lewis. But they finally convinced him he had to dish out the same punishment he had given to Stephens; anything else would be a double standard.

And so Reid became a starter for the second game of his college career, joining Tony Jones in the opening lineup. Lewis, who had not missed a start since his freshman season, and Stephens, who had broken into the starting lineup as a junior, would be on the bench. Keady made the announcement after the pregame meal at the hotel.

"I don't like it," he said. "To be honest with you, it was something that I thought about for a long time before I did it. It's something I don't appreciate, my seniors not being better disciplined than the rest of the team.

"We've got some problems, guys. We've got some big problems unless you get them ironed out. It isn't going to be easy. It's going to be hard. I'm not blaming anybody for things going wrong. I figure if something's going wrong, it's my fault because I haven't convinced you to do it the right way. I'm not blaming anybody. I just want it corrected. I don't get hung up on grudges or worry about whether Troy likes me or not because I'm not going to start him. He should have got up sooner. That's his problem. If he goes to work for IBM, he's going to have to be at work on time. We're dealing with young men here that I respect but I don't think you understand how much I respect you. Because I'm not going to let you cut corners on me doesn't mean I don't appreciate you. That's a very simple thing, guys, let's get it straightened out. It's a fun thing when everything starts clicking. Last year we got things going good and were hitting on all 15 cylinders. Well it's not that way now. We've had some adversity, we've had some injuries, we've had some pressure. But that's OK, it's a challenge. It's going to work out if you have your head right. I don't have any second thoughts about that. But if you walk out of here feeling bad about something, then you've got problems. I don't have the problem, you do. It needs to be ironed out.

"The question tonight isn't the starters. The question is if you have enough courage to fight the things inside of you resisting what needs to be done right. It's never the opponents that are the problem. It's you that's the problem. It's me that's the problem. You've got to get your own things ironed out. Like Scheffler. If you're uptight or inhibited, you've got to become relaxed. I can go right down the line. Everybody has their own problems. I've got my problems. You're not fighting the opponent, you're fighting yourself. You've got to relax and become more aware of what has to happen if we're going to become a good basketball team. That's the challenge of this situation. It's not going to be easy. It's not going to be a lot of fun until we get our heads together.

"OK, you got anything else, coaches?"

Reiter asked if any of the seniors might want to say anything.

There was silence for five seconds. Then Lewis spoke up. He was disappointed over being benched, and a little angry, and wasn't in the mood to be a cheerleader at the moment. But it would have been too awkward if one of them didn't say something.

"I just want to say, we've got to come out and play," he said. "Like coach said, you young guys, the crowd's going to be real loud. It's almost going to be like playing at Iowa. We've got to come out ready to play and forget about all the problems we had. This is a new day and a new game. The Iowa State game's over. We just got to come out and play our game like we're capable of doing."

It was going to be a tough setting to do that in, however. Horton Fieldhouse was a throwback to a bygone era. It was a fieldhouse, not an arena, an old building put together with steel and sheet metal, with a seating capacity of just 7,000. But it was filled to the rafters (it was old enough to actually have rafters) and it was loud; as loud as any place Purdue would play in all season. The fans had two sources of motivation: the chance to upset a nationally-ranked Big Ten team that was already on the ropes, and the ESPN cameras that would broadcast the game nationally.

Illinois State's team didn't figure to be a pushover, either. It had four starters back from a team that had finished 19-13 the season before (although one of them would miss this game with an injury) and the sort of disciplined, intense game from which upsets sprang.

"This one," Keady said after the players left the locker room to warm up, "is going to be a barnburner."

He was right. Illinois State got the joint rockin' by jumping to a 5-0 lead. It still led 7-5 when Keady sent Stephens and Lewis into the game with 14:57 left. But if the senior guards were bitter about starting the game on the seat of their pants, they didn't show it. Lewis fed Stephens with a lob pass for a dunk to tie the score at 9. Lewis then came back with a three-pointer to give Purdue its first lead, 12-11.

Another lift came from a less expected source. When Scheffler picked up his third foul with 3:34 left—McCants already had two—Keady called for Brugos to report in. Brugos, sitting at the end of the bench, was stunned for a second by the command. It would be the first first-half appearance of his career.

But he took advantage, scoring on a ten-foot turnaround jumper in the lane with 2:43 left to give Purdue a 31-27 lead, then rebounding and drawing a foul at the defensive end. He hit both free throws, extending the lead to six.

He finished the half with four points, two rebounds and two fouls, his most meaningful contribution yet.

The game also turned out to be something of a landmark performance for Scheffler. Illinois State grabbed a 52-45 lead midway through the second half, sending the home fans into hysterics and Purdue to the edge of disaster. But Scheffler, who had picked up three fouls and not scored in a tentative first half, scored eight of Purdue's next ten points to pull his team within three.

Purdue took the lead three minutes later when, with the shot clock down to five seconds, Lewis hit McCants with a deft feed underneath for an easy basket to complete a six-point run that made it 62-60. Mitchell missed the front end of a one-and-one free throw moments later that could have added to the lead, then Tony Holifield hit one of two free throws with 1:25 left to pull Illinois State within one.

But poise pulled Purdue through. With the offense bogged down, Stephens drove the lane and hit a floating jumper for a 64-61 lead. Mitchell then rebounded an Illinois State miss, and Tony Jones was fouled with 18 seconds left. Illinois State called timeout to let him think about it. His first shot hit the back of the rim and fell in, and his second glanced off the front of the rim and in. They were ugly, but they counted. The win was assured. Mitchell added an exclamation point with a dunk at the buzzer, for a 68-61 victory.

They celebrated as if they had just won the Big Ten championship, although it was fueled by relief as much as it was joy. It was a great win, coming from four points down in the final 4½ minutes in a tough setting, but more important than that it was a team win, something they badly needed. There was no star of the game, just a constellation of contributors.

"Way to go! Way to go!" Keady shouted over the bedlam.

"Way to play smart, guys!" Brugos shouted.

"That's what happens when you've got veterans!" Reiter shouted.

"That was a team effort!" Weber shouted.

Brugos screamed Scheffler's name. Scheffler screamed Brugos' name. Everybody screamed, period.

They had won. Best of all, they had survived.

5

Homecoming

"Nothing in the world can take the place of persistence. Talent will not; nothing is more common than unsuccessful men with talent. Genius will not; unrewarded genius is almost a proverb. Education alone will not; the world is full of educated derelicts. Persistence and determination alone are omnipotent."

—sign on wall in Keady's office (author unknown)

Gene Keady was born in Larned, Kansas on May 21, 1936, which was not unlike being sketched into a Norman Rockwell picture. A speck on the map in central Kansas, the heart of the heartland, Larned, all 2.3 square miles of it, was home to about 4,000 people, the vast majority of whom qualified as honest, humble and hard-working folks whose lives were rooted to the soil. Lloyd and Mary Helen Keady were perfectly typical.

Mary Helen, whose maiden name was Montgomery, was English by bloodline, but had been born in Mexico. She stayed at home and oversaw the upbringing of their two children, first Gene, and then four years later, Norma.

Lloyd, an Irishman, had grown up on a farm and quit school in the eighth grade to help put his older brother, George, through college. While George Keady went on to earn a business degree and become an executive with General Mills, Lloyd never left the greenhouse where he had first found work; he never wanted to. It was owned by a German immigrant named Sam Gilbert. For many of his first 40 years there, Lloyd Keady earned one dollar an hour and walked to work. He would spend eight hours a day growing, picking, potting and selling flowers, and then walk home. It was an invigorating, stress-free life. When Gilbert, who had no family of his own, died, he willed the business to Keady, and the rest of his possessions to charity.

The Keady's left Larned for five years during World War II, moving 100 miles west to Dighton, Kansas, where Lloyd Keady fulfilled his wartime obligation by working on a farm. Gene, five years old when they first moved, helped out a little and played a lot. Lloyd still remembers vividly returning home one day and finding his son frolicking in the mud with the hogs, minus one shoe.

From Dighton the family moved briefly to Garfield, where Mary Helen had grown up, and then returned to Larned. They stopped along the way to pick up an army barracks in Pratt, Kansas, which they made their home.

The Keady's enjoyed a simple life, short on material wealth but overflowing with happiness. For entertainment, they played cards, went for Sunday drives to visit relatives, listened to the radio, held family picnics and attended movies at the local theater. Meals were a major event that brought everyone in the household together.

It was in that setting Keady absorbed the small-town values that would stick to him, like mud, into adulthood.

"Larned was a great town, because it was small enough I could cover all the areas on my bicycle," he said. "I knew everybody, and everybody knew me. I had a lot of fun and a lot of friends. I was so dumb, I thought we were rich.

"It was a community with a good mix of people. There were a few black people, and they were good friends of the folks, and there were a lot of Spanish people, too. Prejudice wasn't a thing that ever entered my mind. I didn't understand the word. You wouldn't call people nigger or spic, or you'd have a fistfight on your hands. We stuck up for each other.

"I learned discipline and hard work from my dad. Mom taught me about love and how to respect people. I've never seen either of them mad at anybody, except for me. They always liked everybody. My dad scared the shit out of me, though; he was tough. But he wasn't a mean man, he was a gentle man. He just acted mean. He had me buffaloed, I'll tell you that. About the only time I remember him really doing anything was one time when he knocked me through the screen door. I was in high school and I'd said something cocky, like 'You can't do that to me.' And he said, 'Oh, yeah?' Bam!

"The next day he was fixing the screen door.

"I stole an airplane, one of those balsa wood jobs, out of this guy's garage one time when I was five years old. And my mom wore me out—with a verbal lashing, nothing physical. That was the last time I ever stole anything, that's for sure. Boy, she made me feel bad.

"And Dad's as honest as you can get. He worked the cash register at the greenhouse sometimes. From Easter and Memorial Day alone, he could have made a lot of money on the side, and Mr. Gilbert never would have known it. The cash flow was always there to cheat if you wanted to. But he'd knock the hell out of somebody if he caught anyone else doing it. He was really a loyal guy. He was uneducated, but he had a lot of common sense."

Keady grew up to be the spittin' image of his father. Although Lloyd Keady didn't drink, his side of the family was otherwise stereotypically Irish—aggressive, robust and tightly-knit. One of the favored family traits was orneriness, a term Keady refers to often, and a quality he values in his players and friends, providing they know where to draw the line.

Keady crossed the line himself on occasion. He acted up in class and spent time in the principal's office, but was involved in nothing more serious than the typical teenage pranks of the time. Once, he and a few friends moved the cannon that sat in front of Larned's library. Another time he climbed the town's 200-foot water tower and flipped on the power switch that controlled the electrical current for the town's Christmas lights. It probably was a telling aspect of his personality, however, that he never considered climbing the tower and turning the lights off. He had an ornery streak, not a mean streak.

Although Keady almost died of pneumonia when he was six months old, he grew up healthy, inheriting his father's natural athletic skills and temperament. Lloyd Keady was an amateur boxer and part-time pool hustler in his youth, but never had the opportunity to participate in organized sports. He was, however, a natural athlete, with big hands, good hand-eye coordination and a burning competitive fire. He was such an accomplished horseshoe pitcher that Keady would consider it one of the great thrills of what would turn out to be a varied and acclaimed athletic career when, at the age of 35, he finally beat his old man at his own game. But the victories didn't come easy.

"We played 28 games one day before he beat me," Lloyd Keady recalled. "He had to wear me out before he could do it. Then he wouldn't play me again."

Keady's interest in organized sports evolved gradually, through the games beamed to Larned from the outside world. He caught on to football first. In the fifth and sixth grades, he landed a job sweeping up at the Electric Theater in Larned. Newsreels, a major source of information in the pre-television era, were shown before the featured films—dramas and musicals on Sunday, Monday and Tuesday, detective stories and murder mysteries on Wednesday and Thursday, and westerns and comedies on Friday and Saturday—and the reports on the major college football games of the day made his blood boil.

He was exposed to major league baseball in the eighth grade, when his English teacher let the class listen to the World Series on the radio. The New York Yankees won that year, and he's been a Yankee fan ever since.

His interest in basketball was ignited that same year, when Larned High School's team won the state championship for its size classification as if it had followed a Hollywood scriptwriter's outline. Larned, with about 100 students in each of its grades, had been upset in the last game of the season and lost its automatic berth to the 15-team tournament. But it received an at-large bid, and went on to defeat Cherryvale for the title.

Keady listened to the final game over the car radio while working in the front yard one Saturday afternoon. And while the town accepted the championship with tempered exuberance—"It was more important in those days to cure polio or something than win the state title," he said—it left an indelible hunger to become a champion one day himself. The team's five starters became his idols. The following summer, one of them, a 5-8 forward named Bill Hunsinger, encouraged him to try to earn a college scholarship, and that became another goal.

Keady played football, basketball, baseball and ran track at Larned High. His athletic prowess was based on speed, strength and intensity more than finesse, so the only sport he didn't excel in immediately was basketball. He never did earn a starting position, even though Larned had a losing team and the head coach was his cousin.

He was, however, a multi-event star for the track team, which lost the state title by one-half of a point to Haskell High, for which future Olympic gold medalist Billy Mills competed. And he was the starting quarterback for the football team. But it, like the basketball team, wasn't very good, so he escaped the attention of most of the college recruiters. Drake University, in Des Moines, Iowa, and Washburn University, in Topeka, Kansas both offered scholarships, but he had set his dream on playing for a team in what is now the Big Eight Conference. He enrolled at Garden City Junior College to work his way up the ladder.

He continued to excel in football, baseball and track, but continued to struggle with basketball. He played all of about 40 minutes his freshman season. And just as he had received no favoritism from his cousin in high school, he got no sympathy from his father.

"My dad was always for the coaches," Keady said. "He would always say it was my fault if I wasn't playing. He was always pissed because I didn't feed the post more. Really, he's the guy who got me started saying to get the ball inside. That was my dad's philosophy. Most dads come back and ask why you don't shoot more. He'd say, 'Hey, why don't you get the ball into the post, you'll win.'"

Keady obviously was going to have to earn everything he got. Most of his shooting practice while growing up had come in a barn, at a goal nailed to a hayloft, in five-hour sessions of H-O-R-S-E games against his dad and neighbors. He was still shooting the same set shot he had used in the barn, however, so he went to work in search of a jump shot. He attended classes from eight until noon, earned his scholarship money at a local dairy from noon to two, and then snuck in an hour of shooting practice in the school's gym before practice began at three.

Gradually, he built a respectable, if not pretty, weapon.

Keady earned a starting position as a sophomore, and averaged 16 points for a Garden City squad that upset the top-ranked junior college team in the country, Ark City, Arkansas, and qualified for the national tournament.

Football, however, remained his best sport. He was an All-American JUCO quarterback his sophomore year, for a team that finished 8-1-1 and narrowly missed a berth in the Little Rose Bowl, the junior college national championship.

Keady's life nearly took a major detour after he graduated from Garden City. A friend from high school who was studying to become a pilot had planted the idea of joining the Air Force in his head. Full of youthful zeal, and admittedly something of a hot dog, he went for it. The entire scenario appealed to him. He would be paid, he would live in the Rocky Mountains and he would buy time for his athletic career. He would join the Air Force as a freshman, with four more years of eligibility—a six-year athletic career, in all.

But after receiving the required appointment from a Kansas state senator and taking the entrance examination in Denver, Keady was rejected on physical grounds. As a member of his high school track team, he had been hit in the head by a flying shot-put while crossing the infield one day. At the time, he had stood right up and continued on his way. But he collapsed when he reached the stadium bleachers and went into convulsions that lasted three hours. That automatically disqualified him from the Air Force, which rejected anyone who had ever been unconscious for half an hour or more because of the increased risk of passing out at high altitude.

Keady was set to join the Air Force if given the chance, but he wasn't heartbroken by the refusal. By now he had plenty of alternatives. Kansas State, Kansas, Colorado, New Mexico and Wichita State all were offering football scholarships. He narrowed his choice to Kansas State and New Mexico, and finally chose Kansas State, the apple of his boyhood eye.

There, the four-sport star had to settle for mere three-sport fame. He asked Kansas State's basketball coach, Tex Winter, if he could join the team as a walk-on, but Winter had no openings. Besides, the basketball season overlapped with football, indoor track and baseball, the sports at which Keady truly excelled. He was an all-conference outfielder in baseball. In track, he threw the shot-put and discus, and ran the 100-, 200- and 400-yard dashes. He ran a 9.9 100-yard dash.

As always, however, his best sport was football, where his innate speed, toughness and recklessness all became assets. Keady's teammates at Kansas State don't recall much about him today other than that he was a very good player who went about his business. Although free-spirited, he wasn't a troublemaker, and he didn't play the part of big man on campus. Kansas State's head coach at the time, Bus Mertes, who went on to become an assistant coach with the NFL

Minnesota Vikings, recalled "Keady's only problem in those days was that he was too good-looking." Kansas State's football media guide listed him as "the happy-go-lucky sprinter."

He played quarterback, running back, wide receiver and returned punts and kickoffs at various times in his two years there. But just as in high school, his fate was to be a good player on a bad team. Running with the ball at Kansas State in those days, given the caliber of protection, was a valiant act worthy of a Purple Heart.

"You were either stupid as hell or pretty tough," he would recall later.

Still, Keady had a standout junior season. He caught 14 passes for 247 yards, tying future NFL star Charlie James for the conference lead. He also rushed 43 times for 310 yards, scored a team high seven touchdowns, and returned two kicks for 30 yards and four punts for 43 yards.

His senior year, 1957, held great promise. He was used exclusively at halfback, and started the season quickly. After three games, he was among the nation's leading rushers. But he injured his knee in the fourth game, against Colorado, and never fully recovered.

In those days, before arthroscopic surgery, an athlete with a knee injury either quit or rehabilitated it on his own. Keady already was a veteran of rehab. He had injured his knee as a senior in high school, but continued to play. He hurt it again as a freshman at Garden City, and again in spring practice before his senior season at Kansas State. Each time, he worked it back into playing shape by running and lifting weights.

This time he sat out a few games and then tried to return, but was far from full strength. He finished the season with 332 rushing yards on 38 carries, caught two passes for 18 yards, returned six kicks for 95 yards and returned six punts for 47 yards. He was invited to play in the Blue-Gray and Shrine postseason all-star games, but was unable to go because of his injuries.

The Pittsburgh Steelers still thought enough of his ability to make him a late-round pick in the 1958 NFL draft. He tried out as a receiver. It would have been an interesting place for a young receiver to develop, because the Steelers had four quarterbacks in camp that summer who would in later years excel for other teams: Jack Kemp, Len Dawson, Bobby Layne and Earl Morrall.

Keady still believes strongly he could have made the team with a healthy knee. But his injury held him back, and he decided to leave camp. The Steelers saw enough hope for him to ask him to stay, but he was too frustrated. Besides, he had a college degree in biological sciences and physical education and he was married, to the Kansas State Homecoming Queen. (Pat, whom he married shortly after taking the job at Purdue, is his second wife.) Buddy Parker, the Steelers' head coach, advised him to drop the pigskin, take his sheepskin, and run with it.

Keady had but one other desire: coaching. He wanted to coach football, but it was late August when he left the Steelers' camp, and there were no openings. He did locate an opening to coach basketball, however, through an acquaintance from Kansas State who had just been promoted to principal at Beloit High School, in Beloit, Kansas.

Keady interviewed for the job, and accepted the offer two days later. School began just a few days after that.

Keady was used to long work days by then. He had been earning his keep in some form or other from the time he lived on the farm in Dighton. He had earned five dollars once for shoveling wheat for a few hours. Later he set up his own business. He bought 30 chickens for about three dollars, raised them, then sold them for about $100. He was fascinated by the profit-making process, but not motivated enough by money to continue to do it.

He went on to a varied, but unbroken, string of jobs after his family returned to Larned. Besides the sweeping job at the Electric Theatre, he worked at a radiator shop, at the greenhouse for his dad, at a lumber yard, for a plumber, and for the city, painting parking stripes.

At Garden City, he worked for a dairy, a feed yard and a stockyard. He even modeled clothing, for free, for a Topeka television station while at Kansas State.

Now that he was a member of the fulltime work force, the load was greater than ever. His first year at Beloit, over the course of two semesters, he taught classes in economics, general science, psychology, physical education and monitored two study halls. He also was the head basketball coach, the assistant football coach, the assistant track coach and the head golf coach.

Keady's salary for all his trouble was $4,200, not counting a $100 Christmas bonus that would be his last for many years. To help make all the loose ends meet, he also took a job at a local clothing store on Saturdays, for $10 a day, and played semi-pro baseball in the summer.

Teaching and coaching presented a baptism by fire. He was just

21 when he started, only three years older than some of his students. It was all he could do to stay one day ahead of them in preparing the lesson plans and practice schedules.

"You didn't have time to turn around," he said. "There wasn't any time to do anything but coach and teach. It was just a learning process. You just did it. You made your lesson plans out and went to the next class and pretty soon the day was out. The next thing I knew, seven years were gone. And I woke up one day and said, 'Hey, I'm not making any money here.'"

By then, 1964, he had just earned a masters degree in education from Kansas State and turned Beloit's basketball program into a state power. His first three seasons there had been losing ones, but his second team had pulled some late-season upsets and qualified for the state tournament with a 7-10 record, which kept the heat off from the community. His last three teams went 17-3, 21-2 and 20-1, and all qualified for the state tournament.

Keady's infant coaching style was drastically different than what it would become. He didn't emphasize defense much, and his teams often scored over 100 points. He gained a reputation as an offensive coach, and spoke at clinics about shooting.

But there was nothing loose and freewheeling about his discipline. Beloit was a small town, a near carbon copy of Larned, and the basketball team was a community enterprise. Keady regularly attended social gatherings with the players' parents after games and on holidays. It was a place where everybody knew everybody's business.

During his first year at Beloit, the vigilant rookie coach would grab his assistant coach, an older teacher named Blackie Lane, and head downtown on Saturday nights to make sure none of his players were breaking training rules. He wasn't catching anyone, though, and Lane finally convinced him to give it up. "This town's so small, Keady, that if any of the players are out doing anything, you'll know about it by Monday morning anyway," Lane told him.

Discipline problems were indeed rare, although Keady did catch a 6-7 junior who had been the team's sixth man the previous season smoking a cigarette downtown one summer. Keady kicked him off the team. Looking back, in view of all he has had to deal with since then, he wonders if he might have been a little hasty.

During his first few seasons at Beloit, Keady had applied for various head football coaching positions at some of the larger high schools around Kansas. Although he did take over the football team at Beloit one year on late notice when the previous coach unexpectedly quit at mid-summer—he remembers coaching it to a 6-1-1 record—he gradually resigned himself to basketball.

Keady's career took another step forward in 1964 when he landed a job at Hutchinson Junior College, in Hutchinson, Kansas. Again, connections pulled him through. Hutchinson's coach, Sam Butterfield, and president had both been at Garden City when Keady went to school there. Butterfield, impressed by his former player's success at Beloit, promised Keady if he got his masters degree he would bring him to Hutchinson as an assistant coach for one season and then retire and turn the job over to him. He kept his word.

Hutch had a tradition of success, but, like Purdue, it was somewhat handicapped by high standards. The university administration allowed just three out-of-state players on the basketball team, two fewer than most junior colleges permitted, which inhibited recruiting. It also required its athletes to take jobs to earn their scholarships, usually at a local dry cleaner or restaurant. Most junior colleges at that time gave athletes full rides—some even managed to pay extraordinarily well—without making them work.

Keady had to earn his keep, too. He still taught a full class schedule, first biology and then physical education, and served as the assistant football coach. In the meantime, he continued Hutchinson's basketball tradition. Butterfield had been a defensive-minded coach. Keady began incorporating that aspect of the game to his style and kept going. Over nine seasons, his teams won 187 games and lost 48, qualified for the national tournament (played on its home court) six times, and was runner up once.

By the end of that run in 1974, Keady, 16 years out of college, was earning all of $14,000. And he was growing increasingly frustrated by his inability to land a coaching job at a four-year college.

Keady finally found another connection after his ninth season at Hutch. Eddie Sutton, then head coach at Arkansas, had recruited one of Keady's players, Charles Terry. Keady also had known Sutton from playing against him in summer league baseball games a few years earlier. Sutton had an opening on his staff. Keady interviewed for it late in April, but didn't hear from Sutton for two months. Finally, he sat down and pecked out a three-page letter on the typewriter, explaining why he was the right man for the job. The day after Sutton received the letter, he called back and offered the job.

Keady, then 39 years old, was in hog heaven at Arkansas. Finally, he could concentrate all his energies toward coaching basketball. He didn't have to teach. He didn't have to coach anything else. And although recruiting was a primary responsibility, he he didn't have to jump into his car after practice, grab a sandwich, drive 100 miles to scout some high school player, get to the gym at halftime of the game, and then return home afterwards, as he had done so often at Hutchinson.

But Keady was barely less inhibited as an assistant than he had been as a head coach. Sutton jokes now that Keady is the only assistant coach he ever let get technical fouls. Keady also left his mark on the Southwest Athletic Conference referees off the court, displaying one of his primary coaching attributes: the ability to rip someone without turning them against him, by mixing brickbats with bouquets.

"I taught rules at Hutch," he recalled once, "so I knew the rules better than the Southwest Conference officials did. So I was on their ass. I would go out after the game and find them. Eddie didn't even know I did it. And I'd say, 'Hey, you assholes in this league don't know a goddamn thing about basketball, and what we need to do is end up getting this league better. I want one of you guys to be in the Final Four.'

"They'd be pissed off, but then a week later they'd see me at another game and say, 'Hey, you might be right.' And when I left there as an assistant, I had eaten dinner at five different Southwest Conference officials' homes with their familes. And two of them ended up in the Final Four after three years."

Keady also was a colorful whirlwind along the recruiting trail. Decked out in cowboy boots and the brightly-colored leisure suits that were fashionable at the time, he scoured the country in search of talent. He helped come up with three high school players, Sidney Moncrief, Marvin Delph and Ron Brewer, who would lead the Razorbacks to the Final Four in 1978. He also recruited, without success, a high school player at Collinsville (Illinois) High School named Kevin Stallings.

In 1977, after three seasons at Arkansas, Keady received from Idaho State his long-awaited chance to become a head coach at a four-year college. Keady flew to Pocatello for the interview, and, starved for the opportunity, bit on the job offer on the spot. But on the flight to Salt Lake City, where he was to catch a connecting flight back to Arkansas, he began having second thoughts. Idaho State was so isolated, and Keady just didn't see the potential to build a winning program. He called Idaho State's athletic director from the airport and told him he had changed his mind.

The athletic director was mad at him, Sutton was mad at him, and Keady was mad at himself. But the next year, Arkansas reached the Final Four and Keady came up with a better offer, from Western Kentucky. Weber, then 21, joined his staff as a graduate assistant. The Hilltoppers had a fine basketball tradition and played in a good mid-level league, the Ohio Valley Conference. Keady quickly made up for lost time, establishing himself as one of the game's top newcomers to the profession. His first team finished 17-11; his second went 21-8 and qualified for the NCAA tournament.

Keady also gained notoriety during the summer between his two seasons at Western Kentucky at the National Sports Festival, a tournament for high school players and college freshmen in Colorado Springs. Coaching one of the four teams there, he led his group to the championship with an undefeated record.

In April of 1980, Lee Rose left Purdue after coaching it to the Final Four, where it lost to UCLA and then beat Iowa in the consolation game. Rose's two-year stopover had been successful on the court, producing records of 27-8 and 23-10, but he had not fit in with the environment in West Lafayette. Rose was the "southern gentleman" type, a reserved, distant personality who struck the people around Purdue as too arrogant and slick for their tastes.

When Purdue's athletic director George King began his search for a replacement, he had a list of criteria. He wanted a middle-aged coach with a proven track record who would be comfortable in West Lafayette and who would not command a huge salary. He interviewed Bob Donewald from Illinois State, Ron Greene, then at Murray State, Neil McCarthy, then at Weber State, and Gene Keady, whose performance at the Sports Festival had caught the eye of another former Purdue coach, Fred Schaus.

Keady was interviewed at King's house, and knew immediately he wanted the job. The feeling was mutual. King called the next day, and Keady accepted.

Just short of his 45th birthday, he had reached the top of his profession. Persistence had paid off.

For Keady, the game at Wichita State, just two days after the win at Illinois State, would be a sentimental journey. Wichita, Kansas is about an hour's drive from Hutchinson and slightly more than two hours from Larned. Other than playing a game at Kansas State, it was the closest thing to a homecoming Keady could get.

Wichita State had been a distant voice in his ear throughout his life in Kansas. As a boy, he had listened to the school's football and basketball games on the radio. Coming out of Garden City, he had been offered a scholarship to play football there. While coaching at Hutchinson, Wichita State coaches had "rented" him a player for two years.

Not all of Keady's encounters with the university were honorable, however. Wichita State's athletic program has a squeaky-clean image now, but it sports a checkered past. It has been reprimanded or penalized by the NCAA seven times, dating back to the 1950's, and Keady unknowingly played a bit part in two of the episodes.

The football scholarship the Shockers offered him in 1956 included an illegal inducement: $100 extra cash per month, and free laundry service. That was a significant amount of money for a college student then, particularly one from Larned, but Keady didn't consider the offer; in fact, he didn't even mention it to his parents. One year later, Wichita State's football program was placed on probation.

Keady's experience with the school while at Hutchinson was a little messier. It wasn't, and still isn't, uncommon for a four-year college to recruit a player, send him to a junior college to gain his academic eligibility, and then bring him back two years later. Wichita State did that with Rudy Jackson, a star player from New York City, and offered him to Keady at Hutch. Jackson was the only player Keady ever had dropped in his lap at Hutch, and it turned out to be one too many.

Jackson was an instrumental player on Keady's most successful team at Hutchinson, one which finished as the runner-up in the national junior college tournament in 1973. But shortly after the season, it was discovered Jackson had never graduated from high school.

A Wichita State graduate assistant coach had persuaded a counselor at Jackson's high school to break into the registrar's office and steal a blank transcript. He then forged it and used it to gain Jackson's admittance to Hutchinson without Keady's knowledge. Technically, Hutchinson had to forfeit all of its games that year for using an ineligible player, although the school still recognizes the 29-4 record Keady's team accomplished.

Keady, an avid jogger in those days, recalls being so angry after he was told of the scam that he went out and stormed through a six-minute mile, about two minutes quicker than his normal pace. Wichita State was put on probation by the NCAA as a result of that mishap as well.

Most recently, its basketball team was declared ineligible for postseason competition in the 1982 and '83 seasons for other violations.

The only difference between Wichita State and some other colleges, of course, is that it has been caught while others have not. Nobody in college athletics debates whether or not cheating exists, only to what degree it occurs.

Lewis and Mitchell, veterans of many summer tryout camps for various teams that have represented the United States in international competition, were often spellbound by the stories they heard from players from other schools.

"There's two different sections," Mitchell said. "Some schools will cheat to get a player, and once he gets there the buck stops. The marriage is over. Then there's some that do both. I think they're the ones who never really win big, because their kids never have to work for anything.

"I heard one story about a player—there was this Christmas tournament and the coach told him if he got MVP in the tournament, he'd give him $100 for every point he scored. The kid turned out to be MVP and got four or five grand.

"And one guy I heard about checked into his apartment at the beginning of school and found a set of keys hanging from his mailbox with a note that said, 'Drive it in good faith.' There was a 280-Z sitting out front.

"But I think most of the cheating goes on in the summer jobs.

One kid said he worked for this stockbroker's place. He only came in twice a week. He came in on Mondays and Fridays. Every Friday he'd come pick up his check. He was getting like $600 a week. And then at the end of the summer he got a bonus check for like $2,000."

"I think more than half of the teams cheat—seriously," Lewis said. "At the great programs it's the nickle-dime things. At the others it happens more often. I've been overseas with different players and we all sit down and talk. It's verrrrry interesting. I'm like, 'What? You got what?'

"They get cars, shoes, gold rope chains, money, and clothes. Guys say, 'Man, I haven't paid for nothing since I've been here.' Or they might get meal money every day, like $40 or something like that. Or, when they take out recruits, oh, man, they get big bucks—$70 or $80; you're supposed to get $20."

Lewis, like Stephens and Mitchell, had come to believe college basketball players should be paid in return for all the money they make for other people. Purdue's basketball team would earn a profit of $2.1 million by the end of the season, but the players wouldn't share the wealth beyond the standard, although not insignificant, amenities—a free education, travel, first-rate meals and no small amount of glory.

The amount of money a university can legally pay a player who lives outside a dormitory varies, depending on the local housing costs. In a major city, it might run as high as $600 a month. At Purdue, the players received $256 a month to cover room and board. Their apartment rental was automatically deducted from that sum. Lewis and Mitchell, who shared an off-campus apartment, each paid $149 for their share of the rent, leaving about $100 to cover utilities and groceries.

Holding a part-time job during the season, of course, was impossible. For the players, the only means of self-support came from summer jobs, usually set up for them by the athletic department, for the standard labor wages of $7 to $10 an hour.

"You're broke all the time," Lewis said. "I talk to other players, and they get free food sometimes, or an apartment at half price. It's incredible. Like the apartment will say, 'Pay it when you want to.' I hear of guys with 7-11 charge cards and stuff like that.

"When you really look at it. . .you know how much money they make off a big game on national TV. Who are the people watching? They're watching us, you know.

"Coaches say, 'You're playing for the university, and it will be there when you're gone.' But why can't we get a little slice of the pie? The school gets this much. The TV network gets this much. Even with coaches, they get all this money from Nike or somebody, but who's wearing them? We are. We're the ones on national TV wearing Nikes, and we're not getting anything for it. We endorse the shoes on national TV. Nike's loving it. Nike's getting rich. What we get is an education. And that's worth something."

What Lewis wanted, however, was for the rules to be changed, not for them to be broken.

"I'd rather be at a clean program, because then you don't have to worry about it," he said. "Plus, everybody gets treated equal. When you hear stuff about what other players get, right then you're thinking, 'Man, I wish I had stuff like that.' But in the long run, if you're at a clean program, then you have nothing to worry about."

The good guys and bad guys in college basketball weren't easily distinguished, however. It had been Keady's experience that some of the coaches who cheated were nice men, and some of the coaches who didn't, weren't. Keady had agreed to a four-year, home-and-home series with Wichita State, which was now in its second year, when Gene Smithson was coaching the team. Smithson was later fired when the latest round of irregularity was discovered, but Keady remained friends with him.

Smithson, in fact, was one of the many friends who sought out Keady during Purdue's stay in Wichita, joining him when the team ate dinner at its hotel. As the two reminisced about various members of the coaching fraternity, a fraternity Smithson wanted very much to get back into, Keady recalled a line by Colorado State coach Boyd Grant, one of his closest friends.

"He said," Keady recalled, "the guys you think are jerks turn out to be great guys, and the guys you think are great guys turn out to be jerks."

Keady's contract with Wichita State, which called for alternating home court advantages over a four-year period, was unique among coaches at major programs. For a nationally-recognized team to play mid-level opponents such as Wichita State and Illinois State on the road is to court an upset. Most coaches would rather play another national power than a slightly less talented team on the road. Then, at least, a loss isn't as damaging.

But Keady, having been on the other side of the coaching fence for so much of his career, was usually willing to step into the fire. And Wichita State's fans, primed by their rare opportunity to meet up with a national power on their own turf, were more than happy to light one.

The Shockers' second-year coach, Eddie Fogler, had inspired a great amount of hope and excitement among the school's followers. A former assistant at North Carolina, he already had gained a reputation as one of the game's most promising young coaches.

A win over Purdue, then, would make all the hope and promise more immediate. The fans, 10,666 of them, filled Levitt Arena to the brim. As they always do at home games, they stood and clapped rhythmically to the beat of the pep band from the moment the starting lineups were introduced, and didn't stop until Wichita State scored its first basket.

Visiting teams are always intrigued by the notion of holding the Shockers scoreless for the first five minutes or so, just to see how long the fans can go, but Purdue didn't offer much of a test. Just 34 seconds into the game, Sasha Radunovich hit a jumper in the lane. The fans flooded the floor with streamers, then sat down to enjoy the show.

Keady was in midseason form. With just under four minutes left, and Wichita State leading 36-33, he jumped up to protest a foul on Mitchell. "C'mon, Keady, sit down," a man shouted from the stands nearby. "Kiss my ass," Keady said, not loudly. "C'mon Gene, you're getting every call," another man shouted. Keady turned around, smiled, and winked at the man. "You've gotta like a guy like that," the man said as Keady headed back to the bench.

Winning over the fans would be easier than getting a win over the Shockers, however. Radunovich hit both free throws off of Mitchell's foul to put them up 38-33. But two great plays by Stephens, following Scheffler's hook shot that cut the lead to three, brought Purdue back. First, on an inbounding play from underneath Purdue's basket, he soared through the lane to grab a pass from Lewis with one hand in midair and slam it through. Then he knocked the ball loose from behind a Wichita State dribbler, took a return pass from Tony Jones, drew a foul and hit one of two free throws to tie the game at 38. Wichita State was clinging to a 41-40 lead at halftime.

Purdue's momentum didn't carry over into the second half, however. It grabbed a brief lead on Lewis' baseline jumper midway through the half, then quickly fell behind again. And when Dwayne Praylow hit a three-pointer with 4½ minutes left to give the Shockers a 74-66 lead, the season's second loss seemed imminent.

Keady called timeout. The Wichita State fans sitting behind the Purdue bench began chanting, "You're overrated! You're overrated!" Purdue's players seemed dazed. "We're gonna lose this game!" Mitchell shouted in horrified disbelief. Stallings turned to him and offered a calm reminder. "Ten-four Game," he said.

The 10-4 Game was a favorite practice drill of Keady's. The White shirts were given a 4-0 lead and the ball, and the first team to ten won. The idea was to put the starters in a game-like situation and force them to play with poise and intelligence on every possession to pull out a win.

This was clearly one of those moments.

Lewis threw the ball away on Purdue's next possession, but Wichita State went cold. Mitchell hit a driving layup, Lewis two free throws, Tony Jones a driving layup and Kip Jones a swinging hook to tie the game at 74 with 1:10 left.

After Wichita State called timeout, Stephens made another great play: caught by a pick, he raced to block Joe Griffin's jumper with his left hand, then saved the ball to Kip Jones just before it went out of bounds. Purdue now could hold the ball for the final shot. But Wichita State played the odds and fouled Tony Jones, the sophomore who was getting one of his first tastes of final-minute pressure, with 24 seconds left. Jones had a one-and-one, but missed the first shot off the back of the rim.

Wichita State rebounded, and now had its chance to win the game in regulation. It worked the ball carefully, but Purdue's defense closed off the middle. With the clock ticking down, Griffin drove the lane, but Stephens blocked his path. Mindful of the blocked shot moments earlier, Griffin passed the ball back outside, then jumped out to take a return pass. He rushed a three-pointer over Stephens at the buzzer, but missed. Overtime.

Wichita State's fans repeated their pregame ritual, standing and clapping in rhythm as the overtime began. This time Purdue kept them up awhile longer. Radunovich missed the first shot of the overtime, and McCants rebounded. Mitchell later made a nice move across the lane to hit a left-handed layup and give Purdue the lead.

McCants had been nearly invisible in the first half, contributing not a single point or rebound. Keady reminded him of that fact—loudly—as soon as he walked into the locker room to join the players at the break. But now, McCants made two big plays back to back. First, he blocked Steve Grayer's layup out of bounds. Then, after Lewis stole the ball, he slid off a reverse pick underneath the basket, took a lob pass from Lewis, and hit a layup to return the lead to Purdue. The play was one Purdue's coaches had put in specifically for this game; ironically, it was one North Carolina had used when Fogler coached there.

Mitchell hit two free throws with 2:27 left to stretch Purdue's lead to four, then Lewis forced a jump ball on a loose rebound. The possession arrow pointed Purdue's way. It had a four-point lead and the ball with barely more than 90 seconds left. But Wichita State made one more run.

Mitchell was fouled and missed the front end of a one-and-one at 1:07, then Lew Hill hit an 18-footer to cut the lead to two with 43 seconds remaining. Wichita State called timeout to set up a fullcourt press.

Purdue got the ball upcourt, and began working the clock. The Shockers double-teamed the ball, frantically trying to force a mistake. Purdue obliged when, with 20 seconds left, Berning, who had just entered the game, threw a crosscourt pass that sailed over Lewis' head out of bounds.

Wichita State called timeout. It could now tie the game or win it with a three-pointer. Standing in the huddle, Brugos put his arm around Berning, who was shaking over his error. For Purdue, the game had come down to one defensive possession.

Dwayne Prayloh dribbled to his left across the three-point circle, but Lewis cut him off, so he passed back out to Radunovich at the three-point line. Radunovich, unable to find an open teammate, dribbled toward the basket and stopped from 15 feet out. McCants had him covered. He faked, but still had no shot. He then passed back to Prayloh, who, with Lewis hawking him, dribbled to his right and forced an 18-footer just ahead of the buzzer. It missed. Purdue had survived again.

The players instinctively ran to midcourt for an impromptu celebration, slapping hands and exchanging hugs. In retrospect, the
coaches couldn't have asked for a better script in the previous two
games. Not only did they get two victories, they got close games that
had welded the team's framework. Kip Jones, the new starter, was the
star of this game, scoring a career-high 21 points and hitting 9 of 10
shots. Mitchell added 18 points, nine rebounds and six assists. Scheffler, Tony Jones and Berning had all made key contributions off the
bench. And twice, at the end of regulation and the end of overtime,
the defense had held when it absolutely had to.

The celebration continued in the locker room. They had come
from behind to win two straight tough games, both in arenas where
many teams dare not tread. Suddenly, things were starting to come
together.

"How many did Kip get?" Lewis asked as the players undressed.

"Twenty-one," someone answered.

"Twenty-one?" Mitchell shouted. "Kip got some *big* numbers tonight!"

"I had to come back after that Illinois State performance," said
Jones, who had scored three points the previous game.

A few minutes later, as Mitchell made his way from the locker
room to the postgame press conference, a tall, slender man of about
40 stopped him in the hallway. "Hey, Todd. Good game, man," he
said. "My names's Bob Love. I used to play for Coach Keady in junior
college."

The two exchanged pleasantries, then parted. Mitchell took a few
steps, but stopped and turned around.

"Hey, Bob," he shouted. Love, who was heading toward Purdue's
locker room to find Keady, turned around.

"Was coach a bad mother back then, too?" Mitchell asked.

Love confirmed that he was.

The team could have flown home that night on its collective sigh
of relief. After all the dark days of October and November, December
was off to a promising start.

On chartered flights, the coaches sit in the back of the plane, and
the players up front. Keady always sits in a seat facing the rear. Pat,
who had not made this trip, usually sits across from him. The assistant coaches sit on a sofa across the aisle from Keady.

"Boy, that was a sweet one," Keady said as the plane leveled after liftoff. "They had us down and ready to put away, and we kept coming back. We never gave up."

He paused.

"Of course if we had, I would have killed them," he added, letting go with a devilish laugh.

Several minutes later, Stephens, who had played an uneven game, alternating brilliant plays with bad ones, walked back to where the coaches were sitting. Stephens was one of the most unique people Keady had ever coached. He was, if nothing else, one of the happiest players in the country, possessing a child-like charm and spirit that endeared him to everyone he met. An assistant coach at the University of Evansville, where Stephens had paid a recruiting visit while in high school, had actually cried a little while telling Stephens how badly he wanted to coach him for the next four years. Stephens believed it wasn't a put-on.

Most of the time, Stephens could barely contain the party that was brewing inside his head. His cackling laughter was a constant accompaniment to the season, and it was rare to catch him without a smile. He smiled during meetings, he smiled while running sprints, he even smiled—occasionally—while Keady yelled at him.

He wasn't always as tough as Keady wanted him to be, and his concentration was sometimes lacking, but Keady found it impossible to stay mad at him for long.

Stephens was smiling now, too.

"Scoot over," he said to Wood, who was sitting next to Stallings on the couch.

"Where do you want me to go?" replied Wood, who was squeezed in tight as it was.

"On the wing," Stephens said, grinning.

As Wood moved to his right a few inches, Stephens slid in between Wood and Stallings and flung his left arm around Stallings' shoulder.

"Hey, what have the coaches been saying about me?" he asked in a hushed tone.

Stallings was caught off guard. It wasn't often a player came to a coach with such a question, particularly when the other coaches were sitting within arm's reach.

"In regards to what?" Stallings asked.

"How I'm playing," Stephens said.

The two talked quietly for a few minutes. Stallings told Stephens the coaches were happy with his effort, but not with the execution or on-court leadership he had shown from his point-guard position.

"You know," Stallings said later, after Stephens had returned to his seat at the front of the plane, "I think there's been a significant change in our senior leadership."

The team arrived at the Purdue Airport shortly after 2 a.m. Waiting just off the runway was the Boilermaker Special, a truck converted to look like a steam engine. It was a mobile mascot for the athletic program, driven to home and away games as well as pep rallies and other university functions. The Reamer Club, a campus civic organization, was charged with its care.

One man, the only person greeting the team at this late hour, stood by it and sounded its train-like horn.

"Thanks for coming out," Kip Jones said to him as he headed toward his car.

"Thanks for winning," the man said.

The players were happy—and greatly relieved—to oblige.

6

Roller Coaster Ride

With Wichita State behind it, the worst was over for a few weeks. The next five games would be at home, and four of the opponents— Oregon, Colorado, Ball State and Texas Tech— did not figure to offer much of a challenge. Only Kansas State, on December 20, loomed as a real challenge before the team flew to Florida after Christmas for the Palm Beach Classic.

With victory virtually assured, improvement became a major focus of attention. Coaches generally put together their December schedules with just that in mind, lining up a string of relatively easy games, with a couple of tough ones thrown in for good measure, as a prelude to conference play. It's college basketball's version of spring training. The benefits are many: The starters gain confidence, the reserves gain playing time, the team gains wins.

Oregon turned out to be a perfect example. The Ducks had one outstanding player, guard Anthony Taylor, but he was hurt and missed the game. Without him, Oregon was not only a duck out of water, it was halfway in the oven as well.

The final was 88-62, and it was every bit that easy. Kip Jones was outstanding for the second straight game, scoring 17 points, hitting eight of nine shots, and grabbing eight rebounds, both team highs— all in just 26 minutes. Over the past two games, he had now hit 17 of 19 shots.

The game also marked the debut of the three walk-ons, Ewer, Fernung and Rea, who played one minute apiece. For Fernung, it was particularly memorable. He got off a three-point attempt that missed the basket by nearly a foot.

"Hey, Kory," Stephens shouted in the locker room afterwards. "You saw two rims up there, didn't you?"

"Kory thought that rim was *extra* big," Mitchell said.

Stephens put on a befuddled look and offered a joking explanation that Fernung might have given.

"I saw it moving, coach, I swear," he said.

It would turn out to be Fernung's last game appearance of the season.

With the next game, against Colorado, up just two nights later, the team returned the next night to the campus Union, where they meet on the eve of every home game. It's a standard part of Keady's pregame routine, a way of keeping the players off the streets and—hopefully—concentrating on the job ahead. It also is a basic element of his "Together-We attack!" approach.

After watching video and going over the scouting report for the next day's game with the coaches, the players were supposed to go to bed. That sometimes took awhile, however. For them, it was the next best thing to summer camp. If they weren't gathering in someone's room to talk, they were playing games of H-O-R-S-E with paper wads and a wastebasket, or marathon games of Monopoly. Rudd stayed overnight with them to play the part of counselor.

"We've got one week of school left," Weber said as the session broke up. "Make sure you take care of everything."

"Let's not have any surprises academically," Reiter said.

"How you doing with classes, Dave?" Keady asked Stack. "You OK?"

"Yeah, no problems," Stack said.

Keady couldn't say the same about the hours leading up to the Colorado game Monday night. That afternoon, after returning to Mackey from a booster club luncheon at which he and Colorado coach Tom Miller spoke, his car was hit on the highway.

The accident wasn't much worse than a fender-bender, but the news that awaited him in his office that evening before the game hit him a little harder. Waiting on his desk was a program for that evening's game. Inside it was a full-page ad featuring none other than Bob Knight, dressed in his customary red V-neck sweater, stumping for a financial services firm.

Keady, unamused, stormed down to the Sports Information Office to protest.

"It's ridiculous," he said. "We fight our ass off to get some publicity and this stuff happens."

Jim Vruggink, the Sports Information Director, took the matter to George King, who in turn approved the removal of the ad. The sports information staff, with help from its student volunteers, then frantically tore the offending page from all 1,800 programs before the game. It wasn't an unprecedented move. Schools often refused to accept advertisements featuring rival coaches. Indiana surely would have done the same for an ad featuring Gene Keady.

Purdue went on to rip Colorado, 72-54. But what might have appeared to outside observers as a routine win was a matter of renewed concern for the coaches. Purdue hit just 43 percent of its field goals and was outrebounded 41-31. Worst of all, they thought, the players had abandoned the offensive patience that had served them so well in the past few games; they counted seven consecutive possessions when shots were fired after one pass. And the plague of missed free throws had returned. Kip Jones missed all four of his attempts, Mitchell missed both of his and McCants hit just 1 of 4. The team percentage was 58.

The postgame locker room was strangely somber for a team that had just won its fourth game in a row, and by 18 points. But the coaches thought the margin of difference was more reflective of Colorado's ineptitude than Purdue's strength. Overall, they considered it a worse performance than the one in the loss to Iowa State.

Mitchell and McCants came in on their own early the next morning to shoot free throws. But the rest of the day wasn't as encouraging. "The Late Show" was gearing up for another run.

Kip Jones had been late for that afternoon's video session—there was no practice—because he misunderstood the starting time. He was told to run between 25 and 50 stair climbs. He ran 42.

Then, when the players gathered at 6:30 a.m. Wednesday for another special edition free throw practice, Reid was missing. Howat called him at his dorm and woke him up. Reid, panic-stricken, made it to the arena in four minutes, but not early enough to escape his punishment: 100 stair climbs.

That afternoon's practice began at 3:30. But Stephens didn't show up until 3:42, bringing with him a piece of paper and a sheepish grin. He had been stopped for speeding on his way to practice, going 42 in a 30 mile an hour zone. He also had left his driver's license at home. And he had a cracked windshield, which was a violation of safety codes. The officer told him he had rung up a bill of about $270 in fines, but let him off with a warning ticket and an order to fix the windshield. Stephens said later he wasn't sure if the policeman had recognized him as a basketball player or not.

Keady recognized him as late, however, and slapped him with his own fine: 100 stair climbs. With Arnold and Stack still running the stairs on occasion for their preseason troubles, the steps were threatening to become as crowded as the L.A. freeway. And by the time practice ended, Stephens probably wished he had been thrown in jail instead. It lasted three full hours, and was as rugged as any of the season.

Keady set the mood early in the workout when, dissatisfied with the spirit, he put everybody on the end line for a suicide.

The drills continued in quick succession. Fastbreak. Three-on-three halfcourt. Five-on-five fullcourt. When Berning got beat for two loose balls, Keady lined everyone up for a sprint.

Moments later, Kip Jones took his turn in the spotlight when he failed to set a pick properly. "Hold it," Stallings shouted. "Kip Jones, why is it always you? You go down and pick like this [Stallings imitated Jones' lackadaisical pick]. We've been talking about it all day. Why is it always you? Because you leave your watch and your ring in the weight room. Because you come late for meetings. You can't concentrate."

All that was left now was the daily round of free throws. Keady, eager to end practice on a cheerful note, picked his top ten eligible players to shoot, leaving the three walk-ons and Arnold and Stack on the sidelines. If they could hit 16 of 20 shots, practice was over.

Stephens hit one of two. So did Mitchell. Lewis picked up the pace by hitting both of his shots, but Reid put them in a hole by missing both of his.

They had already used up their quota of misses, with seven shooters left. Brugos kept them alive by hitting twice, but Tony Jones took them out of the running when he missed.

But Keady offered another way out. "Okay, Dave," he said, calling Barrett out. "If you hit two in a row, we don't run."

Barrett stepped to the line to encouraging cheers from his teammates. But he missed his first shot.

Keady tried again. All ten players would shoot again, only this time they had to hit 17 of 20. But the first three shooters, Reid, Brugos and Scheffler, each hit one of two, using up the quota of misses. Tony Jones hit both of his shots, but Berning missed his first shot to make it a moot point.

"Okay, we'll start over," an increasingly irritated Keady said. This time he started with the seniors, hoping to get off to a good start and build momentum. Stephens missed his first shot. Keady decided not to count it. Stephens then hit twice. Mitchell and Lewis each hit twice as well. Six-of-six. Kip Jones hit one of two, and McCants hit twice. They were nine of 10.

But the momentum was quickly lost in a pile of bricks. Berning missed, then hit. Scheffler missed twice. Tony Jones hit twice, but Brugos missed one of two. When Reid missed his first shot, they had fallen short again.

Keady, groping for a happy ending now, offered still another deal. "Okay, Dave, if you hit both, we're out of here. If not, we run."

It was his final offer. Maybe.

This time Barrett hit both. At 6:30, practice was over.

Thursday's practice began in sharp contrast to the previous day's purgatory. Keady was loose as the early arrivals shot around, trying a few three-pointers of his own and joking with the players. A few of them imitated his one-handed push shot behind his back, giggling.

The practice went smoothly until Brugos, frustrated by the lack of a foul call in a halfcourt scrimmage and then for being called out for not setting a pick, bumped Lewis hard with a moving screen. Lewis suffered a slightly hyperextended left elbow. Brugos smirked and mumbled something to Scheffler about that being the way they were going to have to play to please the coaches.

"What's so funny, John?" Weber shouted at the top of his lungs. "What are you laughing at?"

Weber, incensed by Brugos' latest display of attitude, grabbed him by his arms. "Get off the court, damnit!" he shouted.

Keady went a step further. He ordered Brugos to leave practice. The rest of the workout went smoothly, and ended with a rare accomplishment. The top ten players hit 17 of 20 free throws. There would be no sunrise service for free throws the next day.

The jolly mood carried over into the weight room, where Keady punctuated the workout with jokes and encouragement. Mitchell told him of one teacher's tough grading scale which required a score of 70 to get a D.

"That's the way it should be," Keady said. "When I was in school, the scale was 94-100 for an A, 86-93 for a B, 76-85 for a C and 70-75 for a D."

"Yeah, but in your day there wasn't as much to know," Lewis shouted from across the room. "They didn't even have computers then. There wasn't a man on the moon or nothing."

"Yeah, but we knew how to shoot free throws and pass the ball on a fastbreak," Keady said.

"You couldn't shoot jumpers, though," Stephens said with a smile, pausing to imitate Keady's one-handed push shot in exaggerated form, much to the delight of his teammates.

"Stephens, I'll shoot you right now for $100," Keady said.

Stephens quickly and dramatically pulled off his shirt, as if accepting the coach's fightin' words.

"Let's make it a car," he said.

"With speeding tickets included?" Stallings asked.

The workout continued amid much laughter and sweat. The tide had turned again—except for Brugos.

A year earlier, when Brugos was going through the same doldrums, Reiter had suggested he think about transferring to a less demanding program. Brugos, however, was adamant. He loved Purdue, he said. But now, nearly halfway through his sophomore season, he was continuing to frustrate the coaches with his ups and downs.

"You try because the kid has some talent," Stallings said at the next day's coaches' meeting. "You try to work with him, but then the kid doesn't even come close to meeting you half way, so you end up saying forget it."

"But he really has tried to do better," Wood said.

"That's why we've tolerated him," Keady said.

"He tried for ten days or so. But he can't do it anymore," Wood said.

"The last two days he's been horrible," Stallings said.

"Yes he has; you're right," Wood said. "But I'm saying he tried, and all that it takes to complete...."

"Quit talking about it," Keady said. "It's a waste of time."

Keady met with Brugos that afternoon after video. It wasn't often that he kicked a player out of practice—Brugos in fact would turn out to be the only one all season—but he would do it when he thought a player had gone out of his way to be belligerent. Stallings, in fact, held the honor of being the first player Keady had booted out of a practice at Purdue.

Keady took pride in not having a "doghouse" to store the players he was unhappy with; every day was a new day in his mind. But he was upset that Brugos hadn't stayed after practice to discuss the matter with him.

"Where were you yesterday after practice?" Keady asked Brugos.

"I went home back to my room," Brugos said.

"What the hell? Why would you go home when you just got kicked out of practice? Weren't you a little bit worried about getting back on the team?"

"Was I worried I should be back on the team?"

"Yeah. You just got your ass kicked out of practice. Don't you give a damn about your teammates?"

"No, that's not the reason why. I knew you were upset; I didn't want you to get more upset."

"Well, you were wrong. You don't tell people to take cheap shots, you understand that? That's bullshit. That's being a psycho, John! We don't operate that way around here. You cheap shot your own teammates? That's not right. I don't treat my players that way, you don't treat your teammates that way. And you know it. Why would you say that? You've got a screw loose. Now prove to me different. Get it tightened up."

"At that time, what did you want me to say, I mean. . . ."

"That you're wrong."

"I know I was wrong."

"Well, what are you going to do about not coming back last night?"

"What am I going to do?"

"Yeah. I consider it the same thing as being late."

"I don't know."

"I'll tell you tomorrow what I'll do. Out of here."

"OK. OK. Can I say something?"

"Sure."

"I didn't know . . . You told me to leave. I just went back home and started working on my homework. I didn't have anything better to do. I didn't know I was supposed to stick around. I have no example in the past that tells me, 'John, when you get kicked out of practice you stay here to see coach.'"

"I understand that. But I'd be worried if I was a player if my status on this team was still intact or not. I'd want to know, 'Coach, am I reestablished on this team?' It looks to me like you're walking off and saying, 'I don't care. I got kicked out of practice, so what?' That's the way I look at it."

"No, I just said, 'Well, tomorrow's another day.' I got in trouble. I didn't think you were going to kick me off the team for something like that. I mean, I went over in my mind what happened and evaluated it while I was sitting in the locker room. I thought, 'Well, I just screwed up. Come out tomorrow and play hard. There's nothing else you can do or say to make a difference right now.' I didn't even want to talk to you guys because I knew it was a hot subject."

"But that's what you should have done, faced the problem. Then it's handled and we're out of here, because I don't hold grudges. All right, get out of here, I'll talk to you about it tomorrow."

Scheffler, whom Brugos was whispering to when the boom was lowered, was waiting around the corner in the lounge to talk with Keady next. He was there to defend his former roommate.

"Steve, you got anything you want to say?" Keady asked.

"John, he had a couple of plays he thought he got bad calls," Scheffler said. "He went in, tried to be aggressive. When he was talking to me, I didn't think he was really serious. He wasn't whispering it to me, he was saying it out in the middle of the lane. He was flustrated. I see it from a different perspective than you guys do. I don't know what happened earlier in practice, but he was flustrated. He thought he tried to be aggressive, and then he was just being sarcastic. Like, 'Well, if they're not going to call a foul, let's go out and. . . .' I don't think he was totally serious about that. I mean, he wouldn't be talking right in front of the coaches in the middle of the lane. I don't think it was the right thing to do, but. . . ."

"OK," Keady said. "I accept that."

Keady never said another word about the incident.

Beating Ball State the next afternoon was easy. The Cardinals had a promising new coach, Rick Majerus, who had been successful at Marquette University, but not nearly enough talent. Purdue led 49-14 at the half, and won 96-47.

It was an all-around good time except for a few scattered exceptions. Kip Jones, after playing so well against Wichita State and Oregon, was struggling again. He had scored four points against Colorado, hitting 2 of 7 shots, and didn't fare much better against Ball State. He seemed to be trying too hard. On the game's first possession, he had caught a pass with his back to the basket and, in one quick motion, thrown up a shot while barely turning to look at the basket. It missed.

"A magician couldn't have done it," Weber would recall later.

A few seconds later, Lewis came in for a rare tongue-lashing, although Keady would have to eat his words. Keady, thinking back to the Colorado game, had placed great emphasis in the pregame talk on offensive patience and shot selection. He also had told the starters to run "30," a play to get Lewis open for a jumper, the first time they inbounded the ball from underneath their own basket.

So with 18:45 still left in the half, they ran "30." Lewis came off a pick on the perimeter and fired a three-pointer that missed. Keady, remembering his pleas for patience, but forgetting he had called the play, jumped up and sent Tony Jones in to replace Lewis.

Lewis hit a layup to give Purdue a 6-0 lead before Ball State called timeout at 18:19 and stopped the clock. Keady glared at him as he returned to the bench. Lewis, who hated being pulled from games to begin with, was especially distraught this time. His expression revealed his exasperation when Jones handed him his warmup.

"Are you questioning me?" Keady said, looking over his shoulder at him.

"Coach, you told me to shoot the ball off of '30' in the pregame talk," Lewis said.

Keady, realizing he had made a mistake, said nothing at the moment. He returned Lewis to the game shortly after play resumed, and apologized to him at the next timeout.

Stallings later would recall it as the earliest Keady had pulled a player from a game since 1982, when a forward named Michael Scearce had fired a bad shot from the corner off the opening tip at Minnesota, moments after Keady had devoted his pregame talk to patience and shot selection.

Keady was loose at halftime, befitting a coach with a 35-point lead. He apologized to Lewis, complimented Mitchell for his hustle, and addressed Jones' game-opening shot.

"Kip, just slow down, babe; you're OK," Keady said. "You've had some great games, you don't have to force everything.

"If you keep forcing things, you're going to force Berning into a starting position," he added, laughing.

The second half was a breeze, except for a few growing pains. During a timeout with 11:28 left, and Purdue leading 74-28, Keady once again stressed offensive patience and execution. On the first play when the game resumed, Reid passed up an open jumper, then took a return pass, dribbled and missed a forced shot.

Keady stood up. "Troy!"

Lewis was already in motion toward the scorer's table before Keady got his name out.

"I know," he said, laughing.

Reid lasted long enough to make a nice pass to Berning for a layup before play stopped and Lewis took his place. Frustrated by his mistake, he grabbed a towel and slammed it to the floor as he sat down.

Stallings kneeled in front of him. "You do not come out of a game and throw a towel or you might not see the floor for three months," he said quietly, but firmly. "He told you at halftime not to dribble and shoot. You passed up a good shot and took a bad shot."

Thirty seconds later, Reid was back in for Lewis. Less than a minute after that, he caught the ball at the top of the key and, without hesitation, swished a jumper.

The frustration only continued to mount for Brugos, however. Entering the game with 7:56 left, and Purdue leading 83-34, he immediately got beat on the baseline for a layup. Keady called timeout and chewed him out, but left him in the game. Brugos finished with six rebounds, but his mistakes were far more obvious: four turnovers, two fouls and a missed shot.

After the postgame huddle, Brugos returned to his locker, sat down and put his head in his hands. He sat motionless for several minutes, pondering all that had gone wrong during the week.

Stephens and Kip Jones walked over and offered brief consolation. Keady, making the rounds to shake hands with the players, stopped by with some advice, too: "Get a haircut, Johnny," he said. "Hear me?" Brugos, still staring at the floor, nodded his head.

At the other end of the locker room, Stallings knew something of what Brugos was feeling. While playing for Rose, Stallings said, he had once been pulled from a game four times within a four-minute span—the final time with one second left in the game.

So maybe it could have been worse for Brugos. But at the moment, it didn't seem like it.

Not only were they now 6-1 and coming off a good performance, they had seven full days to prepare for the next game—the anticipated difficult game—against Kansas State.

That gave Keady ample time to devote to one of his least favorite, but more time-consuming pastimes: rumor-denying.

A story in the December 15 edition of the *Chicago Sun-Times* caught his eye and raised his ire—only mildly, however, because he had grown used to it by now. Amid a roundup of items relating to college sports, there was this familiar subhead: "Keady rumor."

The story read:

"Purdue coach Gene Keady insists there is no truth to the rumor that he wants out, that it is too difficult to recruit against Indiana and he is tired of living in the shadow of Hoosier coach Bob Knight. But the rumor won't die.

"Keady applied for the Arizona job that went to Lute Olson and his name pops up for every major vacancy. The latest rumor? Keady may move to Kansas if Larry Brown leaves to become coach of the new NBA franchise in Charlotte.

"'Gene is tired of competing with Knight,'" one observer said. "'If Knight wants a player, he'll get him. Gene has lost too many good players. For some unexplainable reason, it has been hard for him to recruit at Purdue. He simply hasn't been able to get the best players. Losing Eric Anderson [to Indiana] and Ron Curry [to Arizona] this year really upset him.'"

The story went on to mention that two of the top three juniors in Indiana, Chris Lawson and Pat Graham, were already conceded to Indiana, and that Keady was hoping to land one other underclassman, Greg Graham, and two unsigned seniors, Woody Austin and Chris Lovelace.

The article had about as many mistakes as it had paragraphs. As for this latest rumor that he wanted out of Purdue, it had no known source other than the article itself. Keady also had not applied for the job at Arizona, and it was unlikely he would ever coach at Kansas, the arch-rival of his alma mater, Kansas State. And while Keady had endured some frustrations competing against Knight over the past seven years, he was more enthused by the challenge of stiff competition than tired of it. The article also was wrong about Pat Graham, who at that time was still undecided. And Keady obviously hadn't been unable to persuade Austin to sign in November.

Keady called the story's author, Taylor Bell, to sound off. Bell said he had only been speculating.

"What's the problem?" Keady said. "You guys act like it's a sin when a guy's happy."

Keady had long grown weary of defending his happiness at Purdue. He was comfortable with the campus and community, he got along well with his superiors, he loved coaching in the Big Ten and he was steadily building a national power. He had been frustrated by recruiting on occasion, and the NCAA tournament was becoming a sore point, but that was true for most coaches; changing jobs wouldn't necessarily change that. Still, the rumors that he wanted to leave Purdue had taken on a life of their own the past few years. It seemed his name became magnetically linked with every coaching position that came open. Purdue's coaches found that the rumors often became part of the recruiting sales pitch used by competing coaches. As in, "You don't want to go to Purdue, Keady's not going to be there much longer."

Keady had listened to several overtures from other schools the past few years, but never came close to accepting any of them. Arizona State (not Arizona) had called once. He was attracted by the climate in Tempe, but was turned off by the university's financial package and the fact it could only offer coaches one-year contracts by decree of the state legislature.

Ohio State wanted him badly when Eldon Miller was fired after the 1985-86 season. With minimal recruiting competition from the other Ohio colleges, it was an intriguing opportunity. But Keady didn't feel comfortable jumping to another Big Ten school.

Kansas State's athletic director had called once, too, saying he was under pressure from his alumni to hire Keady, but couldn't match Keady's salary at Purdue. That shortened the conversation considerably.

Houston and USC also had made inquiries. And he had met with the general manager and assistant general manager of the NBA Indiana Pacers in 1984 about coaching there, but the discussion never grew serious. Besides, Keady's instincts told him he wasn't suited to coach in the NBA.

Keady wasn't trying to go anywhere at the moment, except forward. And Kansas State figured to provide a worthy roadblock. The Wildcats had lost their two most recent games, but had won their first five. The coaches figured they would be at least as good as Iowa State.

Keady reluctantly agreed to try a different starting lineup for the game. As a coach who valued stability and consistency, he wasn't one to juggle his lineup unless he felt it was absolutely necessary. But Stallings had been suggesting he start Scheffler instead of Kip Jones for one game. Scheffler had shown continued improvement, scoring ten points in 19 minutes against Ball State and 11 points in 16 minutes against Oregon. Jones, meanwhile, had struggled since the Oregon game.

The idea was not only to reward Scheffler, but give him a taste of starting experience. If someone got hurt later in the season and Scheffler had to start, the experience now would prove beneficial.

The problem was, Scheffler didn't want to start, and Jones did. Scheffler felt more comfortable watching the beginning of the game from the bench, where he could ease into the action mentally. Jones, being a junior, thought his time had come and that he deserved the opportunity. He didn't feel comfortable coming in off the bench, because he worried that his first mistake would put him right back on it. He also had seen his playing time drop from 395 minutes as a freshman to 310 minutes his sophomore year, and feared the possibility of another season in exile if he lost his grip on his job now.

Jones had come to Purdue a highly-regarded recruit. He averaged 30.1 points and 13.8 rebounds per game as a senior at Bellmont, was chosen one of the top 40 high school players in the country by *USA Today*, and was selected to play in the prestigious McDonald's All-America Game. He had further enhanced his reputation with a standout performance in the Indiana-Kentucky high school all-star series.

But college basketball was turning out to be somewhat of a culture shock for him. In high school, where he was the best athlete in virtually every game he played, he had been allowed to roam wild and free. At 6-8, and blessed with a quickness and aggressiveness that seemed to come from a spring wound too tightly, he had been able to do just about whatever he wanted.

But while his game had improved in many ways since he arrived at Purdue, his confidence had declined. A respectable shooter from around 15 feet in high school, he had been nervous his first few weeks of practice and shot poorly, and therefore quickly lost the confidence of the coaches. Now, two years later, he had become what he never could have envisioned in high school: a role player. His job was to rebound, set picks, play defense and shoot nothing more adventurous than a layup or short—very short—jumper.

His performance at the free throw line seemed almost symbolic of the decline he felt in his game. He had hit 70 percent of his foul shots as a sophomore in high school, 67 percent as a junior, 62 percent as a senior, 53 percent as a freshman at Purdue and 49 percent as a sophomore. The slide was continuing this season. He had hit just 5 of 21 free throws in the three intrasquad scrimmages and the exhibition, bounced back to hit 9 of 14 the first five regular season games, but had hit just two of his last nine.

But the game worked out just fine, for nearly all of them. Purdue won, 101-72, putting together what the coaches thought was the best overall performance of the season. Scheffler, nervous from the start, fouled out in just 15 minutes without scoring a point, which put him back where he wanted to be, on the bench. Kip Jones, regaining his starting spot by the beginning of the second half, scored nine points in 25 minutes, despite hitting just 1 of 5 free throws. Mitchell scored 22 points in 27 minutes, hit all ten free throw attempts, and held Kansas State's leading scorer, Mitch Richmond, to 14 points, eight below his average.

It was a memorable game for most of the reserves as well. Tony Jones scored a career-high ten points, hitting 5 of 6 shots. Berning scored six points, hitting all three shots and grabbing six rebounds. Reid had two points and three assists. Brugos tipped in the game's final basket to put the team over the century mark. Ewer scored his first collegiate points, faking and hitting a short jumper. And Rea almost got his, but blew a left-handed layup at the buzzer.

"Man, that's the first time my arm ever got heavy," he said, laughing in the locker room afterwards.

Stephens congratulated Ewer on his basket.

"I almost started to go up, you faked so good," he said.

Scheffler and Kip Jones were laughing as well, each grateful to have regained the position he wanted.

"Gentlemen, that's about as much improvement as we've shown in any game this year," Keady said.

The win was quietly notable for one other player: McCants. In the four games since the one at Illinois State, his play had dropped off considerably; he averaged just 8.5 points and 3.5 rebounds during that stretch. But he had seemed almost rejuvenated against Kansas State, scoring 19 points and grabbing five rebounds in 25 minutes.

McCants knew the reason for both the start and the end of his troubles: academics. As final exams approached, the academic burdens began weighting down his basketball performance as well. But finals had ended two days before the Kansas State game. And when he learned a couple of hours before the tipoff that he had received a B in one of his classes, his spirits were lifted even higher.

McCants grew up in inner city Chicago, on the southwest side. The surrounding neighborhoods had no official names, but were well-known to the residents by nicknames. One area was called "The Dog Houses," another "The Village," and another "The New Homes."

McCants lived in the "New Homes" section. His parents never married, so, although he stayed in contact with his father, he was raised by his mother, Catherine, and his maternal grandmother, Verna. He is so close to his grandmother that he still calls her "Momma," and his mother "Cat."

Both women provided strong influences over him and did their best to protect him from the evils of inner city life. When a coach from a local Catholic high school, Mt. Carmel, saw him play in a summer league tournament as an eighth grader and encouraged him to enroll there, they went along with the idea. It would mean a safer environment, and a better education.

Mt. Carmel won the Illinois state championship during McCants' senior year, but he emerged with more than a ring and scholarship offers. He also had gained the desire to earn a college degree, something nobody on his mother's side of the family, and only a few on his father's side, had ever done.

The poverty that McCants grew up with, however, provided poor preparation for any budding college student. The elementary school he attended near his grandmother's house was not equipped to get a student off on the right foot, and he had been a step behind ever since.

Each semester at Purdue had proven to be a struggle for him. He invariably dropped a class or two, and then picked up the lost hours in summer school. More than once, the coaches had held their breath on the day grades were issued, fearing they might lose their starting center.

But he was maintaining his eligibility with some hard-won victories in the classroom. McCants, by his own estimate, had missed no more than five classes—aside from those he missed while on road trips—in his first 2 1/2 years at Purdue. And one of those occurred when he stayed after class to talk with a professor and arrived at his next one after it had started; not wanting to draw attention to himself by walking in late, he skipped it. Shyness was the only motive that could overpower his responsibility. On the whole, he probably put more effort into his classes than anyone on the team.

McCants displayed the same work ethic on the basketball court. He was an ideal player from a coach's standpoint, a blue-collar worker who showed up every day with a smile on his face and quietly went about his business. And now that finals were over, the smile was brighter than ever.

McCants played well again two nights later in an 82-59 win over Texas Tech, contributing 19 points and nine rebounds in 26 minutes. But the coaches viewed the game much like they did the one against Colorado—a facade, with an impressive front of a final score, but little in the way of good play to support it.

Keady got his first glimpse into the future when he returned to the locker room for his final pregame talk. All the players were still warming up, except for Stephens, who had left the floor early to take care of some emergency business in the bathroom.

"What's wrong with you, Everette?" Keady asked.

Stephens' smile gave him away. He often snacked on chocolate-covered raisins before games. Apparently the laxative effect of the raisins had taken their toll this time.

"I pulled up for a jumper from 20 and something said, 'Oh-oh, you better go to the bathroom,'" he said.

Stephens had to make another emergency run to the bathroom

less than two minutes after tipoff, as he excused himself during a dead ball and ran up the tunnel to the locker room. Tony Jones replaced him.

His teammates, meanwhile, sputtered, running off to a 6-2 lead, falling behind 9-8, regaining an 18-9 lead, then having that cut to four. Reid hit a three-pointer—his first of the season—just before the buzzer to boost the lead to 12 at halftime, but the coaches weren't soothed. Too many turnovers. Too many missed free throws. Too many offensive rebounds allowed. Too much standing on offense.

Keady was frustrated by the pattern the season was taking. Whenever he cracked down, the players responded and played well. When he congratulated them on playing well, they let down and played poorly the next game. When he cracked down, they played well again. Now, coming off a good performance against Kansas State, they had slumped again.

"Every time I kick a wastebasket and raise hell and cuss you, you guys come back and play," he told the players. "Why does it take that? I don't understand that."

The second half wasn't much different. Spurred by the locker room jolt, they outscored Texas Tech 10-2 at the start of the half to take a 20-point lead. From there, the game plodded along listlessly toward its conclusion.

Finally, during a timeout with 3:40 left, and Purdue's lead at 78-49, Keady resigned himself to another one-sided but unimpressive victory.

"Scheff, get in for Mel," he said. "Way to go, Mel. Anybody who gets two A's, two B's and a C deserves a standing ovation."

Keady paused, realizing he had found *something* worth cheering about.

"So let's give him one right now," he said.

The five players in the game stood up from the chairs that had been placed on the floor for the huddle and joined their teammates in a round of applause for McCants.

Keady's locker room report card wasn't as glowing.

"We've got to work to get a lot of things ironed out," he said. "I know you blew them out and I should be happy, and I am happy for you. But we've got too many guys who have too many lapses of concentration. It's got to be a situation where you're the best physically fit team in the league and the most mentally tough. I'm going to tell you, everytime somebody plays defense a little bit, we stand around.

"I want you to have a good Christmas and have a nice time with your family at home for the next three days. But when you come back, you better be ready to go to war. I don't like what happened last summer; you were a better team and didn't get what you deserved. And you were better people and didn't get what you deserved. But it's going to end up the same damn way if you don't stay hungry. You've got to get yourself in a state where nobody's going to beat you because they give a better effort.

"You've done a helluva job here for three years, you seniors. But I don't think you're mentally tough yet, and I don't think you're going to be mentally tough unless somebody draws it to your attention. Because you've got too many people around you telling you you're great. But you can be better. You can be a helluva team, but you're not there by a long shot."

The players dressed in silence. It was another win that felt like a loss. In seven days they would play Wake Forest in the Palm Beach Classic in Florida. Last season's holiday tournament had provided one of the major low points of the season, a 13-point loss to North Carolina that wasn't really that close.

Finally, Stephens spoke up. "Hey, you guys, we've got to come back ready to play," he said. "We ain't going to lose no more Christmas tournaments. Let's come back hungry."

Mitchell smiled. "I know I ain't going to eat anything," he said.

A few moments later, Weber issued another warning.

"You guys need to go to the ramp and sign autographs," he said. "We don't let people back here for a reason, but that doesn't mean you sneak out the back door. Sign the autographs."

Stephens, already tired and frustrated, gave Weber an exasperated look. Weber glared back at him.

"What are you looking at me for?" Stephens asked.

"Because you looked at me funny," Weber said.

"Coach, I'll sign the autographs," Stephens said, a rare hint of anger in his voice.

"Don't talk to him that way," Stallings said.

Stephens sighed. "I'm sorry, coach," he said.

Lewis, lacing up his shoes, rolled his eyes.

"Man, did we win or what?" he said quietly.

Whether it was the rest, the realization that the Big Ten season was less than a week away, or the intense post-Christmas practice sessions, the team reached a new peak in the first half of play against Wake Forest, jumping to a 46-23 lead.

Lewis was brilliant, hitting 8 of 10 shots, including 7 of 9 three-pointers, on his way to 23 points. He owed his performance in part to some timely forgetfulness. He had left the plate he was wearing in his shoe to protect his injured foot at home when he returned for practice after Christmas. He decided to go ahead and try to play without it, and found it took a load off both his foot and his mind.

Stephens also excelled the first half, with eight points, five assists, two steals and a blocked shot. His only missed shot came on a breakaway slam-dunk, when he hesitated and bounced the ball off the back of the rim.

"I couldn't decide if I wanted to dunk like Dominique Wilkins or Michael Jordan, and I ended up dunking like John Brugos," he explained at halftime.

But the game turned out like the season had gone so far. With Lewis getting special attention from Wake Forest's defense, Purdue sat on its cushion and watched it dwindle to the bare threads. With 3 1/2 minutes still to play, Wake Forest had stormed back to within five points, an 18-point turnaround in less than 18 minutes.

The lead was still five with a minute left to play, but Tony Jones hit two free throws, Wake Forest missed four shots on its next possession and Stephens came back with two more free throws to seal the win.

Keady called the first half as good a performance as he had seen at Purdue. But the second half brought more of the same questions. His team had been outrebounded by 14. And Mitchell had been sporadic, scoring 12 points and fouling out after just 25 minutes.

Something else troubled the coaches. As the players left the locker room at halftime, Mitchell's father had leaned over the railing above the door and yelled for his son's attention. He then moved his arm as if shooting a ball; he was telling Todd to shoot more.

That brought up a touchy subject that had first come up the previous season. Charlie Mitchell, the proud parent who wanted his son to have a professional career, thought Todd Mitchell should shoot more. Gene Keady, the demanding coach who wanted his team to win, thought Todd Mitchell should play close to the basket and take his shots within the structure of the offense. They were two headstrong, self-made men who saw things from a different perspective.

The previous season, when the team played in a holiday tournament in Dallas, the conflict had nearly boiled over. During a workout the day before the game against North Carolina, which several alums and parents attended, Keady had cussed at Mitchell for not playing hard. Mitchell responded by viciously dunking the ball on the next play. Keady took it as a display of sarcasm, and lined everyone up for a sprint.

Mitchell's father confronted Keady over the incident after the workout.

"What did you call my son?" Mitchell remembers him asking Keady. "Todd says you called him a prick."

"What?" Keady said. "I might have said he was acting like a prick, but I didn't call him one."

Later that day, after the team returned to the hotel, Mitchell had to talk his father out of going to Keady's room to continue the discussion.

Now the different perspectives of father and coach were coming out again. Keady, who had heard about Charlie Mitchell's advice secondhand after the game, addressed the issue at the next afternoon's meeting.

"It's always amazing to me how some guys when their parents are around are affected by their influence," he said. "I was the same way. It seemed like I always played better football when my parents didn't come to the games.

"It's always been amazing to me, but sometimes the parents get you to thinking things that aren't good for the team. Or good for you. You've got to learn to say, 'Yeah, dad,' then shut them out and do what the coaches want.

"It's not so important what we want done, it's that we do it together. And that's what the key to this team is going to be, team togetherness. It's a matter of you admitting you've got a problem with concentration, and with accepting your role. Some of you, I can tell by your body language that my assistants turn you off. By the way you breathe, by the way you react, I can tell. It's bullshit. Accept it, do something about it. They can tell things about you that will help you. Just listen and go try to do it.

"It's along the same lines as an alcoholic. Guys who never admit they have a problem can't lick it. And then they get worse and worse and finally their liver goes and they die. But the guys who say they have a problem cure it and have a great life. That's where some of you guys are at now."

Whether it was from his father's advice, Keady's or his own inspiration, Mitchell responded in the next night's championship game against Miami with his best performance of the season. He scored 17 points and grabbed six rebounds in just 15 minutes of the first half, as Purdue streaked to a 66-31 lead and did what the coaches didn't think was possible: play better than it had against Wake Forest.

Their fastbreak was awesome. They also outrebounded Miami, with its 7-1 center, Tito Horford, 31-11, shot 58 percent from the field and committed just six turnovers.

If anything could bring a team together that was it. One play stood out as symbolic. Berning, the skinny white kid whose game was based on his outside shooting ability, took the ball to the basket on a fastbreak and dunked over a Miami defender. As he ran downcourt for defense, an impressed Lewis said, "Damn, Ryan, way to get up!"

Now, the question was if they could stay up for the second half as well.

"I think you should go in there and tell them we will practice until midnight if the same thing happens tonight as what happened last night," Stallings told Keady as the coaches met outside the locker room. "That's what I would do."

"Todd was a bitch," Reiter said.

"Why doesn't he do that every game? That's unbelievable," Keady said.

"Say that, coach," Stallings said. "Say, 'You were sensational, but why don't you do that every game?'"

"'And you *can* do that every game,'" Wood said.

"'And you *have* to do that every game,'" Stallings said.

Keady took his assistants' suggestion.

"Todd Mitchell, if you play like that the rest of the season, I can't believe where we'll be," he said after rejoining the players. "You'll be in Kansas City. And there's no reason you can't play like that every minute for the rest of your career. There's no reason. You did a great job."

A few minutes later, Keady called for the huddle to send them back to the floor.

"Did you learn anything last night?" he asked.

"We'll find out," Lewis said.

"Hey, let's play it like we're ten down, man," Mitchell said. "Forget what the score is."

"Hey, guys, you're over a third of the way through the season," Keady said. "This baby's going fast. Tonight you got better, but you've got to get better yet. We need three out of four great halves down here. We've gone south for training camp, now we're going to go back and see what we can do after we play a good second half here.

"Tomorrow night, I tell you, if you play like you did the second half last night, we're going to practice when we get home. If you play like you did the first half, we'll go home, have New Year's Eve and then get ready for the Big Ten. And I don't want to be on the practice floor."

"Let's don't practice, fellas," Lewis said.

Miami made a couple of brief runs in the second half, but could get no closer than 23 points. The final was 110-82. Mitchell finished with 26 points and nine rebounds in 27 minutes, and was named the tournament's Most Valuable Player. Stephens and Lewis also made the all-tournament team. To say the least, there would be no midnight practice when they got home.

"Man, way to play," Keady shouted as he entered the locker room. "Huddle up, guys. That's a great start for the Big Ten. We played for about, oh, 38 minutes anyway.

"Together!"

"We attack!"

"Hey, fellas, listen up," Stephens said, calling his teammates back together. "It was great that we won this tournament. We came out, and we were hungry. We did what the coaches wanted us to do. And most of all, we did what we wanted to do: We had some fun."

The players started to scatter again, but Mitchell called them back.

"Hey, let me tell you something," he said. "Hey, man, the real shit happens on the fourth. The real shit."

"Hey, they [Illinois] want us bad, man," Stephens said. "We got to go in there hungry. Hey. They want us bad. We got to go over there together."

"Together," Lewis shouted.

"We attack!"

Keady, meanwhile, was on his way to the postgame press conference.

"I feel good about the team now," he told the reporters. "I hadn't before tonight. I was very frustrated about the valleys and peaks we had. I think maybe we found a little bit of chemistry tonight."

Troy Lewis

"My older brothers [Kendrick and Scotty] are as good an athlete as I am. But when I was young, I think I fantasized more than they did. I'd lay in my room and read a baseball book and see myself playing in the major leagues. And when I was playing basketball, I'd be in the street and challenge people. 'Can you stop me? I want to do this to you. Try to stop me.' I wanted to make someone look like a fool. That was my whole attitude. I always tried to say, 'I want to be on the team, yeah, but I want to be the best guy.'

"I'm pigeon-toed, and my father and brothers used to ride me hard about it. Whenever we would get together, when I was little, it was always me. They rode me hard. And I'd say, 'Yeah, but I'm better than you are in this.' I thought it was good being different.

"We had a lot of adversity growing up. Our house caught on fire when I was in the second grade. They said it might have been my fault. My brother and I were having a pillow fight and I knocked over a lamp. It was laying on a pillow. Then my mom [Julia] called us down to dinner. The lamp might have started the fire, but they said it might have been wiring, too. My little brother [Rico] was upstairs in his crib and almost died.

"My mom hurt her back once, and had to go on disability. Then that stopped, and she was on social security. There were times we didn't hardly get anything for Christmas. Maybe a pair of shoes or something. My grandfather was working, so maybe he gave us something. But we never complained about it, because we knew that was the best she could do. My mother would give up her last dollar if I said, 'I need a dollar.' She wouldn't say nothing about it.

"My grandfather helped out my mom many times. He kind of became like a father figure when my parents got divorced. He doesn't take anything from nobody. He always gives. He always gives. Like he'd come home from work and be real tired, and I'd say, 'I want a bacon and tomato sandwich,' and he'd get up and cook it no matter how tired he was.

"I started playing basketball in the seventh or eighth grade, but didn't realize that I could play college basketball until I was a junior in high school. Shooting just came natural to me. Nobody ever taught me. I watched a Red Auerbach halftime show when I was little. They had Bob McAdoo on there. Auerbach said if you have backspin on your ball, it will go in. McAdoo was shooting and Red Auerbach was saying if it hits the rim, it most likely will go in. We had a basketball goal. So I went out and started doing it. I used to shoot from my hip and stuff. But I had decent success.

"I didn't really get a shot until I was in the seventh grade. I had this seventh grade teacher, he taught biology, and he was the coach, too. He said we had basketball tryouts in two weeks, and I was scared because I didn't know how good I was. I've always had that fear of how good I really am. I told him I shot the ball down here. And he told me, 'Well, you're going to have to shoot from up here if you're going to make the team.' I thought, 'Oh, God.'

"I went home that night and stood in my room practicing my form, a hundred times, all night long. The same with left-handed lay-ups, just doing them over and over. Then we had tryouts and he called me out. He said, 'Here's how I want you to shoot.' I was surprised. I was in front of *everybody*. But I hit like ten in a row. I was just hitting it. I was like, 'Dang!' I couldn't believe it.

"Baseball was always my favorite sport when I was growing up. Basketball was just something to do in the winter. But I remember watching the state tournaments on TV when I was growing up, and watching them cut down the net after the game and seeing everybody rush the floor. That's what I thought it was all about. I thought that was it. I didn't even think of college then.

"Then in 1981, when I was a freshman, my brother played in the state finals. That's when I knew it was what I wanted to play. I couldn't stop thinking about how lucky they were.

"My junior year, we were playing Gary Wallace in the semistate. There was five seconds left and I was standing at the halfcourt line and it hit me. 'Man, we're going to the state finals!' It was the greatest feeling in the world.

"I got 42 points in the afternoon game of the finals, and 34 in the final game. I missed a last-second shot that would have won the championship game. It was a 15-footer, with a hand in my face. Surprisingly, I went straight to sleep after the game. I guess because I was so tired from having played in the afternoon. But later on it was always in the back of my mind. My whole frame of mind was that I would come back next year, we could still win it again. But now it haunts me a lot more. I think about it a lot even now.

"My senior year we lost in the afternoon game of the semistate to Lake Central. I had a last-second shot again from about 30 feet, with four guys on me. I thought it was going in, but it rimmed out.

"It was funny. When we came back, they had us sit up on this platform in the gym for a pep rally. I had told myself I was going to keep my composure. But I was sitting there and I looked, and we had this one guy, Darnell White, who was really big and rarely showed any emotion. I looked over there and he was crying. I thought, 'Geez.' My best friend was crying, and another guy in my class was crying. I thought, 'Gollee, I wanted this just as bad as they did.' Yeah, I started crying. I had planned not to, but I just couldn't hold it in. That's when it hit me. It was my last game. My last game.

"I don't know how I'll feel when this season ends. It depends on where we end up at. Coach is right. You think you're going to play forever, but it's going to end one day.

"I always had that fear of whether or not I could prove myself in college. I didn't want to come to Purdue and be a total flop and have to go back home. You wouldn't believe the pressure you have going back home. They ride you so bad. Bobby Wilkerson [who played at Indiana] came back after he got cut from the pros. We'd be playing at the Boy's Club and they were ripping him up. 'You ain't no good, you ain't no good.' They got on Ray Tolbert [who also played at I.U.] like that, too, when he got cut. It's just unbelievable. There's so much pressure when you go back home to play. It's all black people. They just like to get on you. They're serious, too. As soon as you're out, you're a bum. I mean, Bobby Wilkerson lasted eight years in the NBA with no jump shot. Give him a little credit.

"The coaches don't understand sometimes. You feel like saying, 'We have problems, too, coach. We *do* have problems.' I might be worried about paying the gas bill or something. Or I'm worried about buying my family some Christmas presents. Sometimes they don't think we have problems, but that's just coach. Coach is like, 'You've got all your life to do those other things.' Well, you never know. You might get hit by a train tomorrow. Life goes on after here. I can't just sit here and say, 'Well, I'll just play basketball, and then when I get done I'll get myself together.' I know he doesn't mean anything by it. But sometimes when I come to practice, I do have something on my mind, you know? Something could have happened at home that's on my mind. Like my grandfather had to retire early last month. I love my grandfather dearly. That was on my mind, and I didn't have a good practice that day. They said I wasn't trying and everything, but that was on my mind. But it was just one day, I'll get over it.

"Coach says, 'How could you be tired?' It's easy. Like when we had two-a-days, I look over there and the coaches are yawning. I'm thinking, 'Man, how do you think we feel?' They say, 'Well, your body can be tired, but your mind can't.'

"But that's their job. And it does make us tougher. After awhile you start to instill that in your mind. 'I can't be tired, or they'll yell at me.' You've got to understand what they're doing.

"I think that's why we're good down the stretch. Because we're tired, but we don't think we are. We just keep going at it and going at it. It's incredible how much talent they have at some places, but they don't be playing. It's got to be coaching. It's got to be.

"It's funny, I was a coach at Five Star [a high school summer camp] last summer, and I got a totally different perspective. I found myself out there doing what Coach Keady does. I used his philosophy, and we ended up winning the whole thing, and we didn't have a great team. Our team was mediocre—we finished 3-3 during the regular part. But we ended up winning the whole thing in the tournament. We just kept going at them. I ran a lot more, but I was yelling about defense all the time. 'Help side, help side, help side!' The players probably thought I was crazy. Coach Weber was there and he was kidding me. He said it was the first time he'd ever heard me yell about defense.

"I did get the other side from doing that. You can really see how you might think you're working hard, but you're not. You might think you're doing it, but you're not. It's frustrating. I know what they see. But as a player you think you're trying, but it's still not good enough. You're thinking, 'What do I have to do?'

7 •

Forward, March

The team flew home from Florida anxious to get started with 1988, and relieved to be done with 1987. Surely the new year would be better than the old one. The loss at Michigan, the tournament loss to Florida, the academic ineligibility, the injuries, the recruiting frustrations, the adjustment to a new style of play, the quest for leadership—the wins in Florida seemed to shift all that to the past tense.

There wouldn't be much time to rejoice, however. Just as it had opened the season earlier than usual with the NIT, it also would play the first Big Ten game of the season, at Illinois, on January 4, for the benefit of ESPN's national television audience.

A Purdue-Illinois game offers a distinct contrast in style and philosophy. Illinois is the acknowledged kingpin among the colleges in its state. Purdue fights to compete with Indiana and Notre Dame for the spotlight. Illinois' Lou Henson is a soft-spoken man who has the reputation of a coach who is able to attract an abundance of athletic talent but often winds up with undisciplined teams that underachieve. Keady has a much more aggressive personality and the reputation of a coach who struggles to recruit the best talent but has disciplined teams that overachieve. Illinois' arena, Assembly Hall, is one of the best in the country for size, comfort and convenience. Mackey Arena, four years younger, is like a smaller, generic version of it. Illinois' pep band plays a vast array of rock and roll music, from golden oldies to heavy metal. Purdue's pep band plays a consistent set of college fight songs and big band music, venturing into nothing more daring than "Sweet Georgia Brown."

Stephens witnessed firsthand a difference among the two programs during the preseason when he drove to Champaign to visit friends. He worked out with the Illinois players while he was there, taking part in their pickup games and even their conditioning program. And while he was impressed with the players' camaraderie and spirit on the court, he was surprised by what he saw when he ran with them. At Purdue, the cutoff time for a two-mile run is 12 minutes. At Illinois, Stephens found the standards a little more forgiving.

"The coaches said, 'C'mon guys, we've got to do it in 12 minutes,'" he recalled. "And some of the players were going, 'Twelve? Make it 14 or 15 or something.' And the coaches said OK. Some of their guys would walk a lap, then run a little, then bend down and stretch some, and then the last lap they'd sprint. And their coach would be going, 'All right, way to run!' And I'd be going, 'Way to run? Shoot, our ass would have another two miles to run if we did it like this.' I couldn't believe it."

Not that Purdue's formula had worked every time. The two teams had split their 14 meetings since Keady took over, and the bizarre had become commonplace.

An 86-43 loss in 1985 was particularly memorable for Lewis, Stephens and Mitchell, who were freshmen on that team. One of the team's traditions when it plays at Illinois is to stop at a restaurant, The Beef House, for lunch on the way to Champaign, and then again for carry-out sandwiches on the way back. Keady wasn't in a patient mood that night, however, because he had called a midnight practice. When one of the student managers ran in to pick up the tenderloins, Keady told him to hurry. The manager returned with the sandwiches, but no condiments or soft drinks. The players started to object. Keady said to forget it, he wasn't waiting any longer. To this day, Lewis, Stephens and Mitchell think of dry sandwiches and a late-night practice when they think of Champaign.

This game had cotton-mouth potential as well. The Illini had better athletes, a fact even Purdue's players acknowledged, so discipline and strategy would be crucial. Keady, who prefers straight-up, man-to-man defense, grudgingly accepted the assistant coaches' recommendation to play zone to exploit Illinois' lack of outside shooting ability.

It worked. Illinois shot just 40 percent from the field as Purdue latched on to the momentum it had initiated in Florida and rode it to an 81-68 victory.

The victory provided several personal moments to be savored.

While Keady stayed on the floor for an interview with ESPN, the rest of the team began the locker room celebration without him.

"Let me tell you what coach is going to say before he comes in here and says it," Stallings told the players. "He'll say, 'Don't get up too high over a win and don't get down too much over a loss.'"

Kip Jones, who had hit 5 of 6 shots and scored ten points, then asked if he could go outside the locker room and visit with his father while everyone waited for Keady to return. It was no small matter for him. Jones' parents had divorced his sophomore year in high school, and his dad, a railroad worker, had moved to Illinois. Jones had only recently resumed communication with him, and this was one of the rare college games his father had seen him play.

A few minutes later, a jubilant Keady returned to the locker room.

"Huddle up, let's go!" he shouted.

"No dry tenderloins!" Lewis shouted.

"Coach, you got to say something; they've been waiting for your postgame speech," Stallings said.

"I'm sorry I couldn't get in here," Keady said. "But hell, I don't want you to get too high over this win.

"Together!"

"We attack!"

"I knew you were going to say that," Stallings said, laughing.

Lewis, who had scored 25 points, and Tony Jones, who had scored a career-high 14 off the bench, then left to meet with the reporters. For Lewis, press conferences were as much a part of the postgame routine as a shower. For Jones, it was a new and somewhat frightening experience.

Jones not only was the team's best athlete, he also was one of its most mature people, a disciplined student with high ambition. When he was seven years old, he flew with his mother to Miami and became hooked on flying. He began buying miniature airplanes and fashioned an airport on top of his dresser. His dream evolved into wanting to become an astronaut until the space shuttle exploded in 1985. After that, he set his sights on becoming a commercial pilot instead. He had chosen Purdue primarily because of its acclaimed aviation program, and had earned his solo license the first month of his freshman year. His dormitory room walls were covered with flight posters.

For him, a tough day of classes was different than for most students. It might mean flying to Iowa and back, and then heading straight to practice with jet lag. Or flying to South Bend, Fort Wayne and Muncie while wearing a visor that prevented him from looking out the window, an exhausting exercise designed to simulate nighttime flying.

He also happened to be shy. Flying an airplane and playing basketball on national television came much easier to him than getting up and talking in front of a group of strangers. He made his way through the press conference without embarrassment, answering a couple of brief questions, and then gratefully returned to the locker room.

"Tony Jones! First press conference," Lewis shouted when they rejoined their teammates.

"Man, I was nervous as hell," Jones said.

Two Illinois players also made unwitting contributions to Purdue's season during the game. Steve Bardo, a notoriously poor shooter, helped make Purdue's zone effective by missing all nine of his field goal attempts. From that point on, whenever Lewis saw someone miss an easy shot, he was likely to shout, "Yeah, Bardo!"

And the next day's video session would reveal a bizarre comment from Lowell Hamilton, a reserve forward. In the second half, Hamilton had taken an inbounds pass underneath his own basket and scored in heavy traffic. He was bumped from behind as he released his shot, and while still in midair shouted, "Get off me, dog." He said it in a lyrical, rhythmic manner: "Ged-off me-dawg." The microphones placed near the basket made it clearly audible on the television broadcast.

The players, watching the replay the next day, were both amazed and amused by it. That, too, became a rallying cry, to be used at any time for most any reason.

Curtis Wilson, Ohio State's senior guard, also had donated a phrase to the team when he and Lewis played on the U.S. team in the World Games the previous summer. One night while the two talked of their upcoming senior seasons, Wilson offered Lewis some advice. "Get yours next year, Troy," he said. "I'm gettin' mine, make sure you get yours."

Wilson was referring to taking what he considered his fair share of shots, something of major concern for many seniors with hopes of playing professionally. Lewis had jokingly made the expression a regular part of his lingo, applying it not only to basketball, but to just about anything that had to do with self- indulgence. If he saw a man with a beautiful woman, a student manager grab the last waffle at breakfast, or a player on television take a bad shot, Lewis would invariably shout, "Get yours!"

Lewis wasn't a selfish player—he would finish the season as the team's assist leader—but he did love to shoot. Scoring had always been the basis of his game, and he was uniquely good at it for someone without superior athletic ability. He was slightly pigeon-toed, which limited his quickness and jumping ability, and although he stood 6-4 in his basketball shoes, he had just one dunk to show for himself over the last three seasons—a baseline dunk against Ohio State his junior season that stunned the Mackey fans into silence.

But he covered his physical limitations with intelligence, a healthy degree of arrogance and a freewheeling nature. He had once jokingly suggested a new team motto to Keady: "Run, gun and have fun." Keady wasn't about to go that far, but he had given Lewis more freedom to shoot than any player he had coached in several years. Still, shot selection was an occasional point of debate. The difference between a good shot and a bad shot can be a matter of opinion, and the players naturally were more liberal in their interpretation than the coaches were.

The issue rose to the forefront three days after the Illinois game, when Ohio State came to Mackey. Mitchell had been personally discouraged at Illinois because he got off only three shots, hitting one. The coaches, on the other hand, were more discouraged by the fact he got only one rebound. Lewis, meanwhile, had been greatly encouraged by the fact he had hit 10 of his 13 shots.

But a few minutes after tipoff, Keady thought he detected both of them exercising the "Get yours" theory of offense a little too freely. Lewis hit a three-pointer to help Purdue to a 5-0 lead. But in the next couple of minutes, he missed a three-pointer, Mitchell missed a hurried jumper and Lewis missed another jumper. Ohio State quickly tied the game, and Lewis and Mitchell quickly took a seat on the bench.

Ohio State kept Purdue off-balance throughout the game with two "junk" defenses, a triangle-and-two and a box-and-one, in which they played zone on the inside and guarded Lewis, and sometimes Stephens, man-to-man on the outside. The strategy worked. Purdue took a 45-36 lead into halftime, but its offense was going nowhere. More often than not it settled for outside shots, and more often than not it missed. Mitchell was 2 of 6, Lewis 2 of 8 and Stephens 1 of 6. The coaches considered the misses a result of poor judgment and execution rather than poor aim.

Keady began his halftime lecture calmly, going over the defensive coverage, and then addressed the more burning issue.

"Troy and Todd set the whole tone for the game because I think they had a meeting over on Elm Street and said, 'Hey, the pro scouts won't let me be drafted if I don't get a shot every time I get it,'" Keady said, his anger growing.

"That's bullshit, Todd! You hunt another goddamn shot and you won't play against Iowa. I guarantee it. And if you don't shoot at all, then I won't play you for a month! You two set the tone for this game, and you two get it uncorked! I'm getting so tired of wrestling with you two on hunting shots it's unbelievable!

"If you just get some movement, Todd and Troy . . . get some movement, you'll get your shots. What'd I write up there before the game? Get the ball inside. Melvin's shot the ball how many times? Four! What's he shooting for the year, 60 percent? What's Scheffler, 67 percent? What's Kip shooting, 61 percent? Right?

"Swallow your pride, Troy and Todd, damnit! You two guys are too good of people to worry about scoring. Swallow your pride and become a basketball player. If you're good enough, they'll find you; you'll make the pros, babes. You don't need to worry about it. There's nobody in America who teaches more fundamentals than we do. Nobody in America works harder than we do in practice. Nobody wants you to be successful any more than I do, either one of you. But you're not going to get it that way; you're going to get our ass kicked.

"Now go out and play with some emotion! Get up and down the court and play your ass off and get the ball to somebody else. Great players make other players look good. I'm not worried about you two. You've got enough talent for 15 guys. Now let's go!"

After the players huddled and left the locker room, Stallings clapped his hands softly in recognition of Keady's speech. "Standing ovation," he said. "Standing o–vation."

The second half was better, but only slightly. The Buckeyes were still within three points with 4 1/2 minutes left, but Purdue scored seven of its last nine points from the foul line to hold on for an 84-76 win. Tony Jones played the key role, scoring ten points and shutting down Wilson (who "got his" to the tune of 20 points) in the final few minutes.

The Boilermakers' record was now 12-1. But Keady wasn't pleased.

"Now I'm going to tell you something right now, guys, if you think you're going to compete against Top 20 teams and play like that the rest of the year, we're going to be out the window," Keady said in the locker room afterwards.

"You seniors better start getting these guys ready to play and get yourself ready to play within the system or we're going to have five or seven losses before we even turn the corner. That display of basketball is simply awful. And most of it is mental mistakes. You two seniors, Todd and Troy. You're good students, you understand the game, but you totally resist any type of smart shot selection and anything to do with what we're trying to do to get the team into a national champion. You just simply resist me all the way. Now if you're goddamn dad is telling you to shoot the basketball, Todd, that's horseshit. You tell him to get his ass in the stands and shut up. Maybe that's not happening. But somebody's messing your mind up."

Keady continued for another minute, then called for the huddle. He was still seething when he addressed the reporters across the hall.

"We simply were not ready to play the basketball game the way I want it to be played," he said. "It's just totally ridiculous. Ohio State comes out and does a few things differently and throws us out of sync and we're not ready to beat anybody. Shoot the ball quick, that's what we want to do. It will not work in this league. We were lucky we didn't get beat tonight.

"OK, questions?"

The reporters were caught off guard by Keady's anger. Seven seconds passed, and nobody said a word.

"Nobody wants to talk?" Keady asked.

Finally, someone asked a question.

The players, meanwhile, quickly and quietly dressed. Mitchell was the first one out the door, hoping to escape unnoticed.

He didn't make it. A reporter and cameraman from an Indianapolis television station stopped him in the hallway and asked for his comments on the game. Mitchell, swallowing his wounded pride, said all the right things and was then led into the interview room. He didn't feel like talking at the moment, but that, too, was part of the game.

A rhythm was developing with the season now, as good performances alternated with bad ones in an almost predictable pattern: Team plays poorly. Keady gets mad. Team plays well. Keady is happy. Team relaxes. Team plays poorly. Keady gets mad. Team plays well. . . .

Why, Keady wondered, did he have to play the heavy to get his team to play well?

The next day, Keady had the players report in two groups, guards in one and forwards and centers in the other, to watch the video replay. Wood and Reiter presided in what turned out to be a mini-course in Shot Selection 101. They went over every possession, calmly discussing which shots they considered good ones and which shots they considered bad ones. Differences of opinion were allowed, and discussion encouraged.

"Now what's wrong with that?" Mitchell asked after the tape played one of his early shots.

"It's a ten-foot shot, leaning, with somebody in your face," Wood said. "Now I understand some people think that's OK. There are a lot of coaches who think that's fine. But I don't think this is the program where we think that. I think we'll prove to you coming up here Todd how good you can be standing still. I'm not saying don't go in there . . . run it back; now see, that's a bad shot, Mel.

"Now, is this a good shot, Todd?"

"Yes," Mitchell said.

"Absolutely. Absolutely that's a good shot," Wood said. "You catch the ball ten feet from the basket, take one dribble and go up. That's a good shot.

"One of the things you have to do is make a constant effort to try to do what we ask you to do and not to fight it," Wood said later. "No matter how much you might agree or disagree—and certainly you're going to disagree, you're human, and you're not stupid—you need to try to do that."

Whether it was the lecture series, Iowa's fullcourt press, the alignment of the planets or the law of averages, the shot selection improved the next evening against the Hawkeyes. But that didn't make winning the game any easier. Iowa jumped to leads of 10-1 and 14-3 as Purdue, unusually tight for a home game, sputtered in the opening minutes.

But three-pointers by Stephens and Lewis fueled a ten-point run that cut the lead to one midway through the half and in turn ignited the crowd. Another six-point spree gave Purdue its first lead with seven minutes left. The lead then grew to eight with just over a minute remaining, but it didn't last. B.J. Armstrong hit a three-pointer to bring Iowa within five. Then, after McCants hit a free throw, Bill Jones dropped a 30-footer at the buzzer to make it 42-39.

That was nothing, however, compared to the excitement at the end of the game.

Purdue, having little trouble with Iowa's press, stretched its lead to 12 midway through the half, and was still ahead by seven with three minutes left. Armstrong then drew a foul from Stephens and hit two free throws. Lewis missed a three-pointer, Armstrong drew another foul from Stephens and hit two more free throws. Suddenly the lead was three, with 1:15 left to play. Mitchell was fouled by Jones with 58 seconds left, but missed the front end of the one-and-one. Iowa had the ball now with a chance to tie. Armstrong missed a three-pointer and Lewis picked up the loose rebound, but Tony Jones missed the front end of another one-and-one with 44 seconds left. Armstrong then hit a short jumper from the baseline to bring Iowa within one point.

The fans were getting frantic. Iowa called timeout to set up its strategy, which was to foul Mitchell. Mitchell, however, swished both foul shots with 28 seconds left to give Purdue an 80-77 lead.

The game seemed to be in hand moments later when, after Iowa missed, Mitchell broke free for a breakaway dunk. Mitchell, however, is a much better jumper off of two feet than one, and this time he jumped off one foot, holding the ball with one hand—and proceeded to slam the ball off the back of the rim. Amid the current debate on good shots and bad shots, it qualified as a bad shot. Keady would have preferred he dribble out the clock.

Iowa grabbed the rebound with 12 seconds left and got off two quick three-pointers, but missed both. Ed Horton's tip-in at the buzzer was futile, leaving Purdue with a highly improbable 80-79 win.

Mixed emotions reigned in the locker room. It was a big win, over one of the league's contenders. But mental mistakes had almost done them in. The players filed in nervously and found a seat. Keady paced the floor for a few moments, sorting out his thoughts.

"We've been telling you guys for four years, win the basketball game; don't be a damn showboat," he said. "We were damn lucky they didn't hit a three-pointer. Todd's not the only one that's done it. In four years, he's not the only one that's done it. He's just the one that missed it this time. But don't ever do it again this year."

"Dribble the ball out and run the clock and they never shoot the ball," Weber said.

"Let's enjoy this one now, though," Keady said, perking up. "Get up here."

"Way to make your free throws, Todd," he added as the players huddled around him. "You would have goddamn got shot if we got beat on that."

Everyone laughed.

"Congratulations, men," Keady said.

"Together!"

"We attack!"

In the postgame press conference, Mitchell discussed the agony of his missed dunk and the joy of his made free throws. Then someone changed the subject. Arnold was due to become eligible for the next game, five days later, against Northwestern.

"Are you looking forward to getting an additional teammate this week?" one reporter asked.

Mitchell paused. He had been opposed to the decision to keep Arnold on the team in October, and he wasn't sure if he wanted him back now.

"Yeah; looking forward to it," he said quietly, unable to muster much enthusiasm. "I'm not sure exactly how it's going to work out. But we're happy to have Jeff back, I think he's going to be a big plus for us."

Neither Arnold nor Stack made it back. Stack's situation was simple: despite his repeated comments that his classes were going well, he failed to regain his academic eligibility.

Arnold's case was much more complicated. Tuesday morning,

two days before the Northwestern game that was to mark his return, Keady dropped him from the team.

Hints of Arnold's impending fate surfaced at Keady's weekly news conference, which included a telephone hookup with out of town reporters and a luncheon that was open to the public. Arnold had been a crowd favorite the season before, and Purdue's fans were looking forward to his return with great anticipation. The team was 13-1 and ranked eighth in the country without him. What could it accomplish with him?

But as questions about Arnold's return began to dominate the news conference, Keady grew increasingly uncomfortable. He was, on the one hand, virtually incapable of lying; yet he didn't want to make a major announcement in this setting. He dodged the questions as best he could, asking to talk about the other players instead.

An hour later, as the players were warming up for practice, word leaked out to the team. Keady addressed the issue only briefly, after Reiter reviewed Northwestern's personnel at the chalkboard.

"He'll be going on to other phases of his life," Keady said. "Worrying about him is over for the team. Worrying as a person, I'll continue to do that and try to work with him. But as far as on this basketball team, he's through. We'll just announce it for personal reasons and go from here. Hopefully we'll keep going like we are as a team and hopefully his life gets better under control and he becomes successful. If you want to talk to me one-on-one, I'll be glad to. OK, let's stretch."

The factors behind Arnold's dismissal were complicated. Rumors persisted around the campus and community that Arnold had failed a drug test given in December. But Arnold, while admitting he had tested positive for marijuana use as a freshman shortly after he arrived on campus, and again as a sophomore while he rehabilitated a broken leg, insisted that had not been the case this time.

He cited more commonplace factors: missed class time, which Keady had warned him about in the preseason, and, most of all, the fact he had resumed frequenting the local bars, which had been at the root of his academic troubles over the summer. With all that had gone on before, the pressure had built on Keady to take more drastic action.

At any rate, the team's roster was now settled for the rest of the season. Arnold and Stack, who had been lingering at the edge of the picture since October 15, neither really in nor out, were now definitely out. And while the bitterness among the other seniors had generally subsided, a potential obstacle toward team unity had removed itself.

Arnold's loss, because of the nature of it and because of the impact he might have made on the season, hit the players the hardest. Mitchell, who had wanted a more severe penalty imposed in October, stopped by Arnold's apartment after practice that day to offer his condolences, although Arnold wasn't at home.

Brugos, one of Arnold's best friends, and a kindred free spirit, was genuinely hurt. His role on the team would now become much more important, particularly in practice. It would be up to him to push McCants and Scheffler. He also would need to assume more leadership of the White squad, which Arnold had done so well in December.

Scheffler, who had surprised the coaches with his improvement, figured to gain the most from Arnold's absence. Arnold's return might have cut into his playing time. But he, too, was saddened. Although they seemed to have nothing in common on the surface they had become close friends. Arnold had helped Scheffler through many of his first-year growing pains, assuming the role of older brother when Scheffler needed someone to talk to.

For Keady, the issue brought back a recurring dilemma. Like so many other times in his coaching career he had gone out of his way to give a kid a break, offering second and third chances while stretching his disciplinary standards to the limit, only to have his efforts backfire.

"The mistake you make as coaches is you give people chances," he told his assistants at their meeting the next morning. "There's a fine line between trying to be compassionate and trying to be realistic. It's the same old thing. You try to help somebody and you end up talking about them instead of the kids who count. I could kick myself in the ass every time."

"You mean you're not going to be compassionate anymore?" Wood asked, in a teasing tone.

"Hell, no," Keady said. "They're gone from now on, the sons of bitches. You just get 15, 16, 17 players that are all equal talent and sort them out, make examples of two or three of them every year and run their ass off. Christ, you try to be nice to them, make them change, but you can't change 18 year olds."

The assistants knew better. Tuesday morning, only a few hours before Arnold's fate had been announced, they had seen him in action with two other team members in his office. Keady's office door is always left open to his players, literally, and he encourages them to come by with their problems. The players are struck by the fact that whenever they walk into his office, no matter the time of day or season, he immediately stops what he is doing to talk with them. If he's on the phone, he says, "I've got to go now, I've got a player here," and hangs up.

That morning, the coaches had interrupted their meeting when McCants stopped by for an appointment Keady had scheduled with him.

"Shoot, you got a 4.04 [grade point average]," Keady said, looking over McCants' first-semester grade report. "Way to go, Melvin!"

"Don't let the fact classes are starting blow your mind and affect your play," Stallings said.

"I won't," McCants said.

"Just go," Keady said. "You've done a great job, Bud."

"Don't let your classes slip, either," Weber said.

"You've got too much going for you now," Keady said. "Now let me tell you what you're getting a reputation for. I've heard you're the world's worst driver. You drive too fast. Slow down."

"Who told you that?" McCants said, laughing.

"You hear me? Slow down," Keady said. "I don't want another David Rivers [the Notre Dame player who had escaped serious injury in an accident a year ago] on my hands. You may not be as lucky as he was.

"OK, I'll see you later; I'm proud of you."

A few minutes later, Reid, who was enduring the typical freshman growing pains, came in. He was wearing a cap.

"Billy. Has coach taught you Mom's Rule yet?" Stallings asked. "Huh?"

"Mom's Rule," Keady said. "The hats come off inside and when the sun goes down."

"Of course with that haircut you might want to leave it on," Weber said.

Reid took off his hat. Keady reviewed his grades from the previous semester, and his class schedule for the upcoming semester.

"How's everything going?" he asked.

"All right," Reid said.

"Anything I can help you with? You've got a lot of talent, Bill. Use it. Think. Use your head. How's the dorm, OK? Coaches, you got anything you want to add?"

"You've got to start improving, Billy," Weber said.

"You had a good October, then things started getting to you because it becomes a heavy load, doesn't it?" Keady said. "A lot of things are going on. The thing you need to know is that we have a lot of confidence in you. But you've got to get yourself back to where you're making progress again. You ever study graphs in Econ? You were playing in October like this, and then you went straight down. Because of the heavy loads. School, coaches yelling at you, the pressure to do good. All those things catch up with people. You've got to start climbing again. It has nothing to do with us having confidence in you, because we do. We believe in you, we like you, and we want you to be a great player here. Any questions? OK."

Reid got up to leave.

"I don't like you," Stallings said, grinning.

"I don't like you, either," Reid said as he headed out the door.

"That's Stallings' opinion," Keady shouted after him. "I like you."

The new, streamlined team that faced Northwestern Thursday night in Mackey showed no hints of the disruption that had surfaced two days earlier. Lewis hit four first half three-pointers, Stephens wreaked havoc defensively, and Scheffler came off the bench to add ten points and six rebounds in 18 minutes to lead an 80-64 victory.

But the next game, two nights later in Minneapolis, was more worrisome for the coaches. Purdue teams had won their last four games in Minneapolis, but each one had been difficult. And Minnesota, an inexperienced team with good athletes, had lost 18 consecutive conference games. That made two streaks that seemed capable of ending at any time.

And out of the ease of the win over Northwestern, a few trouble spots had arisen. Weber reported that Kip Jones, who still had not relocated the groove he had hit early in December, had expressed concern over his playing time—just 15 minutes, less than both Scheffler and Berning—in the game. Jones had been pulled almost as soon as the second half started after missing a forced shot, and then spent most of the period on the bench when the game became a blowout and the reserves filled in.

Berning also seemed to be struggling with his confidence. He had only played five minutes against Iowa, and then failed to score in 19 minutes against Northwestern.

And the subject of Mitchell's inconsistency and shot selection had come up again. After hitting eight of 14 shots against Iowa, Mitchell hit just four of 12 shots against Northwestern.

Keady faced all three issues head-on when the team met in its Minneapolis hotel the night before the game.

"I don't think some of you understand that this is a man's game being played with boy's minds," he said.

"What's happening is, you're resisting my ability to reach you. For example, Kip I understand you were not happy about not playing in the second half. I'm glad you said it. I'm glad you were honest about it. But why, in your mind, do you think Keady doesn't like you? That has nothing to do with it. It has something to do with the time of the game, maybe they were playing a zone, it had nothing to do with you as a person, it had to do with the game itself. Nobody's a bigger fan of Kip Jones than Gene Keady.

"Those kinds of things, guys, you've got to get out of your mind if we're going to become a great basketball team. I can't fight you. I'm getting tired of fighting some of you guys. I want you to come over and get on my boat so I can catch a trout with you. That's what it amounts to. In other words, we're going to be rewarded if we're working together.

"If you keep the game simple, and I'm saying this to Todd Mitchell more than anybody, you can be first team All-Big Ten. Get inside. I saw Mr. Mitchell at Five Star Camp (in high school) and you know what he was best at? Getting the ball and sticking it in their face. My mind still hasn't changed about him. He's still the best two-foot jumper I've ever had the privilege of coaching. But somewhere along the line since his sophomore year, somebody's got in his head and told him he's got to develop his outside game. And that's not going to make us a great team, Todd. You have to become the best player in the lane from now until April that you possibly can become if we're going to go anyplace.

"You know why I'm a little fired up right now? Because I hadn't seen Michigan play this year until the other day. And if we let those sons of bitches kick our ass this year and win the league, we ought to have our ass kicked until we're 65 years old. Because they don't understand the game. You let somebody like this slip on us tonight and beat us, you go to Ann Arbor later and they've got a two game lead on us, those guys are frontrunners and they're going to kick our butt. But if we go in the game tied with them, like 6-0 or 7-1 or whatever it would be, they might swallow the old apple. Let's just test them and see.

"If you do all the basic things right here . . . sure it's going to be tough, hell, it's the Big Ten, they're all going to be tough. But they're not going to be as tough if you keep things simple."

Pure and simple, Purdue beat Minnesota, 82-74. It hammered the ball inside to Mitchell and McCants for its first ten points, then outscored the Gophers 20-2 over the final eight minutes of the period to take a 44-31 halftime lead.

But as was becoming custom, the lead didn't stick. Minnesota pulled to within one point with five minutes left in the game. Williams Arena, the oldest in the Big Ten, began rocking in anticipation of an upset. But Purdue scored its last 15 points from the foul line to hold on.

The simple approach, working the ball inside for close shots, had paid off handsomely this time. Purdue attempted 39 free throws, hitting 30. Minnesota shot just seven.

And Mitchell, taking the ball inside most of the time, but drifting outside for an occasional 15-footer, played perhaps his best game of the season. He scored 30 points, hitting all eight of his field goal attempts and 14 of 16 free throws, and grabbed six rebounds.

The team returned home to a slight drizzle and an empty airport—except for the Boilermaker Special—at 3 a.m. But the rest of the day would be easy. After a morning's sleep, they returned at 3 p.m. to lift weights and do what surely no other college basketball team in the country would do that day: go swimming.

Keady had added swimming to his late-season practice schedule a few years earlier as a means of breaking up the season's grind, both physically and psychologically. The water soothed aching muscles. The relaxed atmosphere soothed weary psyches. For the rest of the season, except when they had a game or a rare day off, they would spend their Sunday afternoons in the university's indoor pool.

Among the many things reflected off the blue-tinted water were the cultural backgrounds of the players. Here, unlike on the hardwood of a basketball floor, the white players were generally more accomplished and confident than the blacks, with the exception of Mitchell and Lewis, who seemed to adapt smoothly to any environment. Tony Jones, McCants and Stephens, three of the best athletes on dry land, were relative walk-ons in the pool. Swimming hadn't been a part of their childhood activities.

McCants was the most foreign to the pool. Having grown up in a corner of downtown Chicago that didn't exactly rival Beverly Hills for its predominance of swimming pools, he couldn't swim when he first arrived at Purdue. His freshman year, he refused to go into water above his waist. Teammates and assistant coaches had lured him into flotation devices and tried to teach him the basics, but his 6-9, 250-pound frame and unabashed fear prevented him from catching on.

By now, at least, he was willing to go anywhere in the pool as long as he was wearing goggles. While his teammates frolicked, he pulled himself along the outer edge of the pool with one hand, carefully and cheerfully dodging whatever projectiles and good-natured barbs were thrown his way.

A few of his teammates tossed around a volleyball. Brugos and Scheffler took Reid up on his dare and pulled off his practice trunks, although he still had his grey cotton shorts underneath. That was more than Stephens had been wearing three years earlier, when some members of the women's swim team were passing by and a few of the upperclassmen took it upon themselves to reveal a part of the freshman guard never before seen in public.

Horseplay, within a reasonable limit, was acceptable to Keady in this environment, however.

"Move around a little bit," he shouted when he noticed half the players standing in the shallow end talking.

Mitchell smiled and jiggled the upper half of his body.

The grand finale was always a relay race, in which the players (except the land-locked McCants) divided into pairs and swam a length each.

Tony Jones and Stephens, both of whom wore fins, paired off. Both could swim well enough to take part in the races, but neither could dive, so they started from inside the pool. Nobody complained, because they weren't going to win, anyway.

"Everette, take off your flaps," Keady shouted.

"But coach, I can't swim without them," Stephens answered in pleading tones. "Come on, let me wear one at least!"

He got to wear both.

The freshman duo of Barrett and Ewer won, Ewer barely edging a rapidly-approaching Kip Jones at the wall. They huddled, and called it a day.

"Hey, Jimmy, can you swim?" Keady asked Oliver, who had been watching, as they headed for the door.

"Sure," Oliver said.

"For real?" Stephens asked.

"Yeah," Oliver said, feigning disgust.

"There's nothing else to do down there," Keady said, jumping to Oliver's defense. "Everybody can swim. What else is there to do? You ever been down there, Everette? You ought to go down there and visit him sometime."

"Are there any beautiful women down there?" Stephens asked. "That's the only thing worth going for."

"You've got to get your mind off women, Everette," Keady said. "Start thinking about your jump shot and playing defense."

As they walked through the underground tunnel back to Mackey, Keady noticed Stephens was wearing only his flimsy practice shorts.

"Everette, are you wearing a jock?" he asked.

"No," Stephens said.

"You're supposed to wear a jock when you swim," Keady said.

"But it feels good this way, coach," Stephens replied, grinning.

The good feeling was becoming contagious. The next opponent, Michigan State, had beaten Indiana the same night Purdue was beating Minnesota, which dropped the Hoosiers to 2-2 in the Big Ten. One of the anticipated contenders for the league championship was already falling by the wayside; the fact it happened to be a downstate rival didn't break many hearts in the Lafayette area.

Wednesday's game against the Spartans would be like a sendoff into a brave new world. Three days later, they would play at Louisville on network television, the start of a harrowing journey that would lead them through five road games in the next three weeks—at Indiana, Michigan, Michigan State and Iowa, too—and no doubt determine their fate in the Big Ten race.

With so much looming off in the distance, playing Michigan State in Mackey seemed more like a roadblock to bigger and better things. The result was an uneven 78-67 victory that left Keady more relieved than pleased. He accepted the win grudgingly, issuing both mild praise and warnings afterwards in the locker room.

Scheffler provided a bright moment to the evening, both during the game and afterwards, scoring eight points and grabbing seven rebounds in 17 minutes, and then regaling the reporters in the press conference.

"Do you have a nickname?" one reporter asked.

"Oh, I've had a lot of nicknames," Scheffler said. "There's a friend down the hall, I call him Barney Rubble and he calls me Fred. And Buffalohead. And Beaverhead. And then Butch. I had a couple friends down the hall last year give me a haircut; I didn't think a butch would be very hard, but they gave bald spots, so I guess that was deserved. There's been a lot of them, especially from the freshman year, but they haven't carried over, too much."

Any that your teammates have called you?" he was asked.

"Buffalohead and Beaverhead, those would be the two favorites," Scheffler said. "Godzuki, Godzilla when I was younger. And Grape Ape. Oh, at Illinois the fans were yelling 'Stiffenstein.'"

"Steve," another reporter said, "five of the next six games are on the road. How important is it to do well?"

"I don't know," Scheffler said. "I don't think I'd be the one to ask. I'm more worried about tomorrow's practice than the next game. I couldn't even think of who we're playing five games from now. I think it's important to win, and keep the winning streak going, but I can't really say."

Jeff Arnold

"I think coach had a lot of pressure put on him by some other people. But he was very fair. He flat out told me at the beginning of the year, 'If I hear of you going to any more bars, or going into any liquor stores, then that's it.' It was a situation where I was here over Christmas break by myself, and I was bored as hell and I went out a few times. He's very justified in doing what he did, and it's very fair.

"He started by asking if it was true. I had to say that it was. He said, 'I really don't know what to do.' That was on Monday. I really wasn't scared going into his office Tuesday morning, because I thought we had gotten everything straightened out on Monday. But he said he had made his decision. I walked the streets for about five hours. I was just walking around in a daze. It was freezing cold, and I was in a daze. I didn't know what the hell I was going to do. A lot of stuff went through my head, like leaving here and getting a job, stuff like that.

"He was very concerned about my drinking. That's why I respect him so much. He could have just thrown me out of his office. This was something he had to do. It was like people were saying, 'Come on, Gene, Jesus Christ, it's time to do what you've got to do.'

"But he was very understanding. He was saying, 'What are you going to do? Don't abandon me, now.' It's strange, but in some ways I was closer than most of the guys on the team were with him. A lot of people think coach is always serious, but he's got a helluva little sense of humor about him. I have a great respect for him, but I think we're friends, too.

"My priorities were definitely screwed up, without a doubt. I had told myself that my freshman year. But it was something where, 'Well, if you can get by with it, the hell with it.' That's just my way of thinking of it. If I had it all over to do now, I think I would have quit drinking a long time ago.

"I came from a lifestyle where I had a lot of freedom. When I was in sixth grade, my mother died of leukemia. My father had a job where he traveled, and I had two younger sisters. My dad's a regional sales manager for Ore-Ida; he's very successful. He's been offered a lot of promotions, but he'd have to move to Boise, Idaho and he doesn't want to do that. He has a lot of free time now, and likes to play the horses and stuff.

"After my mom died, we weren't a very close family. We didn't have sit-down dinners. My dad would cook barbecue stuff, but that was about it. You know how families have a sit-down dinner every night at six o'clock? It wasn't like that with us. After dinner, everybody went their own way. My dad would go upstairs and watch TV, and my sisters would go outside and mess around. In other families everybody sits down in the family room and watches TV and stuff; that's just not the way it was with us.

"It was tough on my dad, because he and I never saw eye-to-eye. I had all these added responsibilities. I had to take care of the house. We had two live-in housekeepers that were supposed to come and cook and help take care of the house, but that never worked out. I learned Hamburger Helper very early in life. The house was my responsibility, making sure the lawn was mowed, and all that. I'm thinking, 'To hell with this, everybody's going to the beach today.' And because of my size, a lot of my friends were older than I was, like three years older. So I was wanting to go out running with them, and I was getting in trouble for missing curfew, or doing this or that. I was always getting grounded.

"Right now, me and my dad are a lot closer than we ever were. But we were always tugging at each other when I was growing up. It didn't help that my friends were older and they had a little more freedom anyhow. I was like any kid.

"I'd say, 'I want to go out, too.'

" 'But you can't. You're not like everybody else. You have responsibilities.'

" 'But I don't *want* these responsibilities.'

" 'Tough. You have them.'

"But I look back now, I just wanted to do the same thing everyone else was doing. I was a normal kid, but then I wasn't, because I had all these added responsibilities, because I had to take care of my younger sisters. One was in fourth grade, and one was in first grade. So I've got a younger sister five years younger, and I want to go do something, but I can't leave her alone. I kind of resented a lot of the responsibilities I had, but I guess it's helped me a lot. I think I grew up a lot in ways other kids didn't.

"I think the first time I drank I was in sixth grade. By my freshman year in high school, I was having keg parties at my house. That's no lie. My friends could get it for me. My father was gone all the time. Hell, he was traveling all the time, and my sisters didn't complain. I'd send them to bed, then they'd come down and sit on the stairs and watch.

"We'd have two kegs going. We had some great parties. We'd have caps tournaments. You get a long table, put a full glass of beer at each end and try to throw a beer cap into the other glass. There's two guys to a team, and you play to three. If you make it, they have to drink a full beer. We'd have tournaments, straight-up tournaments, with brackets and everything. Me and my friend still hold the record; we were 23-1.

"That's just the way it is out there. It's still that way. I was going to high school parties in sixth grade, just because I was so big and all my friends were in high school. Just like people out here get up and slop the hogs every morning, it was part of my life.

"I was to the point where I'd drink a six pack a night. I acquired a taste for beer very, very early. I don't like hard alcohol, but I like beer. I'd come home and drink, six, eight, nine beers after practice. That was a daily thing. To me there's nothing better than after a hard day having a cold beer.

"But it finally got to the point where I looked at it like it was affecting my life in a negative way. I mean, hell, you just got kicked off the basketball team. That's a pretty negative thing.

"Like with my girlfriend. I've been going out with my girlfriend for five years, and every time we get in a serious, heated argument it was because I was all messed up. I'd be talking shit and didn't care."

"Hopefully I'll be able to use this experience to bounce back. Hell, I came in more immature than Todd, Troy or Melvin. I'm trying to turn this all around and make something good out of all of it. Hopefully I can keep lifting and keep the size and strength I want. I just want to lift and lift and lift and get as strong as I can.

"It's weird. I feel a lot more relieved in some ways. That's a helluva burden taken off. I feel so much better; I sleep so much better. Jesus Christ, that's a helluva lot of pressure. And I was getting myself all psyched out, because I was only going to play half the year. I'm hoping it will all end up better in the long run.

"The thing I'm really going to miss is the guys. The guys. One thing I don't miss is walking around and having the label of Purdue basketball on my back. I could care less. I am who I am. That's one thing I don't like about the area out here. It's like the fraternity and sorority system . . . 'What's your name? Oh, you play basketball?' That type of shit. You've got your little basketball groupies, guys and girls. I don't miss that at all. And I don't miss the structure of it. Having to be there at 3:30 or whatever every day and running three laps and squeezing the tennis balls and going to study table. Now I plan my own days.

"But I'm still willing to jump back into their days. No question."

8 •

The Hump Game

The bus ride to Louisville was quiet. Most of the players slept. Barrett read from a textbook, and a few others simply stared out the window.

The only conversation flowed from Kip Jones and Brugos, who kept up a steady banter near the back of the bus throughout the three-hour ride. Jones, who had once tied Scheffler's gym shoes to the seat posts on the way to a practice the season before while Scheffler was dozing, went for an encore performance. He took off the shoelace on Scheffler's left street shoe and put it in his own pocket.

Along with being a starting forward, Jones' position on the team was chief instigator. It was a self-assigned role, and one he relished. Once, after an especially satisfying adventure in tormenting a teammate, he offered a concise, grinning self-analysis: "I thrive on being a prick."

He was a natural for the part. He had the sly grin of a cat that has just dined on fresh mouse, and he wore it often. Even as a kid, he was the mischief maker who was constantly getting in trouble from grade school teachers for cutting up in the classroom. He had the quality Keady thinks so highly of, orneriness, and he had it in bulk quantity.

Jones recalled one incident in grade school with particular pride. It was in art class, while everyone was finger painting. Jones asked the kid next to him if he could have some of his green paint. But when the kid shook the paint off his hand on to Jones', Jones pulled his hand away. The paint plopped on the kid's painting, and ruined it. "I got in *big* trouble for that one," he recalled, smiling.

Jones, more than anyone, carried on the well-established tradition of riding the underclassmen. It was normally a role reserved for seniors, but Lewis, Stephens and Mitchell weren't that interested in it. Besides, it came naturally to him. He even made it a point to needle the seniors on occasion, just to keep their feet on the ground.

Jones had been tagged with all sorts of nicknames as a freshman by then-seniors Mack Gadis and Herb Robinson, and he doled out most of the nicknames for this team, although they weren't in common use. Reid was P.O.W., because of his gaunt physique and crewcut. Scheffler was Beaverhead, because of his thick scalp. Lewis was Potatohead, because of the shape of his head. Mitchell was Cosby Kid, because of his suave appearance and demeanor. Ewer was Coach Weber, with whom he shared a slight resemblance. Barrett was Fishbowl Head, because he wore glasses. Reiter, the intellectual type, was Paperback Reiter.

And Keady?

"Are you kidding?" Jones said, indicating he wouldn't dare go that far. "The Man, maybe."

The team arrived in Louisville just in time to change, get taped and re-board the bus for its 6:30 p.m. practice at Freedom Hall. But in that brief span of time, a couple more examples of its occasional identity crisis were heard, reminders why Saturday's game against the Cardinals on national television would be so important.

As everyone checked into the hotel across the street from the arena, a young woman working at the front desk turned to the man working next to her and quietly posed a question: "Is Purdue in Indiana?" Purdue's name, it often seemed, didn't translate across state lines.

Half an hour later, shortly before the bus left for practice, there was another mild, though well-intentioned, slight on ESPN's "SportsLook" program. Keady already wasn't a big fan of the show, because of a bad experience in October. He had been flown to California to tape a short interview, the kind of thing that was a nuisance to do at that time of the year, but worth doing because of the exposure it offered Purdue basketball.

It didn't go as he expected it would. He wound up answering nonstop questions about coaching in the same state as Knight and Notre Dame's Digger Phelps, a subject he had long since grown bored with. At the time, he had won two Big Ten titles and had one of the nation's top-ranked teams in the preseason polls. He figured he had at least earned the privilege of having some questions asked about himself or his team; perhaps it was even time to start asking other coaches about coaching in the same state as Gene Keady.

And now, Stu Black, who regularly offered commentary in a brief segment at the end of the show, was offering some opinions on the season's Big Ten race.

"For the most part over the past decade, it's been Indiana that's the dominant team," Black told the show's host, Roy Firestone. "I think the team that's going to win this year comes from the same state, but it's not Indiana. I think this is Purdue's year. They have a wonderful coach, Gene Keady, who makes his kids progress every year, and they get better every year. They have some fine players: Troy Lewis, Mitchell, and a kid named Everette Stephens who people have kind of overlooked, but I think would probably be the best NBA prospect they have.

"Illinois has a fine player like Kenny Battle who transferred, but I don't think Illinois will be one of the teams that will really challenge. Michigan, which has the best talent, not only in the Big Ten but I believe in the nation—and some nights when they really get it going look like the Lakers—probably won't be the champion of the Big Ten just because I think Bill Frieder's not quite as good a coach as Keady. He never seems to have the same chemistry in his team, he doesn't seem to get them where Keady gets his teams in March. Now I know that sounds foolish because Purdue has lost the last couple of years very early in the tournament, but I don't think that's going to happen this year."

They were nice sentiments from a Purdue perspective, but there was a catch. Black wasn't able to correctly pronounce the name of this Keady fellow he seemed to respect so much, referring to him as Kee-dy rather than Ka-dy.

Ka-dy wanted this game very badly, as was evident during the team's workout Friday night. He began it by lining up the players for ten sprints. The coaches had recently instituted a new policy of having the players run a sprint for every offensive rebound they allowed above ten. Michigan State had come up with 20 in the previous game.

That was only the beginning of a grueling 2½-hour session filled with fullcourt drills. Two hours into it, Keady exploded and ordered two more sprints for everyone when Brugos bumped Lewis excessively hard and then cursed at Stephens when Stephens asked him what he was doing. Keady also scolded Lewis for overreacting to Brugos' bump.

After practice, the team then returned to the hotel, showered, ate a late dinner, and met in Keady's suite to watch video and go over Weber's 11-page scouting report. It was 11:30 by the time they went to bed.

The next day brought breakfast, the shootaround, lunch, 20 more minutes of video and another meeting before the 4 p.m. tipoff.

Keady reminded the players of the impact this game would have. A national television audience would be watching, and media from all over Indiana and Kentucky would be on hand. It was a chance to take another step into college basketball's mainstream by defeating a more recognized national power. Keady didn't say so, but maybe it would teach people which state Purdue is in, and how the head coach's name is pronounced, as well. It also might be a factor in the team's seeding in the NCAA tournament.

Louisville was sure to be ready. The Cardinals were 8-5, and looking to shake the doldrums that had haunted them the previous season, when they had finished 18-14 in a disappointing followup to their 1986 national championship. A win over Purdue, they thought, would put them back on the right track heading into the heart of conference play.

Beyond that, they felt they had a score to settle, as their All-America center, Pervis Ellison, had indicated to Lewis during the Pan-American Games tryouts the past summer. Louisville's players, Ellison said, had felt "shown up" when they lost to Purdue 88-73 at Mackey Arena in a nationally-televised game the season before. Purdue had broken out its gold uniforms for that game, and 10,000 gold pom-poms were distributed to the fans to add to the fever pitch. The Cardinal boosters made sure they weren't outdone for the return engagement. Red pom-poms and a cardboard sign featuring the team's mascot and the words "Wild Cards" were waiting on each of the 19,000-plus seats as the fans filed into Freedom Hall.

Among the points of emphasis Keady wrote on the board for the players before the game, the most important was rebounding. They had been outrebounded by five of their last six opponents, and Louisville figured to be a good rebounding team.

"Let's get after these guys!" Keady said, calling the huddle together. "It's not anything compared to what's going to be happening over at Bloomington next week—that's a helluva lot more important game—but this game might be a factor in whether you're going to get a nice draw or not. So let's get after these folks and play our butts off!

"Together!"

"We attack!"

After the players left to warm up, the coaches milled about the locker room, discussing the game plan, and the game, one more time.

"I just want to play good," Stallings said quietly. "We need to play well, win or lose."

"We sure didn't two years ago," Weber said, recalling a 77-58 loss to the Cardinals in Freedom Hall, a game in which Kip Jones, then a freshman, had to start at center because of injuries to McCants and Arnold.

"But we were young pups then."

They were big dogs now, but they showed some growing pains. The coaches' worst fear, a slow start, was realized as the Cardinals jumped to a 10-4 lead in the first three minutes. The players seemed uptight. Worse than that, Ellison was dominating inside and McCants had picked up two quick fouls.

But patience, execution and Everette Stephens gradually took over. And it was almost by command. Trailing 26-25 with seven minutes left, Keady stood up in front of the bench and shouted at Stephens, who was waiting to inbound the ball. "Everette, take the ball at them and dominate!"

That had been Keady's wish for the past several weeks, when Stephens' play had been agonizingly inconsistent. He had played well against Illinois, but poorly against Ohio State and Iowa. He had played reasonably well against Northwestern and Minnesota, but poorly against Michigan State. Keady, in one fit of frustration during a coaches' meeting, had even talked of starting Tony Jones in his place, but not seriously. "Jesus, if he could play good and get us going, I'd have a damn party for a week," Keady had said.

So now, he was asking again: "Take the ball at them and dominate!" And he got his wish. With the shot clock down to five seconds, Stephens nailed a three-pointer that gave Purdue a 28-26 lead. He later added a driving jumper from the baseline that made it 33-30, and then made what might have been the biggest play of the game: He stripped Louisville's freshman guard, LaBradford Smith, at midcourt and glided in for a highlight-film variety dunk that pushed the lead to 38-32. The emotional lift it gave the team was more important than the points.

He went on to add an 18-foot jumper and two more three-pointers, including a 22-footer with seven seconds left in the half that provided a 48-40 halftime lead.

He had scored 17 points, tying his season high for an entire game. Keady, if he had meant his earlier promise literally, could have rushed out to buy party hats right then.

Lewis got things started nicely in the second half when, on the opening possession, he threw a lob pass to Stephens that was off-target—so off-target that it fell through the basket. "Holy cow!" Keady shouted in disbelief, falling back in his chair. It counted as a three-pointer, and pushed the lead to 51-40. McCants' layup on a quick feed from Stephens and Kip Jones' breakaway layup a minute later on a pass from Mitchell made it 55-40 with 18:26 still to play.

Mitchell led another surge midway through the half. He scored eight of his team's ten points through one stretch, including awesome back-to-back dunks on Ellison.

The first of them gave Purdue it's largest lead of the game, 75-56. From there, it was a matter of hanging on for dear life. Kenny Payne came back with three consecutive three-pointers and two free throws in the next 90 seconds to cut the lead to 77-67. Two jumpers from Ellison later reduced the lead to six, with 4:43 left, and suddenly it was a game again.

The Cardinals hung tough, narrowing the lead to four with 2:55 left, but Purdue held on for a 91-85 victory.

The locker room celebration was the wildest of the season, an exercise in unrestrained joy. Kip Jones stood at the door and greeted everyone as they walked in, slapping hands. Keady made the rounds, pumping everyone's hand. Stephens, CBS's Player of the Game, was whisked off for a quick interview.

Amid the bedlam, Keady called for the huddle.

"Way to go, men! Together!"

"We attack!"

"Hey, wait!" Lewis yelled quickly, getting everyone's attention.

"We seniors have been here for four years and this is the first time we *really* got over the hump of doing something, fellas! Let's keep it going!"

Like the win over Miami, it was a melting pot sort of victory, one that brought everyone together because everyone had played an important role. Lewis finished with 23 points, 15 in the second half. Stephens added 19 points and eight assists. Mitchell had 16 points and 10 rebounds. McCants, playing just 20 minutes, had ten points, and Kip Jones added eight points and nine rebounds. The bench also had sparkled. Scheffler had relieved McCants and hit every shot— three field goals and two free throws—for eight points. Tony Jones had six points and four assists. And Berning, in seven minutes, added a point, three rebounds and two assists.

There was one more vital and impressive statistic: Purdue had outrebounded Louisville 41-26, and allowed just nine offensive rebounds.

After a tough loss, a trip to the postgame press conference can be as dreadful as a sip of sour milk. But after a big win, it's a sweet moment, a chance to relive the glory for public consumption.

Lewis, Mitchell and Stephens went first, lining up behind a podium in front of a crowded room full of reporters.

Mitchell was asked about his back-to-back dunks on Ellison.

"Well, against Pervis that's the only way you're going to get anything accomplished, unless you're 7-foot," he said. "I'm not 7-foot, so the best thing I can do is take the ball right at him."

"You're lyin'," Stephens deadpanned. "You told me at the beginning of the game you were scared!"

They were asked about their national ranking, which was fifth entering the game. Where did they want to be ranked?

"Tenth, 12th, 15th, right around there," Lewis said.

"And then at the end No. 1," Stephens said.

And they were asked about next week's game, at Indiana. When would they start thinking of that?

"Right now," Lewis said. "We can't help it, because when we go home everybody's going to be talking about Indiana."

"Everybody else will make *sure* you think about it," Mitchell said.

About 50 fans were waiting for the bus when it returned to Mackey that snow-covered evening. The Boilermaker Express was there, too, blaring its horn. Keady addressed the players one more time before they got off.

"You did a great job, guys," he said. "You went undefeated in December and you have a chance to go undefeated in January. And that would really be sweet, considering who you play next week. Get some rest, stay out of trouble and go to class."

Everette Stephens

"I was an innocent little dude, but I liked to be having a good time.

"I have four older brothers and sisters. They used to tell me all kinds of stuff, just to see me get upset. Like my birthday is October 21. I have an uncle whose birthday is October 21. They were always teasing me, saying, 'Your birthday is with your uncle, but my birthday is with Doctor J.' I'd go to my mom crying and say, 'Mom, can I get my birthday changed?' They were always teasing me, just to see me get upset and run back to mom.

"The good one they used to get me on was that I wasn't a part of the family. They'd say, 'You're adopted, but you can't tell mom.' It was incredible how you believe that stuff. They'd say, 'Look, do you see how everybody else in the family looks like each other?' I look like them, too, but when your brothers and sisters start telling you this, it starts going through your mind.

"Herbie and Tony's birthdays are close together, and Sharon and Gail's birthdays are real close, too. They'd use that as an example why I wasn't a part of the family. I'd be thinking, 'It's true, their birthdays are only two months apart, they're together. And where's my birthday? It's way over here.' They really got me on that.

"My brother Herbie was a big influence. He'd tell me to stretch and do push-ups, and I'd do it—like before I'd go to bed, or if I knew I was going out to a movie later that night, I'd get them out of the way during the day. I listened to what he said. He'd ask me how many pushups I could do. I'd say 15, or whatever. And he'd say, 'In two weeks, I want you to be able to do 35 pushups.' And in two weeks, he might catch me off guard, and I'd only be able to do 26. He'd say, 'You haven't been working out.'

"He was the only one who would take me out to play with older guys. He'd tell me to play good defense and not let my man score, and not get any turnovers. And if I'd shoot, to make sure I had a good open shot. I was happy just to do that. He would sneak me into gyms where you had to have a membership or whatever, and he'd let me go in there and play. Sometimes he'd sacrifice not playing, like say, 'You're going to have to play without me if you don't let my brother play.' He was always doing something extra for me. My other older brother, Tony, he wouldn't take me anywhere. I'd go crying to mom, so she'd make him do it.

"I first started playing basketball in the backyard. My neighbor, Kenny Hicks, would come over and we'd bend a hanger into the shape of a hoop, and screw it into the tree. We'd even get nets for it. We'd play so much it got to the point where we could shoot 20-foot J's and it would be nothing but net—with tennis balls. It was incredible.

"We'd go one-on-one, and we'd make it as real as possible. My mom would come out and sing the national anthem. This was in the sixth grade. We'd stand there and look at each other and get ready to play. We had tip-offs and timeouts. It would be the Celtics against the Lakers, something like that.

"I was always one of the better athletes in grade school. I remember this one time, everyone in gym class got a certificate of accomplishment. I didn't even receive one, and I thought I was the best one out there. They called out everyone's name after class, and I didn't even get one. I went back in to class and everyone had their things. I was acting like I wasn't mad or anything, but I was real mad. I went back in and I was crying and everything. I went to my home room teacher and she asked me what was wrong. I was really crying; I was having one of those *deep* cries. She took me out in the hall and said, 'You've got to promise not to tell anyone I'm telling you this, because I'm not supposed to do this.' She had this paper on who was supposed to receive awards at the banquet in the next few days. And it had my name for the best athlete in the school. That's why I hadn't received one of those awards. She told me that, and after that, man, I was all right. Yeah! I got a trophy!

"I didn't play much my freshman year here [166 minutes]. But the reason I didn't was I thought I was a good ballplayer, and I thought everyone expected so much out of me. So when I missed a jump shot, I felt bad. I thought I was supposed to have a perfect game. When I went to the free throw line, I just didn't feel right. I was thinking, 'Damn, I should be doing better than this.'

"I was putting added pressure on myself, because Todd and Troy were playing a lot. I knew that I was at their level of play, yet I was changing to a new position. They were playing their normal position. For some strange reason whenever I went into a game—every time—I felt the crowd expected something out of me. I wasn't even comfortable shooting a free throw. I'd go up for a jump shot and all I'd be thinking about was the crowd. 'I've got to make this shot. I've got to make this shot.' Every time. There was only a few times where I'd shoot the ball normal and feel good shooting it. It's really unexplainable. Have you ever been in a situation where it's a tie game late in the second half and you're at the free throw line? You know how nervous you are? That's how I was the whole time. I could have had a good freshman year if I hadn't thought the way I did.

"I'd have a lousy practice where I was working hard and things just didn't go right for me. I was just so tired. I'd be working so hard on defense. Then they'd want me to be the best offensive player, too, just be perfect all the time. I'd think, 'Gollee, what you want me to do, be a computer? Why don't you put a computer in my head?' It was just real frustrating, trying to keep up with school and everything.

"But I alleviated all that pressure my junior year, because I had worked so hard that summer. I worked so hard, I wasn't even thinking about it. I just went out and played. I developed that confidence. I'd get up at 6:30, and run this hill. Then I'd go to work for this ventilating and sheeting place in Chicago. Then after work I'd go to the gym and work on my shooting and ballhandlling. It was incredible how much I improved in one summer, because I was working out hard. I wasn't going to the park and playing five-on-five with the fellas. I was just working hard on my own, five days a week.

"I laugh a lot at different things because I visualize them. If coach says something like, 'Johnny, you're playing like you're halfway to Mars,' I'll picture Johnny on some damn airplane going to Mars. And that makes it even more funny.

"The thing I get a big kick out of is watching the other guys get introduced before the game, just watching the way they run out there. Some guys, like Melvin, got a funny run and all. It just makes me happy. It's kind of hard to say why.

"But I hate the fact I don't get a chance to go home for Thanksgiving and Christmas. I really enjoy watching cartoons of the Grinch and all that stuff, doing all the things you normally do when you're young, like when it's Easter and you're looking for eggs and stuff— just that feeling you get. You really don't get that a lot here, unless you're on the road. There's nothing like being home with your family.

"It's hard keeping up with your classes. I remember last year, when I was on [academic] probation. Probation is a 3.8, and I had a 3.86. I was doing good in basketball and I was just so scared I was going to be ineligible. I just went by myself driving around one day. I went to this school in the parking lot and started praying and crying. I was literally crying. I had worked so hard. I'm not as smart as lots of people in my class who don't participate in sports, but I work hard to get what little I have. It just hurt so much. I prayed, and it's just amazing, things just went peaches and cream after that."

9

•

Going South

The win over Louisville was intoxicating, lifting everyone's spirits to a new high. Keady gave the team Sunday off, and Monday's workout was limited to weightlifting.

Along with rest, the week brought more respect for the program. Purdue was now ranked second in the latest wire service polls, behind Arizona, and was number one by a computer ranking service published by the *Chicago Sun-Times*. Those ominous days of December seemed a long time ago now. The team was riding a 16-game winning streak, tying a school record, and still stood alone atop the Big Ten with its 6-0 conference record.

The challenge now was to avoid a hangover from all the excitement and get back to work—a strange concern given the fact the next opponent was Indiana.

The rivalry between these two schools is perhaps the premier rivalry in all of college basketball. It dates back to 1901, encompassing 150 contests and some of the great names in the history of the game. Purdue has won 90 of those games, and can boast that it has won more Big Ten games and championships than the Hoosiers. But Indiana has the not-so-small matter of five national championships, three in the previous 12 years, to back its arguments for superiority.

But the quality and equality of the series is best reflected by the respective all-time records of the two schools in conference play. Through the end of the 1986-87 season, through 82 years, Purdue had won 610 games and lost 441, a winning percentage of 58.039. Indiana, in 80 years of play, had won 629 games and lost 456, a winning percentage of 57.972. Over 87 years, the difference in the quality of the programs has been that minute.

Since Keady took over at Purdue, however, the rivalry had escalated to a new level. Keady and Knight each had won seven games against each other. The previous season, each team had won on its home court by 11 points, an appropriate measure of the growing equality of the programs.

The games themselves usually made for gala events, but they were often spiced by fireworks displays as well. During Keady's first year at Purdue, Knight had fanned the flames of the rivalry by bringing a donkey on his Sunday morning television show, dressing him in Purdue clothing and introducing him as a Purdue spokesman. Then, in the first Keady-Knight matchup, in Bloomington, Knight stood up a few minutes into an already heated battle, grabbed a referee who was blocking his view by the back of his belt and pulled him out of the way. The referee nearly stumbled to the ground. Keady, enraged that a technical foul wasn't called, stormed onto the court in front of the scorer's table, and was promptly slapped with the technical he thought Knight should have gotten. After the game, a 69-61 Indiana victory, Keady, who was seething because he thought Knight had successfully intimidated the officials, greeted the press corps with an announcement.

"You guys don't know me very well yet, but I won't take that shit," he said as he entered the room from behind the assembled reporters. "I'll fight their ass until the world falls in." It was with precisely that attitude Keady's teams had managed to play Indiana on even terms over the years, despite having less talent most of the time.

The best remembered game between the two teams in recent years, although hardly the best-played, came in 1985. Knight, who had coached the U.S. Olympic team to a gold medal in the boycott-riddled games in Los Angeles the previous summer, was riding a ragged edge with the Hoosiers that season. They were 14-9 overall, 6-7 in the Big Ten. Purdue, with a freshman class that included Lewis, Mitchell and Stephens, was 8-6 in the conference when the two teams squared off on a warm Saturday afternoon the first week of March.

With Lewis starting his fifth collegiate game, and Mitchell his first, Purdue jumped to a 11-2 lead. Five minutes into the game, I.U.'s Daryl Thomas slapped the ball from Purdue forward Mark Atkinson at the top of the key. The ball rolled loose, and there was a brief scramble on the floor before I.U.'s Marty Simmons was whistled for a foul. Knight began screaming for a jump ball, gesturing wildly. His anger mounted when Thomas was immediately called for a reaching foul on the ensuing inbounds play. Knight continued his tirade, and just as he was sitting down, was hit with a technical foul. He then stood up, picked up the red plastic chair he had been sitting on, and slid it across the floor. It passed about eight feet in front of Steve Reid, who was preparing to shoot the technical free throws, and stopped in the corner of the floor. Reid jogged over to pick it up, but an usher grabbed it first. Knight would be hit with two more technicals in the arguments that followed, and was kicked out of the game.

It would stand as the most publicized incident in a long line of incidents for Knight. A few of the fans were so caught up in the bedlam inspired by Knight's ejection that they protested other officials' calls by throwing coins toward the floor as the game wore on. One of them bounced off a fan and hit Pat Keady in the eye, forcing her to wear a patch for a few days afterward. Purdue held on to win, 72-63.

Through it all, however, Knight and Keady had managed to maintain a civil, often warm, relationship. After all, they had considerable common ground to stand on: hard work, discipline and adherence to NCAA guidelines. Knight had been one of Keady's coaching idols when Keady was coaching at Hutchinson. Keady, in fact, had raised a few eyebrows the day he was presented as Purdue's new coach in April of 1980 when he was inevitably asked about coaching against Knight.

"You guys might not want to hear this," he said, "but I like the guy. I like the way he goes about things and the way his teams play."

The two established a solid friendship in the early years of their rivalry. Once when Pat Keady was hospitalized, Knight sent her flowers. Knight, who normally avoids the social gatherings that many schools have on game days, also appeared at a Lafayette booster luncheon when Indiana played at Purdue in 1984, and exchanged compliments with Keady.

They even became golf partners, for awhile. Keady and Purdue's golf coach, Joe Campbell, would play with Knight and Sam Carmichael, the pro at a country club just north of Bloomington, at the end of each summer before putting up their clubs for the winter.

But a funny thing happened as Keady's teams began winning

more consistently against the Hoosiers. After Purdue beat Indiana twice in the 1984–85 season, Knight suddenly lost interest in the golf outings. Keady had been warned of that occurrence by Illinois coach Lou Henson, and it turned out to be right.

That, along with a few other matters, had soured the relationship in Keady's mind. Knight, Keady thought, became involved in far too many petty matters that were not becoming of the profession, played too many mind games with too many people, and took himself much too seriously.

"You can't have fun with the guy any more," he often said.

A minor incident reported in *A Season on the Brink,* John Feinstein's bestselling book on Knight and Indiana's 1985–86 season, probably didn't help their relationship. After Keady had confronted Knight over the fact Indiana's players were only willing to shake hands after games Indiana won, Knight, according to the book, had told his players "I'm not very big on the people up here, including their coach. . . ." Keady wasn't particularly bothered by the quote, realizing it was something a coach might say in the privacy of a locker room. But it still was the kind of comment a competitor tends to remember.

Keady didn't need any help keeping his competitive instincts sharp for this series, however, if for no other reason than the fact he was continually being compared with Knight. The story of Keady as the under-recognized coach struggling to meet the challenge of competing against one of the game's most dominating figures was beginning to wear thin in his mind. Every season, it seemed, another army of reporters lined up at his office door and fired the same line of questions.

Many people around West Lafayette believed the depth of Knight's popularity in the state was at least one significant factor in Lee Rose's decision to leave Purdue after taking it to the Final Four in 1980. Keady, too, had been warned of it. Before accepting the job at Purdue he had called Al McGuire, the former Marquette coach. McGuire advised him not to take the job, thinking the obstacles of competing in the same state as Knight and Notre Dame's Digger Phelps, whose programs were nationally renowned, would be too great for anyone to overcome.

Notre Dame had turned out to be an obstacle only in the case of a few recruiting battles. It was no obstacle on the court, because Phelps refused to play Purdue. Keady, baffled why two in-state powers shouldn't play one another, called once and proposed they renew the series that had been dormant since 1966, but Phelps said no. "The roads don't lead from South Bend to Lafayette," he explained once, when asked about it at a banquet. Keady never brought it up again. "It's like asking a girl out," he said. "I only get turned down once."

The media and general public kept bringing up the question, but Notre Dame wouldn't budge. As Purdue's success grew, its followers delighted in joking about Notre Dame's unwillingess to stand up and fight. Once, when Reiter sent a video of a common opponent to a Notre Dame assistant for scouting purposes, he added a reminder that Purdue would like to get a game up sometime. The Notre Dame coach wrote back, thanking him for the tape and adding: "I talked with Coach Phelps and he is not interested in playing Purdue University in the near future, but if we can ever be of assistance to you, don't hesitate to call." Reiter tacked the letter to his bulletin board as a souvenir.

Backing down from a challenge had never been an issue with Keady. By this point in his coaching career, his problem had become getting everyone to recognize he was meeting the challenge successfully and shut up about it. Since his arrival at Purdue, his teams had won just three fewer conference games than Knight's and had played Knight's teams on even terms in head-to-head competition. But Indiana's NCAA tournament championships and Knight's headline-grabbing manner always seemed to stand in the way.

The Hoosiers' championship the previous season had been particularly difficult to live with, considering Purdue had tied them for the Big Ten title. Just when it seemed Purdue's seven-year sprint had finally pulled it even with the Hoosiers, it had to sit back and watch them run off and win the national championship.

Keady, for one, refused to do it. A couple of hours before Indiana tipped off against Syracuse in New Orleans, he and Pat flew to Las Vegas. It turned out to be a winning move. He won $4,000 at Keno as soon as he hit town, and continued his hot streak through the evening. It was at least some consolation.

Keady's frustration with Knight and the circumstances of the rivalry surfaced occasionally. During one Sunday afternoon practice in

October, Dave Stack had made a bad decision on a fast break. "Stack, I hope you go into coaching someday," Keady shouted. "And I hope you get a job in Bloomington. Then they'll have two idiots down there."

Another time, after a Purdue home game, Keady was signing autographs for a few teenaged boys, one of whom was wearing an Indiana sweatshirt. A few days earlier, Knight had pulled his team off the floor during the second half of an exhibition game against the Soviet Union. The move had shocked Keady; quitting was a foreign notion to his way of thinking.

"I can't believe you would cheer for a quitter," Keady said as he signed his autograph.

"I don't like the coach, I like the players," the boy said.

"Well, I can buy that," Keady said. "He's got good kids."

Still, Keady respected Knight professionally, liked him personally, and got along with him whenever the two were together. In many ways he didn't mind losing to Indiana as much as he did to other teams in the league, because of his respect for Knight's coaching ability.

Although the history of the rivalry and the recent quality of the teams dictated that each game between Indiana and Purdue would be special, this one promised to be unique from Purdue's standpoint. For the first time in several years, Indiana was a legitimate underdog on its home floor.

The Hoosiers were in the throes of the kind of puzzling slump that historically follows Knight's greatest achievements. They had opened their conference season with losses at Iowa and Northwestern, barely defeated a weak Wisconsin team at home, and then lost at Michigan State—this from a team that had three starters back from the previous year's national championship team.

Ricky Calloway and Keith Smart, two of the starters from that team who figured to be fixtures in the lineup, had been benched in favor of two freshmen, Jay Edwards and Lyndon Jones, highly-recruited guards who had led Marion High School to three consecutive state championships and shared the state's Mr. Basketball award. It was an odd state of disarray for a team that seemed to have so much raw talent and experience going for it.

Always, a goal in sight.

Gene Keady and Steve Scheffler embrace a Big Ten championship.

Todd Mitchell adds an exclamation point to the victory over Indiana.

Everette Stephens puts on his "donkey ears" for Todd Mitchell after the tournament win over Memphis State.

Bruce Weber, Gene Keady and Kevin Stallings find the action hard to watch.

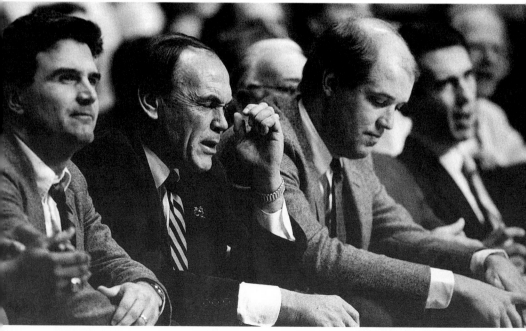

Todd Mitchell, Gene Keady, Troy Lewis and Melvin McCants enjoy a "pressing" engagement in South Bend.

Gene Keady in a contemplative moment before the game.

The White shirts gather for advice during a practice scrimmage.

Preparing for the attack—together.

Ryan Berning and Gene Keady keep their eye on the ball.

Troy Lewis, Gene Keady, Todd Mitchell and Everette Stephens rejoice after the season's final home game.

Troy Lewis finds a seat in the sold-out Athletic and Convocation Center.

Troy Lewis and Todd Mitchell deal with the weighty issues of the day.

Bruce Weber takes the plunge, courtesy of Everette Stephens and Troy Lewis, the day after the Big Ten title-clinching victory.

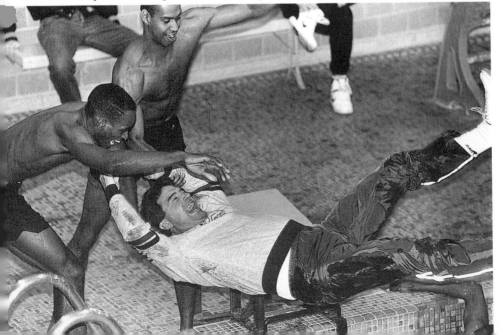

The Big Ten championship in hand, Melvin McCants, Troy Lewis, Everette Stephens and Todd Mitchell head for the bench in the final seconds of the Michigan game.

Sometimes the video replays are entertaining, although Gene Keady isn't so sure.

Gene Keady demonstrates defensive techniques
before tipoff.

The first version of the 1987–88 Purdue University basketball team:
Row one: Kory Fernung, Tony Jones, Todd Mitchell, Everette Stephens, Troy
Lewis, Dave Stack, Billy Reid, Dave Barrett. Row two: Gene Keady, Dave Wood,
Bruce Weber, Eric Ewer, John Brugos, Ryan Berning, Melvin McCants, Jeff
Arnold, Steve Scheffler, Kip Jones, Tom Reiter, Kevin Stallings, Dale Rudd and
Ed Howat.

But Purdue's coaches viewed the Hoosiers as a stick of dynamite. There simply was too much powder at Knight's disposal for an explosion not to go off before long. Smart and Dean Garrett, after all, had played on the U.S. Pan American team the previous summer, and appeared to be certain first-round NBA draft picks. Calloway had pro potential, too. Jones and Edwards were two of the best freshmen in the country. Even the far end of Indiana's bench was filled with former Mr. Basketballs and All-State prep talent.

The hope was to get in and out of town before somebody lit the fuse.

But Keady, at the moment, was looking for a fuse to re-ignite his team. The emotionally-charged victory at Louisville, the win streak and the general well being of the team was making it difficult to re-introduce nose to grindstone. It hadn't been long ago that games against Indiana were the cornerstones of the season for Purdue. Now, it almost seemed as if this one was an afterthought, a stepping stone toward bigger and better things.

The week's practices reflected the relaxed mood. Wednesday's workout in particular was listless, and Scheffler had come down with a sore elbow in his shooting arm. As if that wasn't warning enough, Indiana sounded another one that night by winning at Ohio State, 75-71. It was a win that seemed to smooth over many of the Hoosiers' rough spots. Purdue's coaches had hoped another loss might send them deeper into their doldrums and make them easier to beat. Now, they probably would come into Saturday's game with renewed enthusiasm.

And that was precisely the ingredient Purdue suddenly seemed to be lacking. After Thursday's video session, and before practice, Keady tried to snap his team back to attention. He talked of confidence, of knowing your role, of focusing on continued improvement regardless of the win streak. But it had little effect on that day's workout. The play was sloppy, and not much more spirited than it had been on Wednesday.

Keady, his patience already worn thin, went after the White shirts first. They responded, and he went after the Blacks. "I'm going to tell you something, guys!" he shouted, at all of them. "You are so horrible today I can't believe it. It looks to me like you didn't learn a damn thing from the game at Michigan last year. If you want to go to Bloomington Sunday and get your ass kicked, it's OK with me. But I don't want to. If we don't start something, we're going to be 6-6 at the next turn."

Keady yelled, he cursed, he kicked a ball into the stands, but it didn't make any difference. Brugos in particular was deep into his funk, offering only token effort on defense against McCants. Arnold was gone, and Scheffler was now hurt, so he was having to fight more of the battles inside for the White shirts. It didn't take long for his frustration to mount and his effort to fade as he faced what he saw was a hopeless situation. Weber was just about to tell him to get off the floor and step in to play himself when Stallings spoke up.

"You give less effort than any player I've ever seen here," he said.

The practice concluded a few minutes later in the weightroom. Keady sat in his customary spot on the countertop and gazed at the floor while his players stoically went to work around him.

"We've destroyed everything we've built up the last 12 weeks," he said quietly.

Stallings and Weber were still angry with Brugos' showing. Weber stepped out and demonstrated the statue-like manner in which Brugos had been guarding McCants, allowing him to turn and shoot without resistance.

"It was like a layup drill," he said.

"Well why don't we get rid of him?" Keady said.

"We can't, coach," Weber said. "We need the body."

Keady knew full well he would never drop a player, either during or after the season. He took pride in his ability as a coach to extract a player's potential, and to get rid of one, no matter how great the frustrations imposed, would be admitting failure in that regard. Besides, he had already proven many times that he didn't have the heart to drop a kid from his team unless he had no choice.

He would prove it again the following morning. As the coaches' meeting broke up in Keady's office Friday, Fernung, the freshman walk-on, was waiting outside the door. Fernung had been granted a spot on the team after his mother, who had already been told by Purdue's assistants that her son wasn't good enough to play in the Big Ten, called Keady and made a heartfelt plea. Fernung, whose only game appearance had been against Ball State, when he fired the three-point attempt that was wildly off the mark, had since hurt his knee and been sitting out for several weeks. But he was rounding into shape now and was anxious to play. The past couple of days in practice he had begun substituting himself into fullcourt scrimmages, literally running onto the court from the sideline and jumping into place. He even ran sprints with the White squad, voluntarily.

It was a sticky situation. The coaches knew Fernung lacked the raw athletic ability to make it in the Big Ten. The assistants, in fact, had told Fernung's parents that the previous summer, when they asked if he could try out. Only because Keady couldn't say no was he given a shot in the first place. Now, with the injury, and with Rea's emergence as a valuable practice player, it seemed time to part company. To keep Fernung along for the ride would be unfair, both to the players and to Fernung, and Keady had told the coaches he had no choice but to drop him.

"What's going on with your knee?" Keady asked Fernung. "I was surprised to see you out there. I didn't know the doctors had given you approval to play yet."

Fernung said he had been cleared to participate in some of the less demanding drills.

"Well that's not what I had heard," Keady said. "Let's get it checked out. That's all I've got."

He couldn't do it.

One of the challenges in playing Indiana, Purdue's coaches figured, would be in not allowing the importance of the game to be blown out of proportion in their own minds. In the leaner times of previous seasons, a victory over Indiana would be a season highlight. But the program had advanced beyond that now. A loss to Indiana this season would hardly be the end of the world, given all that had been accomplished already, and all that lie ahead.

In retrospect, the coaches wondered if they might have overreacted the previous season when Purdue had lost by 11 points in Bloomington. Keady had responded that day the way he usually reacts to a loss, with raging disgust, and it was amplified by the fact it had come to such a big rival.

The sour mood had turned perversely comical on the ride back to West Lafayette when McCants passed gas in the back of the bus. The odor hovered in the air for what seemed like forever, as the players exchanged nervous glances and stifled laughs. Keady, sitting in the front of the bus, wasn't amused, particularly because his wife was present. He didn't say anything until the team gathered for the next workout, when he scolded them for the breach of etiquette.

He continued to ride them hard until the next game five days later, a homecourt win over Wisconsin, and then loosened his grip a bit. The Wisconsin victory turned out to be the first of eight straight that cleared the path to Purdue's portion of the Big Ten championship.

This year, however, the unofficial emphasis for the coaches would be to look at things from a broader perspective. The game at Indiana would be followed by a home game with Wisconsin, and then the most crucial stretch of the season: road games at Michigan, Michigan State and Iowa. It was important now not to let the team's momentum and confidence be shaken by one loss, no matter who it might come to.

"Our attitude's got to be in these next five games, if we get our ass kicked, we've got to come out of there and keep going," Keady had told the coaches. "And I've got to be the best one at it, not the worst."

Stallings laughed at that one.

"If we get beat on Saturday, it'll be a miracle to see you come out of there smiling," he said.

"Yeah, I'll be pissed," Keady agreed. "We shouldn't get beat Saturday."

"But we could," Weber said.

"Sure," Keady said. "Anybody could beat us, coach. That's what's so scary about this team. Anybody can beat us, because we don't have a dominating player."

Like it or not, however, this game, like all games against Indiana, was going to have some added emphasis. If nothing else, the Purdue fans demand that it be that way.

Keady and some of the players had been receiving many letters of encouragement in the days leading up to the game. And there was a sendoff rally when the team left Mackey, complete with the Boilermaker Special and cheering fans.

Playing in Bloomington almost demands a greater emotional investment than most games for every team. The arena itself, Assembly Hall, can be an intimidating presence. It's a mammoth, awkward-looking limestone structure filled with corridors and stairways, balconies and basement rooms, nooks and crannies. Except for foldaway bleachers at each end of the floor, the fans sit to the sides of the court, in red-cushioned theatre-style seats that rise steeply in two levels, giving the appearance of a set of jaws waiting to clamp shut on its victim. To get to the playing floor from outside the building, one must walk through a hallway, down two flights of stairs, and—if Indiana is practicing—through black curtains. It is a dungeon-like atmosphere that often mystifies first-time visitors. What unspeakable acts could be going on in the basement behind those curtains?

Indiana was wrapping up its practice when the Purdue traveling party arrived late in the afternoon. A few of the players and support personnel stuck their heads through the curtains for a quick and curious glance, which brought a student manager scurrying over to stand guard.

"You know what I ought to do?" Keady said as Purdue's players filed into their locker room to change clothes. "I ought to just walk out there and tell Bobby to get the hell off the court. What do you think he'd do?"

A look of terror swept over the face of the student manager—until Keady smiled and let out a gleeful chuckle.

A few years earlier, someone had written a message on a chalkboard in Purdue's locker room when it arrived the day before the game: "Keady, we're going to kick your ass." Keady wasn't sure who was responsible, but he suspected one of Indiana's players. Not that it bothered him. That was the sort of blunt, competitive attitude Keady loved, the kind of "knock-this-stick-off-my-shoulder" challenge he thrived upon.

When Purdue began its workout, Knight came back out on the floor to talk with Keady. The two chatted amicably for several minutes, then Knight walked over to talk with Pat Keady. He thanked her for sending flowers when his mother had died earlier in the season, and then returned to talk briefly with Keady awhile longer.

The festive mood lasted through most of the practice this time, an improvement from the previous few days. The Black shirts were playing much better, and the White shirts were offering some resistance. The coaches were encouraged, given the workouts of the past few days.

When the practice ended at 7 p.m., Indiana's players were waiting around the corner by their dressing room to come back on for their second session of the day. Mitchell stopped to talk briefly with Garrett, then joined his teammates in the locker room, where

Stephens was joking with Weber about the latest emphasis on staying positive.

Stephens reminded him of the coaches' reaction to the loss to Iowa State.

"We were positive after the Iowa State game," Weber said.

"Yeah, positively chewing our ass off!" Stephens said, bursting out laughing.

"Yeah, PosiTIVEly chewing our ass," Mitchell added, illustrating the joke by jumping behind Stephens and pretending to chew on his behind.

Purdue's coaches had gambled a bit in making the hotel reservations for the weekend in Bloomington. They decided to have the team stay at the Inn of the Fourwinds, a resort hotel in the countryside south of Bloomington, about a 30-minute drive, mostly along winding, two-lane roads from Indiana's campus. Keady subscribed to the popular coaches superstition that a team should never stay in the same hotel as the previous year if it happened to lose. And while Keady's teams had won twice at Indiana, in 1984 on their way to a share of the Big Ten title, and again in '85 in the infamous chair-throw game, their six losses had exhausted all the respectable hotels within Bloomington's city limits.

The only problem with staying so far from campus was that the game's 2 p.m. starting time would make it unfeasible to drive to Assembly Hall Saturday morning for the customary hour-long shooting practice and return to the hotel for the pregame meal and meeting. But the coaches decided a break from the normal routine might be good preparation for the NCAA tournament, when normal routines become fond memories and games begin anywhere from noon to 10 p.m. to please the Godfathers of college basketball, the television networks. They skipped the shootaround.

By game time, everyone was restless. It had been a long week of practice, and all the anticipation had made it seem even longer. It was a relief to have the game finally at hand. One more time, Keady wanted to set the record straight.

"It's no disaster if you can't get out of here with this, but it certainly would be great to continue what you've got going," he said. "It would be awful nice to step on those golf tees next summer and not hear any bullshit from the white and red. That's a minor thing with me, but it's still nice."

Assembly Hall normally isn't one of the louder arenas in the country. The acoustics absorb much of the noise, and the comfortable seats don't inspire rowdiness from the fans. But for this game, the place rocks. The ovation as Indiana took the floor could be heard clearly from Purdue's locker room as Keady finished his pregame talk. Purdue's players were greeted with boos. No matter what the coaches or players might want to think, this couldn't be just another game. It never would be.

"Nobody told me about this, and nobody can explain it," Reiter, the Wisconsin native, said as the teams warmed up. "This rivalry is something."

And so, it turned out, was the game. Something else, in fact.

From a tie at 4, Indiana took complete control as it beat Purdue's fullcourt press easily and stymied its fastbreak. It grabbed a 10-4 lead. Keady called for a switch to a matchup zone, but it didn't help. Edwards missed, Joe Hillman rebounded, and Magnus Pelkowski hit an 18-footer. Stephens missed a three-pointer, Garrett rebounded, and Hillman hit from the baseline.

It was 14-4, with 14:47 left in the half. Keady called a timeout to stem the tide, and the red sea of fans in Assembly Hall erupted. It didn't matter. The lead grew to 19-6, then McCants missed two free throws and Scheffler fouled on the rebound.

A television timeout followed. Keady tried to calm his players, but the worst was yet to come. Scheffler, showing no effects of his elbow injury, sparked a brief rally with a basket and two rebounds that helped close the gap to 21-12, but it didn't last. Lyndon Jones hit from the baseline. Edwards picked off a lazy pass from Mitchell, then made a beautiful pirouette to get past Tony Jones and hit a layup. Scheffler missed, Mitchell fouled on the rebound, and Todd Jadlow hit a 15-footer. Lewis forced a jumper, the rebound was tipped back to Purdue, but McCants was called for charging when he turned and shot over Garrett.

Keady, livid with the call and the general course of events, stripped off his coat, slammed it to the floor and paced in front of his bench. For Indiana's fans, starved for success in recent weeks, this was ecstasy. It was as if they were standing atop their in-state rival, the Big Ten leader and a newcomer to the neighborhood of national powers, and grinding their heel in its chest.

The Hoosiers weren't done yet, either. McCants picked up his third foul on the next possession, and Garrett hit both free throws. Berning, fresh off the bench, missed a three-pointer. Garrett got inside Scheffler and hit an eight-footer. It was 31-12 when Keady called another timeout. The fans erupted again.

This time Keady spared no words.

"Goddamnit, this is just like Michigan!" he shouted above the din of the fans and the pep band, which was playing Indiana's school song. "You guys get in a game that means something, and you fold! Now let's get our ass in gear! Where's your pride?"

Weber started to offer instruction to the guards, but Keady wasn't through. "Hell, they're going to skin your ass if this keeps up!" he shouted. "This is an embarrassment to the whole damn state, even to Indiana's fans! Now let's go!"

The response wasn't immediate. Kip Jones threw away a cross-court pass to Berning, and Garrett scored his sixth straight point on a tip-in. Indiana now led by 21, with eight minutes still to play in the half.

Stephens finally threw a bucket of water on the raging fire with a three-pointer, then added another after Kip Jones' steal at the end of a good defensive series. The lead had quickly been sliced to 15. It shrunk as low as 12, and was 13 when Mitchell hit a three-pointer with 18 seconds left.

But even that basket was an indication of how ragged things were for Purdue. Taking over the ball with 59 seconds left, the coaches had called for Laker. The plan was to get a quick shot within about 10 seconds so that they would get the ball back after again Indiana's possession. But the play had broken down, and the 45-second clock was nearing its expiration when Mitchell was forced to shoot the three-pointer.

Hillman then delivered a parting shot at the buzzer, shaking loose from Berning and hitting a baseline jumper to return the lead to 15 at the half.

Knight would later call his team's performance, except for the final few minutes, the best half of basketball he had seen any team play up to that point of the season. It was certainly good enough to dominate the number two-ranked team in the country. The Hoosiers had shot 64 percent from the field, forced nine turnovers, and grabbed seven offensive rebounds.

The coaches gathered first outside the locker room in a back hallway. They were a bit dazed, and spent the first few moments reflecting on all that had just gone wrong before Wood snapped them back to attention.

"Hey! What do we have to do to get back in this?" he asked.

The answer was to get more movement in the offense and get the ball inside. Indiana had successfully gummed up Purdue's offense by dropping off of Kip Jones at the top of the key on Early Break and was having its inside defenders switch to lessen the advantage of Purdue's picks. With it then more difficult to get the ball inside, the guards had responded by settling for outside jumpers. Lewis in particular was frustrated, and wasn't cutting sharply. Mitchell wasn't getting into the flow of the offense, and was having trouble guarding Edwards, so it was decided Tony Jones would start in place of Kip Jones, moving Mitchell inside.

Keady was alternately cool and hot with the players in the locker room. He called for more patience and movement on offense. He scolded them for their lack of defense and mental preparation. The practices had been foreboding.

"What'd you think they were going to do, guys, come out and play dead?" Keady said. "You watch them on television, you watch Michigan State beat them and you think they're no good? Are you that stupid? These guys have got more talent than anybody in the league, and always have except for Michigan and Illinois. Always!"

It was time to go again.

"You cannot get back in the game by shooting it quick," Weber shouted as they huddled. "Gain four points every five minutes and you'll win the game."

"Together!"

"We attack!"

"Chop it down, chop it down," Lewis said as the players exited the locker room.

They chopped it down. McCants scored inside to open the half's scoring. Garrett missed with McCants in his face, Tony Jones rebounded and Mitchell scored inside again over Garrett, who was nursing three fouls. Seventy seconds into the half, and it was an 11-point game. Garrett hit a turnaround jumper, but Mitchell scored again inside, this time with his left hand. Stephens knocked the ball loose from Lyndon Jones to Mitchell, who hit Tony Jones for a layup. Now it was a nine-point game, with 17:48 left. Garrett scored again on a turnaround jumper, but Lewis came back with a three-pointer, his first points of the game, cutting the lead to eight. They were ahead of schedule.

Indiana gradually rebuilt its lead to 12 points as Garrett continued to dominate inside, but Lewis scored along the baseline and Stephens stripped the ball from Hillman and stuffed the ball to make it an eight-point game again with 11:17 left. One minute later, Stephens hit another three-pointer to cut it to five. Garrett missed, Kip Jones rebounded and Lewis dropped another three-pointer from the top of the key to cut the lead to two. Kip Jones later would recall a feeling of incredible oneness during this stretch, a sensation of almost mystic perfection. It was at the very least the magic level Keady so often mentioned.

Indiana called timeout.

Garrett's rebound basket after the timeout made it 69-65, but Kip Jones slid through the lane and hit a layup to make it a two-point game again. Both teams were getting a bit frantic now. Indiana missed four straight shots, but Purdue couldn't capitalize until Lewis drove the baseline and hit a running one-hander.

They had come all the way back now, from 21 points down in the first half to a tie with more than 6 minutes left. And they weren't finished. Indiana missed three shots on its next possession, then McCants rebounded. Purdue worked the ball patiently, and McCants scored inside. Purdue now led for the first time, with 5:10 remaining.

Edwards answered with a three-pointer to give Indiana a 72-71 lead. McCants was fouled, and hit the second of his two free throws. Tied again. Hillman missed, Kip Jones rebounded and Mitchell, now working the lane like a maestro, scored again over Garrett, who had four fouls now. Purdue led again, 74-72, with four minutes still to play.

Edwards hit another three-pointer to return the lead to Indiana, but Kip Jones drove the lane and scooped in a basket to make it 76-75, Purdue, with 3:30 left. Edwards then missed, and Kip Jones rebounded. Seconds later, he took a pass from Mitchell and scored in the lane, but was called for charging.

There was a timeout. Purdue had a one-point lead and the ball with just a few minutes remaining. Earlier that week in practice it had worked on this sort of situation.

"We've fought all the way back!" Weber shouted above the screaming masses, whose joy had turned to panic. "We've got to win this one at the free throw line."

"Get a shutout and a rebound, and their ass is in a sling!" Stallings added. "They can't win the close ones!"

"We can't lose!" Mitchell shouted, his face locked in a glare, as the huddle broke.

It didn't seem as if they could. They had, after all, come so far. And they had such a good record in close games.

Indiana was even cooperating now. Lyndon Jones drove around Stephens and passed off to Garrett, who missed a jumper in the lane. Pelkowski grabbed the rebound, but missed underneath. Mitchell and Garrett both grabbed onto the rebound for a jump ball, but the possession arrow pointed Purdue's way.

Purdue had a one-point lead and the ball. But Lewis' pass to Mitchell was stolen, and McCants fouled Garrett at the other end. Garrett hit the second of two free throws, tying the score at 76. Stephens, however, ran off a pick and nailed a three-pointer over Lyndon Jones from the left wing, giving his team its largest lead of the game, 79-76, with 1:50 left. Stephens looked at Tony Jones as they ran back on defense, clenched his fist and shouted. "Yeah!" It was all coming together.

Garrett worked his way free at the other end and went up for a dunk from the left baseline. Mitchell met him in midair and appeared to block it cleanly, but was called for a foul. Garrett hit both free throws. Purdue's lead was now one, with 1:27 remaining.

Keady called for the control game to drain the clock. Stephens, Lewis and Tony Jones dribbled in a weave out front. With the shot clock winding down, Stephens broke to the basket around Lyndon Jones and drew a foul as he went up for a layup. Purdue had the ball out of bounds, underneath its own basket.

Lewis couldn't find an open teammate to pass to, however, and had to call timeout. During the break, Keady called for Auburn, a play for Mitchell to come off a pick in the lane.

But it never had a chance. Lewis, again unable to find an open teammate, quickly passed the ball to the corner as the five-second limit neared its expiration. But he didn't fake, and Edwards, who was standing in front of him and waving his long arms, deflected it to the corner and ran to pick it up.

Indiana had the ball now, with a chance to regain the lead. Purdue's defense was solid, forcing the Hoosiers away from the basket. Stephens nearly deflected the ball away from Lyndon Jones at the top of the key, but Jones passed to Garrett. Garrett started to dribble to his left into the lane, but his path was blocked by McCants. Garrett passed back to Jones, who dribbled to his right and went up for a shot from 18 feet. He was off-balance, however, and quickly passed back to Garrett, who, with the shot clock down to its final seconds, dribbled to his left again and rushed a 15-footer over McCants. It fell off the front of the rim. Lyndon Jones, who hadn't been blocked out, grabbed the rebound right in front of the basket and rushed another shot from midair that rolled around the rim and out. Mitchell grabbed that rebound, and was fouled by Edwards.

Purdue led by one, with 15 seconds left. Mitchell would have a one-and-one opportunity from the foul line. If he hit both, Indiana would have to hit a three-pointer to stay in the game. Knight called timeout to let him think about it.

"If they tie it up, do you want us to call timeout?" Lewis asked in the huddle.

"No. If they tie it, run Boilermaker," Keady said.

"This is our game!" Weber shouted. Mitchell's teammates slapped him and shouted encouragement as he left the huddle. He had hit five of his six free throws in the game, and played a brilliant second half.

But he missed the free throw. Shooting into a backdrop of screaming, red-clad fans, Mitchell's shot hit the back of the rim and fell into Garrett's hands. Indiana then rushed the ball downcourt without calling timeout, and fed Garrett inside. He turned immediately to his right, fired, and scored from seven feet, giving the Hoosiers the lead again with four seconds left.

Purdue called timeout. Mitchell pulled his shirttail out of his trunks and staggered back to the bench, holding his head in his hands.

Purdue's coaches gathered at the edge of the huddle to set up the final play. Stallings quickly drew up a fullcourt out-of-bounds play, and Keady accepted it. Tony Jones would inbound the ball, while

Stephens, McCants, Mitchell and Lewis would line up across Indiana's free throw line. McCants was to pick for Stephens, who would take the pass and dribble upcourt along the sideline. Mitchell was to pick for Lewis downcourt, giving Stephens the option of creating something on his own or passing off to Lewis.

Indiana called a timeout after seeing Purdue's setup. Stallings flip-flopped Stephens and McCants at the foul line, and the teams returned to the floor.

But the play never came off. Stephens, who was supposed to run to his left off McCants' pick, headed to his right away from the ball. Tony Jones had no choice but to pass to McCants, who immediately threw the ball back to him. Jones, who was sprinting upcourt, was caught off-guard and traveled.

The game was over. The long comeback had been wasted in the final two minutes. Indiana got a layup on its final inbounds play, finishing off an improbable 82-79 victory. The players from both teams, numbed by a game that had been both physically and emotionally draining, shook hands and headed to their locker rooms.

The rivalry between Purdue and Indiana is too fierce to be contained by the final buzzer, however. As Keady was walking off the court, an overweight, middle-aged man wearing a red and white striped rugby shirt jumped in front of him and called him an obscene name. Keady stopped, turned and tried to grab the man by his shirt just below his neck, but Purdue's senior manager, Ed Howat, intervened. Keady turned and continued into the locker room.

Such an encounter between fan and coach wasn't unprecedented. The season before, after Purdue had beaten Indiana at Mackey, a Purdue alum from Indianapolis had shouted a sarcastic comment at Knight as he headed toward his locker room. Knight turned quickly toward him, but was stopped by his assistant coach, Joby Wright. Purdue officials, embarrassed by the incident, responded by closing off the area to fans, a practice they continued to enforce.

The locker room was like a funeral parlor. Most of the players sat in the folding chairs and stared at the floor. Mitchell, his jersey stripped off, paced the floor. Outside, the crowd could be heard singing the school song, adding a verbal exclamation point at the end of it: "I.U.!"

Now the pregame declaration not to let a loss become too devastating, to walk out with heads held high and focused on the future, was an ugly reality for Keady. He paused a moment, then turned to his players.

They had just had a remarkable comeback fall short. Knight, talking with friends after the game, would say he felt like he "was bleeding to death, but couldn't do anything about it." They had hit 18 of 21 field goal attempts in the half, including four of six three-pointers. But they had hit just two of five free throws. Mitchell's game was a perfect summary. He had been splendid in the second half, finishing with 24 points and hitting nine of his ten field goal attempts. But he had missed the one-and-one free throw opportunity that might have won the game.

"Well, one thing you can say, guys, you were men, you were courageous and you came back," Keady said. "You couldn't win it when you had to, but you came back and made a helluva game out of it. What can you say? You've just got to come back, learn from it and not get off to bad starts again and get ready to play.

"It's a shame we have a time getting ready for good teams. You've got to get that worked out in your thinking some way if we're going to be anything in March. Because either we're tentative or we're not ready. That's just something we've got to learn how to do better. Let's huddle up. Let's go!"

The players stood up slowly, silently, and brought their hands together above their heads.

"You showed good courage, men; you can't battle any more than that," Keady said. "We should have won it and we didn't.

"Together!"

"We attack."

Mitchell, still agonizing over his missed free throw, leaned against the wall outside the shower as steam poured out around him. Keady headed for the post-game press conference for the unpleasant task of explaining the loss to the media who had poured in from around the state. He congratulated Indiana, said his team hadn't deserved to win, and would go back to work from here.

"Were you surprised at their starting lineup?" one reporter asked.

"Are you shitting me?" Keady shot back. "Nothing ever surprises you down here!"

The reporters laughed, and Keady returned to the locker room. His joke aside, he was in no mood for levity. His approval of the inbounds play with four seconds left still burned in his stomach. They had tried a play they hadn't practiced. Sometimes such things work. This time it didn't.

"You don't run things you don't practice!" Keady said with disgust as he took off his coat and sat down in the back of the locker room. "That's ridiculous. That's our fault."

Weber, standing next to him, started to bring up other factors that had contributed to the loss.

"Oh, bullshit!" Keady shouted. He stood up, grabbed the folding chair to his left and slammed it to the floor. "You don't run things you don't practice! You deserve to get beat if you do that!"

Keady sat down again, rubbing his face with his hands. The only sound now was Stephens' high-pitched voice slicing through the steam-filled air in the shower.

"You come all that way back and lose," Stephens said, speaking to nobody in particular. "That's unbelievable, man. You work so hard and don't win.

"We lost that game in the first half. We'd score and they'd score. You can't get in no damn shootout with them. That's bullshit. We were just running up and down the floor."

"Hey, Everette," Keady said calmly, sticking his head into the shower area. "Cool it. I know you wanted to win."

Indiana's fans weren't finished celebrating their victory, however. As Purdue's team bus made its way up State Road 37, winding through the rock formations north of Bloomington, a black Thunderbird pulled in front of it. Two red pom-poms hung out the windows, and a sign was taped to the rear window. It read: "Purdue sucks." The car slowed down, from the speed limit of 55 to about 40 miles an hour, forcing the bus, which was penned in by traffic to its left, to slow with it. It continued at that speed for a couple of minutes, then sped on ahead.

After stopping at a traffic light, the same car pulled in front of the bus and slowed down again. The bus driver called the police on his C.B. radio this time, and reported the car's license number. The car then swerved to the right onto the shoulder of the road and sped ahead, passing several cars.

Purdue's team bus was now becoming a major focus of attention

on the highway. The players were like the prisoners locked into stock-
ades and set out in the public squares of Colonial America. There
was nothing they could do but sit there and take the abuse.

A parade of cars loaded with ecstatic I.U. fans passed by. Some
honked and extended their middle finger. Others held up Indiana
sweatshirts to the window. Those Purdue players not sleeping gazed
out the window at them with blank faces.

A few moments later, as the police department called back to the
bus driver to report an officer was on the way, the black Thunderbird
pulled off the road onto a strip of asphalt connecting the two sides of
the divided highway for use by emergency vehicles. The man driving
the car, who appeared to be college-aged or slightly older, got out and
held up another sign, this one reading, "Bye bye Purdue." The
woman riding with him was shaking her pom-pom, jumping up and
down and cheering as the bus passed.

A few minutes later, as the bus neared Indianapolis, a limousine
drove by. The rear passenger window dropped down, a man clutch-
ing a beer can stuck his head out and held up his middle finger.

"How about that?" Pat Keady said from her seat in the front of
the bus. "A chauffeur-driven limo and a man sticks his head out and
gives the finger. Is that class or is that class?"

"That's what you get when you get beat," Keady said matter-of-
factly.

Steve Scheffler

"I found out I had dyslexia when I was in the second grade. My brother had it, too, so that made it easier to diagnose. I had to go to a different school, a public school, for my English class, and then back to the parochial school for the rest of the classes. I was already bigger than everybody, so that made me stand out that much more.

"I was a big target for bullies. I can't even remember all the names people gave me then. I think your mind wants to block it out. I can't pick out a particular incident when I got teased, but yet there's something in my mind that tells me, 'Yeah, Steve, you've been teased before.'

"I used to be extremely shy and quiet. I definitely think it had an effect. It made me more timid in certain ways. I have a very difficult time. . . I love to tease people, absolutely love it, but I never tease them in a way that would hurt their feelings, you know what I mean? I have strong feelings against that.

"I used to be real scared about having to read out loud in class. And I remember being in spelling bees. I liked it when I got a hard word, because if you miss a hard word, it's all right. It's embarrassing to miss an easy word. But you can't spell right when you have dyslexia. I remember once in fifth grade, the teacher said, 'Well, look it up!' But how can I look it up if I don't even know the second letter? I'm not even sure what the first letter is sometimes.

"Even now, sometimes, I'll try to proofread my own papers, and I won't even remember what word I'm trying to spell. Sometimes I give one of my [complimentary] tickets to a guy down the hall for proof-reading my papers.

"In high school science, I'd take advantage of it sometimes and say like, 'I know the word starts with a G. Is it Gugama?' And the teacher would say, 'Well, glycogen, close enough.' But I also got burned a lot of times when I knew the answer but I spelled it so wrong I wouldn't get credit for it. So I think I lost more than I gained from it.

"Another thing that presents a problem...A lot of people think if you can't remember their name it's just because you're a basketball player and you don't think they're that important. But there are very few guys in our hall that I know the name of. It's surprising how long you can carry on a conversation with someone and never know their name. And after you talk to them for three months, you can't ask them what their name is.

"It was like in the training room, with Audrey. One day I was the last one in there getting my ankle taped, and she asked me, 'What's my name?' I turned all red. That was this year, and I had known her all of last year.

"But that's just the way it is. When I was on the football team in high school my sophomore year, my teammates would get mad at me. I'd come up to the line and the quarterback would be going, 'Red, Blue, 52.' And I'd go, 'Uh-oh.' I'd forget when I was supposed to go. The guy next to me would look at me and go, 'DT.' That meant double team. That was a classic.

"By the time I got here last year, I was used to having people tease me. It wasn't anything new. You become callous to that stuff after awhile.

"Last year it bothered me. Then I wondered if I should even be playing basketball. Sometimes I think it all gets too negative. A lot of it depends on who's saying it and what context. If Jeff would bug me about something, it would be funny. But other people...Or if people would bug you about something constantly, then it would start to bug me some.

"By the end of the season, I was worn out mentally. I was getting teased a lot, and practices seemed a lot harder then. When the fun goes and you start getting motivated because you don't want to have coach get on us...You can whip a horse to make it run, but if it wants to run, you're better off.

"I was wondering, 'Why am I out here? Why am I rooting for these guys? They haven't been very nice to me. Why am I even playing basketball? The coaches say I don't have any basketball savvy. All this, for nothing. What is this big circus?'

"Last year I thought about switching to football. But that wouldn't have necessarily been any better. Some friends from back home and I were talking. We could just go to a small NAIA school and play basketball, all three of us, and get scholarships and not even worry about it. Just play and win. It wouldn't be very much challenge, but that crossed my mind. But I didn't want to just quit.

"If I quit, it just wouldn't seem right. I don't know. This might be a weak answer, but I've always done it for as long as I can remember. And God gave me the skill to play basketball. Unless you can think of something better to do that would be more appropriate and not just waste it... There's a lot of good things you get out of playing, but I don't think you appreciate it fully when you're in it.

"I've gained a lot of confidence this year. I actually go out and have fun during the games now. It's been a gradual thing. I've been surprised. Last year I could not envision myself playing, even as a senior. I thought, 'It's going to be a sorry four years on the bench.' But you just keep working and hope something happens.

"I don't feel near as scared or as anxious. This is my job I have to do, I'm going out to do it the best I can. If that means diving on the floor...you know what I mean? But I'm far from being able to prepare myself mentally. I'm very much on a roller coaster, I'd say.

"I'm just an emotional person. Sometimes I'll cry, but inside I'm still in control. Sometimes I wish I wasn't that way. Like last fall in the weight room, Coach Keady told me to see him in his office the next day. I was really anxious about it, wondering 'Why is coach having a meeting with me?' He didn't yell at me or anything like that. I sat down in the stairwell and thought, 'What did coach try to say to me?' I had tears coming to my eyes. I couldn't figure why I was upset. Even if he would have yelled at me, that wouldn't make me upset.

"That's just the way I am. In the third grade, I think I was on my way to an ulcer. Before a test, I'd get so worried. And I remember one time, I was all upset. I was afraid I wouldn't go to heaven. It said somewhere in the Bible that if you want to be forgiven, you have to forgive everyone else. So I sat by the front door next to the telephone and watched everyone walk in. And I'd sit there and say, 'I forgive you for everything you've done. And I'm sorry for everything I've done wrong.' It was embarrassing. I had just read and didn't understand it. That scared me.

"Maybe that's part of why I'd get so nervous in games: I'd be worrying about different things. When I was a freshman, I'd practically hyperventilate when I got in the games. Some of these guys in Indiana play in big high school gyms. But I'm not used to that. I got scared more than excited when I got in.

"I remember the Michigan players last year at the end of the game when we played up there. They were going, 'Come on, white boy; come on, white boy; shoot it, shoot it.' I'm thinking, 'Man, I'm scared enough as it is, you don't have to be saying that.'

"I really thought about it, the whole thing of college basketball, last summer. If all of a sudden you're getting attention, then all of a sudden you're paying attention to other people less. I think that's definitely bad. That's one nice thing about my philosophy minor. You meet people who say, 'Yeah, Purdue does have a basketball team, don't they?' They're hardly aware of all this. I think there is too much ...there's a point where attention is good, but I think it's definitely bad most of the time.

"Even when I was little—I must have been thinking deeply or something like that—it dawned on me that people are just regular people. After growing up more you come to realize that more. There's no difference. I mean, why is that person so special? All they do is sit there and dribble a basketball around. So what? Or, sure, that person can sing music real well and makes a lot of money, but he is still a person. It's nice to get some attention, but...hey, put this in the book. I wish girls would pay more attention. Beautiful girls. I never get that. That would be the nice way to get attention. People see me play and say, 'He doesn't do it pretty out there,' I guess that's the problem. But the football players are saying, 'Yeah, good job.'

"I know a lot of girls. I'm terrible with them, though. I don't know how Brugos...he's great at this. Let's say a girl's just sitting there somewhere. He can go right up there and just talk to them. I see other guys, how they treat their girlfriends, they don't give them any respect or anything. And yet they've got all these girls. If they're in a class where I can get to know them, then I don't feel that uncomfortable. Once I got pressured into talking to this girl. I knew in the first 30 seconds it was a big strikeout. How do you get out of it without saving face? I'm terrible at that. That's one thing I wish I could learn how to do.

"I usually pray before games, unless I forget. It's so easy to drift away, especially in the atmosphere where everyone around you . . . you know what I mean? It's easy to pick up the habits of everyone else. It takes an effect slowly but surely, to an extent.

"A couple of games I started to drift away from that. Michigan State, Michigan I prayed. I can't remember the games before that. But at Iowa, I was really worried about winning or losing that game, and that made me think something was wrong. What are you setting your perspectives on? I sat down and tried to think about that. But now you get down to the end and can sort of see the Big Ten championship, especially when you're going against Michigan. When that becomes more of the focus, it's harder to focus on God and things like that, and I don't think that's good. That builds up a lot of anxiety and a lot of things. I don't think that's why I should be playing the game.

"So I pray that that will be my focus, just to have God let me do what He wants me to do to glorify Him. It's a combination between prayer and meditation. What would God want me to do in this situation? I might pray, 'Please, God, put this in perspective, this is only a game and this is only a short little segment of your life. I realize it seems important to me now, but please, if we win or lose, give me the perspective of what this actually is.' Different things like that. But, I've prayed at free throws, especially when someone else is shooting. 'Please, Lord, I realize this is only a small little thing, but I sure would appreciate it if it would go in.' "

10

•

Shakeups and Shakedowns

Keady backed his words about not overreacting to the loss. He even waxed poetic, handing out a mimeographed poem called "Winners vs. Losers," by Janna Weir. He then congratulated the players again on their comeback.

But, he sounded a warning as well.

"All I want today is good hard work in the weight room, swimming and we'll get out of here and get ready for practice tomorrow," he said.

"But I'm going to tell you one thing, gentlemen: if we don't kick Wisconsin's ass bad, then I am going to become a bear. I'll take all the heat as far as the losses are concerned, because that's my responsibility. But I don't think we should have to worry about that anymore. It has to be up to you to perform and execute. How many times have we told you not to be casual? How many times have we told you to make crisp passes? How many times have we told you to take squared-up jumpers? How many times do we have to keep telling you? Well, we'll keep telling you until we get it right."

To help get the message across, Keady brought in an old and dear friend, Bud Presley, that week. Presley was something of a cult figure in college basketball circles, unknown to the general public but a legendary elder statesman to veteran coaches. He had never gained much fame as a coach, only respect.

Presley, 66, had coached 12 seasons at Menlo Junior College in California. It was there he met Keady, who was recruiting one of his players for Arkansas. Presley went on to serve as an assistant to Jerry

Tarkanian at the University of Nevada-Las Vegas before retiring in 1984. A chain smoker all his life, he suffered a stroke a month after retiring that left him partially paralyzed on his left side.

Keady felt a strong kinship with him. They were both Irish, for one thing, and shared the same outlook on basketball and life: fundamental, hard-nosed, emotional, ornery. Keady had been amazed by the way Presley's teams played all-out for 40 minutes, particularly on defense. Every day, every minute, even in practice, his players never stopped getting after people. Presley would drive them, cuss them, challenge them, but they loved him back. No doubt Keady saw a lot of himself in Presley.

Presley was considered one of the game's defensive gurus, an innovator and teacher without peer. He even worked as a special defensive consultant to the NBA's Golden State Warriors for a few years. But his no-nonsense approach also kept him from moving up in the coaching ranks. He was a non-politician, as likely to tell off the college president as he was his freshman point guard, and in just about the same tone of voice.

He also was one of the game's great characters, a man who was funny without trying to be funny. He spoke with a raspy, cigarette-worn voice, and called everyone, players and coaches alike, Kid. Those who knew him well could spend hours delighting in Presley stories. At Menlo, for example, he had owned an old Renault that he loaned out to the players when they needed to run errands. They were free to take it whenever they needed it, the only stipulation being that they pay for their own gas.

One time, on the day of a game, Presley—a notoriously bad driver, but that's another story—ran out of gas after one of the players had used the car and not refilled the tank. But he didn't say a thing about it until the game started and the first timeout had been called that night. As his players gathered for the huddle, Presley was hot—but not about what had just taken place on the court. "Goddamnit!" he shouted, "Who forgot to put gas in the Renault?"

Keady flew Presley in to spend a week with the team as an adviser, and to demonstrate some of the more intricate defensive principles to the players. He also wanted to get him back in the game, if only briefly, to let him sit on the bench again and feel the excitement.

Keady's primary concern following the loss at Indiana was his team's emotional lapses. The dry spells that had marked so many of the victories at the start of the season had finally caught up with them in the first half in Bloomington and cost them a game. This was never going to be a rah-rah group, the coaches realized, but somehow they wanted to find a way to avoid the slow starts that had been plaguing them.

"What would you do?" Keady asked Presley.

"I know one thing, you're not going to motivate them consistently by getting all over their ass and giving them passion talks before the game," Presley said. "It's a habit, like anything else. You've got to program that by the intensity in your practices. Every practice has to be emotional and with great intensity and with defensive drills and with great hustle and that will consistently carry over.

"If anything, my kids had to be calmed down before a game, they were so jacked up from practices. They were like Pavlov's dog. I had to calm them down or they'd knock the damn door down and kill each other getting out of the locker room."

Keady's practices were hardly exercises in gentle persuasion as it was, but practicing with a frenzy, from the very beginning, became the emphasis that week. Keady adjusted the schedule to begin with more intense drills, to get the players going immediately.

That was easy to do on Monday, because the players owed him seven sprints for the 17 offensive rebounds allowed against Indiana. (Purdue had grabbed just four.) Keady lined them up, and sent them on their way.

It turned out more like a marathon. McCants, who always took a long time to get warmed up anyway, didn't finish the first one in time. Everyone made the second one, but McCants was late on the next two. He was late on the one after that as well, but Keady counted it anyway. The next two, everyone made. They still had three to go, but were getting more and more tired.

"That's just like you are in a ballgame; you're not ready to play," Keady shouted. "I'd like to get some work done on defense, guys. We wouldn't be doing this if we had blocked out."

They went again, but didn't make it. They went again, but still didn't make it. It was getting hopeless now, because they obviously weren't going to get any faster. Keady gave them a short break, then struck a bargain: Make one more, and they would go on to something else. They made it, barely.

After a water break, they went to work on halfcourt defense. On the first possession, Lewis deflected a pass and then dived on the ball. It was a wondrous sight for the coaches, something Lewis rarely did, and they cheered him wildly. For Lewis, however, it was more of a slick public relations gesture. He knew what mood the coaches would be in following the loss, and he knew what they wanted to see. So he gave it to them right away, to ease the pressure for everyone.

"That's what they wanted," he would explain later. "You've got to do that once in awhile. When you lose, coach goes back to the basics. You've got to do that a couple of days in a row, then when you win, everything's fine again. You just do it so everyone won't get yelled at."

Lewis continued to carry the banner throughout the rest of the practice. This was the type of situation when his leadership was strongest, when the players needed an example and a voice. He volunteered to go first in drills, and continued to encourage his teammates.

Not all of them responded the way the coaches wanted, however. When Mitchell was too slow getting into position to start a new drill, Keady whistled everyone to the line and ordered a double suicide in 1:15. As they continued with the workout, going four-on-four fullcourt, the players began to drag. Mistakes began to mount.

"Right now you're tired," Keady said. "You've got to stay positive and work hard mentally every game for what three things? Purpose, performance and pride. Remember that? It's the little things that hurt you. What little things in the game hurt us? I don't want to hear any answers, just think about it. A pass here, not blocking out there."

A few moments later, Scheffler didn't block off for a rebound. The Black shirts ran 2 1/2 lengths in 30 seconds. Shortly after that, Mitchell didn't block out. Everybody ran this time. Not long after that, Keady sent them all to the line again, for not being alert enough.

When it was over, the coaches considered it a good practice, but the players just thought of it as exhausting. One of their favorite topics of discussion after workouts such as this one was the coaches' commands that they weren't tired. "You're young, how can you be tired?" Keady would often ask. The players thought it was easy to get tired, actually. In more reflective moments they realized that it was all a method of building mental toughness, and they knew it paid off; that was the added ingredient, they figured, that allowed them to beat teams such as Michigan and Illinois despite having less raw talent.

But that didn't mean they had to like it.

"They tell you, 'You can't be tired, you can't be tired,' Mitchell said in the locker room after practice. "That's the thing that gets me."

"Hell, I don't know what it is to play tired," Lewis said. "They always take you out before you get tired anyway."

"Coach Wood told me I play much better when I play 31 or 32 minutes," Mitchell said. "I say, 'OK, hold me out of practice some, and I'll be a bad mother then, too.'"

Tuesday's practice was no easier. And for Mitchell, it was much worse. Keady turned the first 15 minutes of it over to Presley, to teach new techniques of on-the-ball defense. Presley demonstrated the methods himself, his words tumbling out as he fought to catch his breath. What he was saying made a lot of sense to the players, but his style—here was some old man with a limp who seemed ready to keel over at any moment trying to show them how to guard somebody—nearly made them laugh.

"I know the game pretty well," he said. "I've scouted and coached a long time. And you've got enough ability to go as far as you want to go. You've got to have some breaks, too. But to win the Big Ten, you've got to use your ability with great intensity every day.

"Now defense is 80 percent desire, but it's also 20 percent technique. And I watched your game at Indiana, and your technique was the shits. They beat you with dribble penetration, and that should never happen."

Presley demonstrated the proper way to slide backwards and cut off a dribbler.

"My wife's a spastic, but she can slide to the back foot side," he said. "Where you guys got hurt in the Indiana game is you crossed your front foot. Learn to do this. Push off the front foot. Push, push. I'm an old fat-assed wimp, and I can still do it. Push, push. It's just a jab push."

The players worked on the steps, as well as other Presley techniques. Then they went to work fullcourt. Mitchell, however, wasn't going hard enough to please the coaches. He had a slight cold, but that didn't count as an excuse.

For whatever reason, he was struggling. And given the mood of the times, it wasn't long before he heard about it.

"I'm going to tell you something, Todd, and it's a true statement," Keady shouted after Mitchell didn't get back quickly enough on defense. "We're going to drive your ass to first team All-Big Ten, but it's not because you want it. If we let you do it your way, you wouldn't get anything done!"

It went on like that for much of the practice for Mitchell. Afterwards, he approached Keady to plead his case. Keady told him he wasn't practicing hard enough. Mitchell said that he was sorry, but nothing he did ever seemed to be enough.

"Coach, you never say anything positive," Mitchell said in a pleading tone. "Just once, I'd like to be told when I'm doing something right. Just once I'd like to know when I've had a good practice."

Keady waved Mitchell off, and headed for the showers. But his anger grew as he walked up the ramp. Finally, he turned and yelled to Mitchell to meet him in the locker room.

Mitchell walked into a raging storm. "I'm fed up with your bullshit!" Keady shouted. "Why don't you just quit this team? We've been babying your ass for four years now. As far as I'm concerned you can quit this team!"

Keady kicked over the large, plastic wastebasket set by the door, spilling its contents onto the floor. He then stormed out of the room, shoving the door so hard that he broke the metal support at the top that automatically closes it.

Mitchell was stunned. By his own estimation, he'd been yelled at more than anyone during his four years there, but this was something new. He followed Keady out of the room and headed the other direction, fighting back tears.

Word of the incident spread quickly among the players as they filtered back into the locker room. Rea, who had caught the tail end of the explosion, gave his account of it as his teammates gathered around the tipped-over wastebasket. Lewis was among the last to walk in. Kip Jones sent him to find Mitchell.

The two roommates sat together in a hallway on the other side of the building for nearly half an hour. Lewis told Mitchell to shake it off, that whether he had deserved it or not, he had to stay focused on the business at hand. No matter what he thought about it, it wouldn't do him any good to rebel.

But Mitchell wasn't easily consoled. For one thing, he didn't think Lewis knew how he felt. Lewis hated to be yelled at, and was adept at avoiding it. Although hardly one to play with reckless abandon, he rarely loafed, either. And he seemed to have a knack for knowing what to do (such as diving on a loose ball at strategic moments) or say to stay on the coaches' good side. He was so good at not getting yelled at, in fact, that Stallings had once started to yell at him about the fact he never got yelled at.

"Troy, you don't know what it's like," Mitchell said. "You get down when Coach Weber just gets on you a little bit. You have no idea what it's like to get hollered at."

Lewis had to agree. But the fact remained, Mitchell had no choice but to forget about what had just happened and go on.

Keady showered and left for his weekly radio call-in show immediately after the outburst. One of the characteristics of his temper is that it always falls within the context of the game, and it burns out quickly—he can be livid one minute, laughing the next— which is why the players don't resent his style. On his radio show, he gave no hint of what had just happened at the end of practice—until one woman called in with a compliment.

"I appreciate the fact you don't shove your players and you don't publicly humiliate them," she said. "Someday they'll appreciate it. I imagine they appreciate it now, but when they're as old as I am, they'll appreciate it even more. I appreciate the positive reinforcement you use, so keep up the good work."

It was true that Keady had never physically abused or publicly embarrassed a player. His encounter with Mitchell that afternoon was as violent as he ever got, and that was rare. But the irony of the call didn't escape him.

"I'm sure I've got a couple players tonight who would disagree with that," he said, chuckling.

The team gathered again at the Union that evening. It was playing Wisconsin, which was 3-4 in Big Ten play, the next night. There had been little talk about the Badgers the past few days, both in the coaches' meetings and in practice. Most of the conversation was about the previous game at Indiana and the one coming up Sunday at Michigan. The plan against Wisconsin was simply to play hard and be fundamentally sound, and let the rest take care of itself.

Keady didn't talk with Mitchell directly about the afternoon's events, but he did address the issue to the team as a whole that night.

"Guys, I'm not interested in how people feel toward me, I'm interested in you becoming a guy that plays up to your potential," he said after the video session. "When you're an athlete 18, 19 or 20 years old, and you think you're playing hard, and you got a coach who tells you you're not, and you're in a program like this where people care about you and love you and have compassion for you, then I'd make my ass do it. I wouldn't even question it.

"There's not a player we don't respect and appreciate and know what your families are like. If I don't feel like you're playing up to your potential, it's got nothing to do with having a personal vendetta towards you, because if I didn't like you I'd get rid of your ass.

"Just like tonight, I had a player tell me I never praise him. Well, I praise and protect my players from the media and do those things that I think makes this a first-class family. This is like a family to me. You're my sons and my brothers and nobody challenges me and what I do in my system—except my assistants. The players are young and don't know what the hell it takes to win. I can tell you right now, ten years from now you'll say, 'Why didn't I do it like coach said?' if you don't go as far as you wanted to. So that conversation is ended.

"We've got a lot of things going for us, guys. And just because we don't say we're proud of you doesn't mean we don't feel that way in our hearts. So we've got to get after folks."

Keady wanted to get after Wisconsin immediately. He wanted to see the players come out in the frenzy he had talked about so much in the past few days and take control of the game early, unlike what it had done against Indiana and Louisville.

"What did the referees say, Troy, anything special?" he asked as the players returned to the locker room for the final time before tipoff.

"They said they're calling handchecking," Lewis said.

"Oh. How about knocking the shit out of each other in the post?" Keady asked.

"They didn't say anything about that," Lewis said, laughing.

"OK, let's do it, Mel; get after 'em," Keady said.

All hopes for a quick start, however, collapsed in a heap at the foot of Purdue's fullcourt press. The Badgers' first ten points came on layups, and the 12th on a 3-foot jumper. It wasn't until midway through the half, after the press had been called off and Wisconsin had taken a 26-23 lead, that the momentum shifted.

Mitchell, playing hard and alert, hit a 14-footer to get things started. McCants followed with a free throw, Kip Jones with a breakaway dunk and Mitchell with a tip-in to give Purdue a 30-26 lead.

Tom Molaski interrupted with a basket for Wisconsin, but Lewis and Stephens hit back-to-back three-pointers to start another ten-point spree that pushed the lead to 42-28.

The rest was a formality. Purdue won rather routinely, 86-62. Although hardly a work of art, it was a successful follow-up to the loss.

Mitchell led the scoring with 17 points, hitting 7 of 11 shots in just 30 minutes. He also had five rebounds, two blocked shots and just one foul. Keady told him afterwards it was the smartest game he had seen him play.

But the contributions from the bench stood out even more. Scheffler had nine points and six rebounds in 18 minutes. And Berning tied his career high with nine points in just 12 minutes.

Brugos, however, stole the show, scoring a career-high six points and grabbing two rebounds in eight minutes. Despite scant playing time—he had played only 45 minutes all season going into the game—he had become the "people's choice" of the home fans. That was partially because he rarely played, partially because he showed flashes of potential, and partially because he knew most of the students in the arena. If Brugos wasn't always aggressive on the basketball court, he showed great enthusiasm and finesse around the campus social circles. His intelligence allowed him to keep good grades without spending much time studying, which in turn gave him more time to socialize.

He got a rousing ovation upon entering the game with 12:34 left, and scored almost immediately, on a fluke shot that was deflected high into the air and fell straight through the hoop. He was pulled from the game a minute later, and then returned after another minute on the bench. He quickly hit a turnaround jumper in the lane from Lewis, and later added a 12-footer on an offensive rebound.

Brugos' performance earned him an invitation to appear at the postgame press conference across the hallway. It was the first of his career—such a novelty, in fact, that he had to ask where it was held.

When he stepped before the reporters, Brugos was asked if the evening's performance had shown him some light at the end of the tunnel.

"I don't feel like I'm in a tunnel, actually," he said. "I like to play basketball and I'm not maybe as dedicated and serious as some of the guys on the team, so in that aspect I can understand why some people get to play ahead of me. I just like to play the game. Every day I get to play against the number two team in the nation, so it's really fun. It doesn't bother me too much to sit on the bench."

Presley left the next morning, but not before leaving behind several yellow legal pad pages full of suggestions and remarks. Among them was praise for Kip Jones, who had scored five points and missed three layups against Wisconsin. Jones, Presley thought, was the kind of player he had won with at Menlo, one who made up for whatever skills he lacked with effort.

But Presley was relieved to get out of town. Being back on the bench for a game, even as an analyst, had drained him. He got stomach cramps, he was smoking more, and he said Keady made him nervous. Weber had seen him gulping Rolaids before the game and thought at first they were nitroglycerin tablets for his heart.

"I thought, 'Oh, geez, don't let him die here,'" Weber recalled.

But if it had been rough on Presley, it had done Keady's heart good.

"I want to thank you for the way you treated Mr. Presley," he told the players after the next day's video. "You made his stay very comfortable and he told me to tell you guys you were the best bunch of people he had ever been around as a group; that's quite a compliment.

"Of course he worked for Tark [at UNLV] for two years, so they weren't too hard to beat," Keady added, laughing. "No, he was serious about it and he said you guys were gentlemen and he enjoyed working with you. I'll tell you right now, you made his year, not just his week. Because when you quit coaching and you're not around young men any more—you know we're always chewing your ass and yelling at you when we're with you, but when you're not around the players you miss it. You're not as alive as a person when you're not with young people. So you made his day. And I appreciate the way you treated him."

The mood would have to get less friendly in the days ahead, however. Thursday morning brought a double dose of bad news. Berning, who had played so well the night before, had come down with back spasms, and would be out indefinitely. And Michigan, the next opponent, had pounded Iowa 120-103 that night in Ann Arbor.

Friday morning, Stallings reported early to watch video of that game.

"What do you think, Coach Stallings?" Wood asked as he walked into the room.

"I think we're headed for a blowout," Stallings said.

He meant the receiving end.

John Brugos

"The Region [the area surrounding Gary, Indiana] was a great place to grow up, because I learned about every lesson I could possibly learn. I knew every possible ethnic person. It was a melting pot. When the mills opened up, they didn't care if you were white, black, green, purple, if you could do your work. The mills at one time were a great institution as far as labor. But now it's declined. So there's all these people who came there living in their cardboard houses hoping they'd make more money, and all of a sudden they're cut off at the wrists and bleeding. And they're still in the cardboard house and all of a sudden that cardboard house is costing more and you've got kids, so you've got to learn a lot of things just to get by. And the easiest way to get by is to devote yourself to bad. The easiest way to something is always the bad way, more than likely.

"If you're just going to assimilate into the group, you're not going to get anywhere. You have to be an individual, be a free-spirited person to get out of there, or you're just going to be another number at the mill.

"Marvin and I call that area G.I., for Gary, Indiana. There's a whole G.I. attitude. It's an immoral, nasty, 'get yours' attitude. Get over, get by and get out. Don't put more effort in anything than you have to. If you can get by by stealing something and get by by earning it, you'll steal it every time. Take every break you can get and take it as far as you can. A very selfish attitude about everything. That's the way I was raised. That was my environment.

"Growing up, I played basketball in the biddy leagues and on the seventh and eighth grade teams, and just dominated. I played junior varsity when I was in ninth grade, and then played varsity as a sophomore. But I wouldn't go out and play in the summer unless all my friends played. I went to basketball camps, but my parents more or less put me there. I liked it, but it was more or less recreational. I didn't enjoy the intensity of it. And I hated the losing feeling of it. It got to the point I didn't even want to play any more. There was a time in my life when I was a lot bigger, faster and stronger than everybody. I just dominated. Then it got to the point everybody caught up to me and it was more work. And I've never liked work.

"I didn't want to go to college then, because I had never worked for anything. I was happy just where I was. I didn't want to grow up. I got my 20 bucks a week, I didn't care about anything else. I was just living for the present, I never looked to the future. I worried about waking up the next morning as much as I worried about anything. I was worried about what I was doing a half hour from now as much as anything. But I looked at college like going to the zoo in Chicago when you're a little kid. You don't know what's there, but you want to check it out.

"I got kicked off my high school basketball team so many times. Hell, the day I signed my letter of intent with Purdue, that night I had a party at a friend's house next door. Me and about 50 of my friends got arrested and taken to the police station in a school bus. The party started at nine and we got busted at 9:30. No one was drunk. There was a full keg of beer sitting there, it was barely tapped into. Maybe everybody had one glass. All our neighbors were waving at us as we got taken away. I'm waving out the window at my parents, going 'Bye!'

"It was funny in a way, but it wasn't funny. That event probably cost me my career here in a way. If there's a problem with me, it's accumulative, my past gets brought into it. I don't have a clean slate. They're leery of me, very leery. I like that in a way, because they can never figure me out. As a person I like that, but as a basketball player I don't. I want them to know they can trust me and put me in. In the back of my mind, my subconscious won't let me give in to what they want me to do. It just won't. Because I'm too much of an individual. I'll con them enough to where they think I'm really doing it. But if I had a million dollar question, I'd say, 'Hell, no, I'm not doing it.' I've tried to do what they want me to do, but it's not really working out. I've really tried to assimilate into it, but I'm having a hard time, because I'm dealing with guys who devote just everything to this damn team and basketball. Ryan and Steve go to bed at 9 o'clock and say, 'Damn if I'm going to drink.' But hell, I'm up at 3 o'clock. Who knows what I'm doing sometimes?

"I know if I worked harder I could do better. I know if I put myself forward more and tried to achieve more, I'd do better. But I'm not necessarily unhappy with my life. I'm kind of just having a good time. I think the more pressure I put on myself the harder it will be. At this point I'm kind of living three lives at once. Obviously I'm well-known socially at Purdue. Whenever I get in the game the crowd goes nuts. I have a million friends there; I like that a lot. I'm not going to give that up. It takes a toll because I'm out and about sometimes when I shouldn't be. But that's just kind of the way it goes. That's part of my life's philosophy.

"I'm a good player, not a great player. Potentially, I look at myself and I could be a great player. If you want it bad enough and go out five hours a day, you're going to do it, because physically and mentally your body will just do it. But I'm not going to do it. I have other things going. I have a couple of other lives going on. I'm juggling all kinds of things. That's just me. You can't say it's good or bad, it's just the person I am.

"I have so many views on coach it's not even funny. There's a chance he's lucky to be in the position he's in, or there's a chance he's worked hard and earned it. So you can't necessarily respect someone for who they are. You have to evaluate how they got there. I think Coach Keady has honestly worked for everything he has. So I respect Coach Keady. I don't know if I'm to the point where I'd take a bullet for him, but I would do just about anything less than that to protect him and what he stands for.

"I go to about a third of my classes. The most I've ever studied before a test is three days. The intellectual ability I have in school has allowed me to have more free time, because I just knock it out right away and don't have any more problems with that class. That just kind of melts into everything else. I'm thinking, 'I don't want to be in this damn gym for three hours, we can get this done in an hour.'

"I think I'm too intellectual for my own good sometimes. I've read all the works of the great masters of philosophy. Some I really disagree with and some I really agree with. As far as some theories of nonconformity and withdrawing from society, I really agree with them sometimes. You can't let people push you around. It's your life and you're on this earth one time. That's my art major talking there. You're free, you're creative. My science major, which is a realistic thing, all facts and knowledge, that really brings you back to what's going on. If you want something, you've got to work for it. Who wants to go live in a cabin up on the mountain? What's that going to do? But then there's that part that says, 'You should be away from all these people telling you what to do all the time. Just do what you want.'

"I'm trapped that way. I always have these intellectual battles with myself. I think the left side of my brain definitely dominates the right side. I'm a very up and down person, too. I have a really hard time being leveled off.

"I call myself Captain Contradiction. I can wake up in the morning so happy, then come out of the shower and just be shitty. It's kind of scary, because in our family history, we've had a lot of people who ran away. A lot of poets and artists. A lot of people who have been craftsmen, built things with their hands that people couldn't even imagine. That's just our genetics. One day I'll be the most sensitive person, the next day I'll be a bear. It's hard to do something consistently in basketball every day, when you're like that. Some days I'll go into practice and just kick ass. I'll say nobody's going to stop me. Then some days you won't even know I'm there. I can't wait until 5:30. I'm like that, I really am. I won't even be thinking about practice because there's something else I'm worried about.

"I've come close to quitting so many times. I've walked 15 miles from Lafayette, down I-65 and realized, 'What am I doing?' and turned back. I've done that at home, too. My dad found me 80 miles from home one time. I just took off. I took off down Highway 41 one time, just walking. I had already signed with Purdue, and people are filling the damn gym to come see me play. I'm feeling all this pressure and I'm thinking, 'Why did I do all this to myself? I don't want people watching me.' That was the last thing I wanted. So I get involved in a problem. The coach doesn't have evidence against me, but assumes he does, and says, 'You're off the team until you get your shit solved.'

"I was just gone. I left. I didn't think my parents could understand what happened. I thought it was going to eliminate me from going to Purdue and eliminate me from being the person the whole earth thought I was. It was a situation involving something I don't even like to bring up anymore. It was a problem I had, and I said, 'Hey, I'm taking me and my problem and I'm just going to leave everyone else alone so there is no problem.'

"But about halfway gone I realized I had just made the problem worse. I had 38 cents in my pocket and holey jeans and an army jacket on. Where was I going? I'm 17 years old. Then my dad pulls up next to me and we just sat there in the car. He's like, 'Now, really, where are you going?' All I could do was laugh.

"I felt really bad about that, because my mom lost her brother at the age of 19. He went to Purdue for two years and played football, and he left. We just made contact with him a few years ago. He's one of the most artistic, creative persons I've ever met—almost to the point where he's like Van Gogh. Van Gogh died because no one understood him. My uncle is very much like that. Right now he's down in Florida, building ships out of wood, by himself, in the Keys. He wanted no more of it. His grades were fine, but he couldn't deal with the responsibility of being on his own and having other people tell him what to do.

"I have the exact genetic code that he has, more than likely. It's scary. It's like, 'Oh, shit, all this stuff's happening to me. What time is it? It must be time for me to go.'

"Up until about a week ago, I really hated basketball—*this* kind of basketball. I just wasn't enjoying basketball. "But the Wisconsin game gave me hope. Because all the people I'm involved with really came out and supported me. They were all truly happy to see that I was doing good. That gave me inspiration. It was like, 'Hell, these people love you, man, how can you turn away from them? You've got to do your best now.' It brought me back into basketball a little bit. I had a couple interviews, and a couple people on campus say, 'Nice job.' Stuff like that. It made it more fun. It wasn't just a job any more.

"I'm a person that lives day to day. I don't even look at tomorrow. I never do. But I might look ahead 20 years. So I think, 'John, stick it out.' I've got a double major going now, and I'm doing really good in school, which is surprising me. In 20 years I'll be able to be my own person again. I think everybody has to be challenged and put through a trial period."

11

•

Breaking a Curse

As rocky as last year's trip to Ann Arbor had been, this one didn't seem any more promising when the team gathered at the Purdue Airport Saturday morning. The temperature was hovering defiantly around zero in both West Lafayette and Ann Arbor, and was bolstered by a stiff breeze that made it feel even colder.

While a few of the players were still fighting colds, Keady and Stallings had been walloped by a virus. Both were nursing temperatures at around 102 degrees, and looked as peaked as they felt. For Keady, illness was a rare enemy. He had missed just one day of work since launching his coaching career at Beloit in 1957, that coming when he was struck by the flu on the very first day of school his first year. Since then, he had always maintained the upper hand in germ warfare, running up a string of consecutive appearances on the job that would have made Lou Gehrig proud.

But this time the streak would have to be kept intact with a considerable amount of suffering. Keady, his wife, Stallings, Wood and the players boarded one plane. The other assistant coaches and the rest of the traveling party—the healthy branch of it—piled into the other, smaller one.

For both groups, the flight was a roller coaster ride through the clouds, a wind-blown journey punctuated by unexpected dips and turns. Most of those who didn't already have a head-start on feeling bad soon caught up. Brugos spilled his soft drink in his lap after one sudden jolt. Stephens let out a high-pitched shriek that in turn frightened everyone else. Reid vomited in the aisle as the plane began its descent.

By the time the passengers from the weather-beaten planes regathered gratefully on the ground in Ann Arbor and boarded the bus that would take them to the hotel (as in Bloomington, the coaches had made reservations with a different hotel because of the loss the season before) everyone was woozy.

Reid, pale and drawn, came in for the most abuse. "I heard him, but I thought he was just coughing," Kip Jones recalled of the souvenir Reid left behind.

Stephens took his share of kidding as well. "Everette, are you white now, or are you just scared?" Weber asked.

Keady and Stallings sat sideways on the bus, their heads propped against the backs of their seats, on the way to the hotel. The players, shaken by the flight, were unusually quiet. All in all, they hardly had the look of a team preparing to play its biggest game of the season to date on national television.

Aside from Indiana, Michigan probably generated more of a gut reaction from Purdue fans than any other Big Ten team. Michigan's coach, Bill Frieder, had taken over his job the same year Keady started at Purdue, and the series had followed a rugged, unlikely course from that point. Keady's teams had won the first eight games, including two single overtime victories and one triple overtime affair, all in Ann Arbor. But that streak came to a crashing halt as Michigan rebounded to win the next four games.

The series had progressed from warm to hot the previous season. Purdue won the first game in West Lafayette, as Lewis scored a career-high 39 points. But when the two teams later met in that fateful finale to the regular season in Ann Arbor, the Wolverines administered a 104-68 whipping that went a long way towards ruining Purdue's season and a good part of its summer as well. The lingering aftereffects of that loss, in fact, were still being felt, if for no other reason than the fact people kept talking about it.

That trip, like this one seemed to be, had been bad from the beginning. Keady had a virus then, too, and could barely talk— an ironic punishment, because it turned out there would be a lot to shout about. Stack missed the flight and had to catch a ride to join the team. And the practice session in Ann Arbor the day before the game was one of the worst of the season.

Michigan, playing its final home game of the season on national television and fighting for a berth in the NCAA tournament, knocked them cold with a 27-point halftime lead, and spent the rest of the afternoon dancing on their heads.

The loss had been particularly painful for Lewis, who was made to pay dearly for his 39-point outburst in West Lafayette. Frieder assigned his point guard, Gary Grant, one of the nation's best defenders, to him the second time, and Grant made it a personal mission to stop Lewis. He succeeded, holding him to five points on 2 of 12 shooting and taking him completely out of his game. It would be the only time in Lewis' final 67 college games he failed to reach double figures.

The game also bruised Keady's relationship with Frieder. Frieder, perhaps trying to impress the NCAA tournament selection committee, or perhaps merely enjoying the spectacle, left his starters in the game much longer than Keady thought necessary. Keady's feelings were aggravated by the fact that in the two seasons prior to that, when Michigan won back-to-back Big Ten titles, Frieder would call him when Purdue was about to play a team contending with the Wolverines and give him a pep talk. "You've got to beat those guys, so we can win the Big Ten," Frieder would say. And more often than not, Purdue did. Keady didn't consider Frieder's laziness in getting his starters out of the game that day an appropriate way of saying thanks.

Keady's emotions boiled over after the loss, setting up one of his rare brushes with controversy. Talking privately with Purdue's radio play-by-play announcer, Larry Clisby, outside the locker room about an hour after the game, Keady unloaded his frustrations.

"You know what ------- pisses me off," he said. "Why doesn't ------- Michigan play like that every ------- game? You know why? It's because they got no ------- character."

It wasn't an unprecedented critique. The season before, Knight had said much the same thing in the postgame press conference after Indiana had been dealt an 80-52 defeat under nearly identical circumstances. The Wolverines, in fact, along with Illinois, had become stereotyped around the league as an undisciplined team that failed to consistently take full advantage of its bountiful raw talent, frequently losing to inferior teams.

Keady's remarks, however, weren't quite as private as he thought. Jeff Rush, a reporter from Michigan's student newspaper, was standing around the corner in the hallway leading to Purdue's locker room and overheard them. He included them in his column the following Monday.

Frieder clipped the column and mailed it to Keady, jotting a short note that sarcastically thanked him for helping out a "young, struggling" coach. Keady, shocked that his vitriol had been reproduced in print, was embarrassed, apologetic and angry, and said so at his weekly news conference before the tournament.

Much to Keady's regret, the story proved to have a lasting shelf life—into the 87–88 season. The same night Purdue was beating Wisconsin, Michigan hammered Iowa by 17 points in a game not even that close. Rush re-introduced the story to the Michigan fans in his column the next morning.

"Purdue Coach Gene Keady's worst nightmare came true last night," his column began.

Rush went on to recall Keady's infamous quote from the previous season, this time bleeping out the profanity.

"Uh-huh," Rush wrote. "You ever hear about how crimes of the past catch up with you, Gene?

"The Michigan team that he complained had no character showed again last night that they had plenty of it. And you know the Wolverines will remember what he said last year after the Wolverines slashed the Boilermakers in the final conference game."

Just in case their players didn't remember, Michigan's coaches went in for some creative interior decorating in the locker room to remind them. Michigan's locker room was routinely decorated before home games, as if it was to be the site of a 5-year-old's birthday party. Blue and yellow streamers swept across the room from overhead. Crudely drawn posters hung from the walls and lockers, featuring pictures of players from the opposing teams and made-up quotes about what they were going to do to specific Michigan players. On Grant's locker, for example, there was a picture of Lewis, with this fictional quote: "I'm not going to stop at 20 points or 30 points, I'm going for 40 points." The idea was to help Michigan's players slip into their game faces.

And, just to make sure everyone was properly motivated, a photocopy of Rush's column was taped to each locker, with the crucial paragraphs highlighted by a yellow marking pen.

Regardless of its physical condition, Purdue was going to have to be at its best mentally for the game. The Wolverines, in fact, had the look of an NBA team in waiting. Grant was an All-American guard—some thought the best in the nation. Glen Rice, a sophomore, was probably the best forward in the Big Ten, talented enough that he was seriously considering turning professional at the end of the season. Rumeal Robinson, a guard, and Terry Mills, a forward, had sat out the previous season as Proposition 48 victims, but had been two of the best high school players in the country two years ago and already had proven themselves as legitimate Big Ten players. Loy Vaught and Mark Hughes were interchangeable in the other starting position, both were imposing forces at 6-9 and about 225 pounds.

Purdue's coaches believed the way to beat the Wolverines was to break the game down to a halfcourt test of wills, then execute fundamentally and exploit their youth and lack of discipline. To get into a track meet with them would be disastrous. And there were encouraging precedents. Michigan's two losses so far had come to teams that had displayed those very qualities, Arizona and Ohio State.

Nobody wanted to call the game a make-or-break affair, but that was the unspoken line of thinking. With both teams clinging to a 7-1 conference record, the winner would take command of the Big Ten race—particularly if it was Purdue, since a win on the road over the co-leader would be even bigger.

Despite Michigan's success in basketball in recent years, the crowds at Crisler are relatively tame by Big Ten standards. Frieder had complained about it himself, going so far as to adopt a "Frieder Meter" to rate the noise level after each home game. But there would be no problem turning up the volume for this one. The national television lights always seem to bring out the animal tendencies in college students. And if that wasn't enough to get them riled, Keady's well-documented remarks from the previous season had helped, too.

While the teams warmed up, the Michigan fans behind Purdue's bench began taunting Keady, who was wearing a gold sport coat.

"Hey, Gene, nice coat!"

"Hey, Gene, watch your language after the game."

"Hey, Gene, watch those cuss words after the game. We'll have our tape recorders going, because we have no ------- character."

Keady, who had been sitting quietly in his chair, got up and walked a few steps to his left to a security guard wearing a bright yellow jacket. "If you don't shut them up, I'm liable to go up there myself!" he said.

As Keady returned to his seat, the hecklers continued.

"I'll come up there right now if you want!" Keady said, although probably not loud enough for them to hear.

The security guard reached the offending fans before the debate could continue, and quieted them. Already, it was clear this wasn't going to be an ordinary game.

The players, however, had seemed typically oblivious to the pressure all weekend. The evening before, after dinner, all 12 of them and Howat had piled into the hotel elevator to get to their fifth-floor rooms. They obviously had exceeded the elevator's weight load, but they were in a silly mood and nobody felt like waiting for another one. Before anyone realized the situation, the doors pinched together and the "Sardine Express" began its ascent.

Tony Jones had hardly had time to give a quick tap to the emergency bell button, as he always did, when the elevator stopped with an awkward jolt. It was stuck between floors. But because they were packed in so tightly and talking among themselves, they didn't immediately realize what had happened. There were some nervous giggles. Brugos laughed and bounced up and down a few times.

It didn't take long for reality to set in. "Hey, guys, shut up!" Tony Jones said. "We ain't moving." A hush fell over the group. The air supply obviously wouldn't last long. Scheffler tried to pry open the doors, without success, then felt around the ceiling to see if there were any panels that could be budged to let in oxygen. There weren't.

Barrett, who had claustrophobic tendencies anyway, was on the verge of panic, and his teammates weren't far behind. Finally, after about a minute that seemed like an eternity had passed, the elevator returned to the ground floor and the doors opened. A few of the players gratefully jumped out and waited for another ride.

The morning of the game, during the free throw contest at the close of the shootaround, Lewis had noticed an ABC technician attaching a microphone to the basket support.

"Are you doing a mike check?" asked Lewis, a communications major.

The man said he was.

Lewis walked over to the mike and leaned up toward it. "Get off me, dog!" he said. His teammates cracked up.

And, just a few minutes earlier in the locker room, Stephens had taken Keady aside to ask a burning question. "Coach, I didn't know how to ask you this, but I've been wanting to say something to you for a long time," he said. "Can my mom sing the national anthem at the Minnesota game? She really wants to."

Keady, expecting a more serious topic of discussion, said it was fine with him.

Now this same group of young men was going to play a crucial game before millions of people across the country, many of whom revered them, on national television.

And they were ready. Purdue led 11-6 at the first television timeout five minutes into the game, and clung to the lead for four more minutes. Then Michigan exploded with a fury, shifting its fast break into gear and dominating the inside. The Wolverines ran off ten straight points for a 26-19 lead, and then came back with another eight-point spree capped by vicious dunks from Rice and Vaught that made it 39-29 with four minutes left in the half. Crisler was ignited to rare hysteria. Michigan seemed on the verge of delivering another knockout punch, just as it had done the year before.

But Purdue stayed calm. Mitchell started the trip back by picking up a loose ball in the lane and dunking it. He then deflected a pass defensively, and, on a play that had been set up in the intervening timeout, took a lob pass from Stephens, faked, scored, was fouled and completed a three-point play. Rice then missed a turnaround jumper, Scheffler rebounded it, and drew a foul. He hit one of two free throws.

With Purdue stepping up its defensive intensity, Michigan's offense began to unravel. Vaught fired an air ball from 15 feet. Lewis then hit from 17. Vaught missed again, and Mitchell drove the baseline for a reverse layup to tie the game at 39. In 2 1/2 minutes, they had erased a ten-point deficit.

Rice and Stephens exchanged a pair of free throws in the final minute, but Robinson gave Michigan a two-point halftime lead when he faked Lewis into the air and hit a 17-footer at the buzzer.

"Don't worry, Gene, we can't win," a Michigan fan yelled at Keady as he walked to the locker room. "We got no ------- character, just like your coat!"

Keady ignored the heckler, but he couldn't forget Robinson's basket. Through his four seasons at Purdue, Lewis had heard countless warnings about skying up on fakes. But in the heat of battle he had done it, and given up a basket.

The coaches were part instructors, part cheerleaders when they met with the players.

"Here's what's going to make the difference in the game," Keady said: "Free throws, our turnovers and our ball movement."

"I know this," Wood said. "We did a good job. We had a good half. The same good half and we get beat. We've got to get better. We've got to be three points better than they are for 20 minutes. And I've got news for you. We are three points better than they are."

"All the little things have to go for us," Keady said. "Get loose balls, block off and hit the free throws."

"Play with a lot of confidence," Weber said. "Tony Jones, you went in there and it was like, 'Well, should I dribble, should I do this, should I do that?' Take the ball. You've played before."

"You don't have to be careful, Tony; play, babe," Keady said. "Just like at Northrop [Jones' high school]."

"They've got great individuals, but we've got a better team," Wood said. "And we're going to win. It's not going to be easy, but we're going to win."

Mitchell evened the score immediately, stealing a pass and streaking downcourt for a dunk on the first possession of the second half. After Robinson missed two free throws, Stephens ran off a pick at the free throw line and dunked a lob pass from Lewis to give Purdue the lead again. A minute later, after Mitchell had worked his way inside for a layup, Lewis hit Stephens with another lob for a layup. The play looked like a carbon copy of the first one, but was slightly different. One was called Mystifier, one was Chicago. Michigan's players, however, were equally confused by them, and began bickering among themselves about who was responsible for stopping them. "I felt like saying, 'Hey, man, it's two different plays,' " Mitchell would recall later.

Stephens' layup gave Purdue a four-point lead, but Michigan ran off five points in the next 30 seconds to regain the lead. From there, the momentum teeter-tottered the rest of the way. Purdue built leads of four, and then five, but Michigan continued to fight back. At the third timeout of the half, with 7:54 left, the Wolverines led 74-73. Purdue regained the lead, lost it, then with 2:05 left edged in front 86-82. Michigan called a timeout. Purdue huddled joyously, while Michigan's pep band played the Wolverines' school song to pump up the fans.

Keady: "We've got a long ways to go, guys."

Mitchell: "It ain't over yet, fellas."

Keady: "It's like an eternity. Listen. You know what beat us at Indiana. Mental mistakes and missing our free throws. So we've got to be cool as cucumbers and take care of the basketball and don't force anything. And rebound! For heaven's sakes, rebound, Kip! And know where 41 [Rice] and 25 [Grant] are."

Stallings: "Hey. This is the biggest defensive possession of the year right here. If we stop them, we've got their ass."

Keady: "Together!"

The players: "We attack!"

"Stay down on shot fakes!" Weber yelled as the players returned to the floor. "And contain the dribble."

Some instructions were adhered to, some weren't. The echo from all the instruction in the huddle had hardly died off when Mitchell went for Grant's shot fake. Grant missed, but Rice scored on the tip-in. It was 86-84.

Purdue ran its control game, then moved into Laker. The play was getting nowhere, but with the shot clock down to five seconds, Stephens took a pass from Lewis on the left baseline and swished a 15-footer, returning the lead to four.

Robinson then rushed a shot in the lane and missed, and Lewis rebounded. With Michigan pressing desperately now, Lewis passed to McCants, who was fouled with 41 seconds left. Michigan called timeout.

McCants missed the front end of the one-and-one, but Michigan tipped the rebound out of bounds. McCants, after taking the inbounds pass, couldn't find an open teammate. He finally tried an awkward pass, using his right hand when he should have used his left, and had the ball intercepted by Mills. Rice quickly hit a three-pointer, pulling Michigan within a single point with 26 seconds left. Michigan called timeout again, and the crowd erupted as the band played the school song yet again.

The Indiana game was happening all over again. Keady sat in his chair, dazed, as the players returned to the bench. Weber grabbed him and pulled him up.

There wasn't much to say at this point but the same things that had been emphasized all day, all season. Make good passes, make sharp cuts, hit your free throws, keep your poise. All the timeouts remained. If you get in trouble, don't force a pass, call timeout.

"Take control of the game," Weber said. It sounded more like a plea, now.

The huddle broke, but some uncertainty had replaced the enthusiasm so obvious earlier in the game. Michigan set up its press fullcourt, hoping for a quick steal. Tony Jones worked free for the inbounds pass, however, and was immediately fouled by Griffin. There were 23 seconds left.

That morning, Jones had been the first player eliminated from the free throw contest when he missed his first attempt. Now he was going to shoot his first free throw of the game into a sea of screaming fans waving yellow flags.

Jones blocked out the shimmering backdrop, but not the deafening roar as he toed the line. He stopped, aimed and fired. Swish. The lead was two points now. But his second shot bounced off the rim, and Mills rebounded. The Wolverines would have another chance.

They worked the ball around the perimeter, but Purdue's defense was giving up nothing. Finally, Mills, standing at the free throw line, passed inside to Vaught, who tried a jump hook from five feet on the right baseline. Replays later would show Vaught could have simply turned and shot a near-layup over McCants, but in the heat of the moment he didn't notice he had McCants beat. The shot bounced off the back of the rim and was tipped outside, where a mad scramble ensued 15 feet from the basket. Finally, Tony Jones emerged with the ball and was fouled.

Only three seconds remained now. Jones again had a one-and-one. He needed to hit one to guarantee an overtime, two to clinch the win. He hit both this time, rattling the first one off the rim and swishing the second. The game was over. They had held on, beating one of the nation's most talented teams on its homecourt on national television after a long, rough weekend.

Everyone who played had contributed. Mitchell scored a game-high 22 points. Lewis, shaking off the demon named Gary Grant that had haunted him a year ago, added 20, along with six rebounds and six assists. Stephens had 16 points and seven assists, McCants 15 points and Kip Jones six points. Scheffler came off the bench to score eight points and grab six rebounds, while Tony Jones added four points and four assists.

The locker room celebration was wild, even louder than at Louisville. Everyone forgot about spreading germs long enough to exchange hugs, high-fives and handshakes.

"Way to go, guys, way to go!" Keady shouted after the noise died down. "This is maybe the biggest win since I've been here in eight years. I'm very proud of you!"

"Hell, yes!" Lewis said.

"Way to go!" Keady shouted, raising his arms. "Together!"

"We attack!"

The celebration continued, with shouts of congratulation and sheer joy—and no doubt some relief, too.

Weber: "You did a hell of a job, guys! Keep it going now!"

Brugos: "That's a big one, boys!"

Stallings: "Hey, you guys played your ass off, way to go! You sure know how to make a guy feel unneeded. If I had been here yesterday, you bastards would have lost."

And, of course, Rea: "Get off me, dog!"

Lowell Hamilton wouldn't have believed what he had started.

The victory was only one of the impressive things Purdue's players saw that day. As they waited on the bus directly outside the arena, they saw Mills, wearing a fur coat, climb into a new, white Nissan 300Z sports car. A college basketball player wearing a fur coat and driving a new sports car, particularly a sophomore, is sure to invite skepticism regarding compliance with NCAA rules.

"Hell, if you go to Michigan or Illinois, you don't want to go pro, because you got to take a pay cut," Mitchell said.

The plane ride home was much smoother, much more pleasant, than the one to Ann Arbor. They were alone in first place, a game up on Michigan. And the next game between the two teams would be played in a much more comfortable place, West Lafayette.

"Hey, Everette, where do we play next," one of the players asked Stephens on the plane.

"I don't know," Stephens said.

"You mean you don't know?!" Mitchell said, faking amazement.

"Hey, coach schedules the games and I just play 'em," Stephens said, making sure Keady could hear. "Then if we lose, I call him into my office and have a talk with him."

"If we lose, I kick your butt," Keady corrected.

But as high as the team's spirit was on the flight home, it wasn't prepared for what it saw upon arriving in West Lafayette. An estimated crowd of about 1,500 fans, braving the bitter cold and snow, greeted the team at the airport, surrounding the main terminal and filling the hallways. Many more were turned away by police officers. The players were cheered wildly as they filed out of the plane, gathered their baggage and headed for their rides home.

It was a different world than the one they had left behind the day before.

Tony Jones

"When I was about four years old, I flew to Birmingham [Alabama] with my mother. I can barely remember it, but my mom says the stewardess took me up into the cockpit.

"When I was about seven, I flew to Miami with my mom. For some reason, I just started liking planes after that. Going through the clouds, feeling how fast we were going, I just couldn't believe it. It was amazing. It's fun, being up there by yourself in another state. Just up there looking down. I told my parents after that I wanted to be a pilot, a doctor or a train engineer. I liked traveling, and I like the kind of things you don't see every day, like a train or an airplane.

"I used to buy these small planes and make an airport on top of my dresser in the room. And when I used to ride in the car, I'd hold my hand out the window, and pretend it was an airplane. And I remember going outside with my dad to look at the moon when one of the flights was going there; not the first one, but one of the others. I wanted to be an astronaut until the space shuttle exploded. Then I decided to become a commercial pilot.

"The courses you have to take aren't as difficult as engineering or something like that, but you still have to know a lot of math and science. And you have to study. You either know it or you don't. I'll be qualified to be a pilot as soon as I graduate, but you usually don't get hired that quick. You usually have to fly a commuter airline, fly cargo, be an instructor or go into the service. But being black should increase my chances of getting hired, because there aren't that many black pilots.

"I don't know what I like better, basketball or flying. I like 'em both. But they help out both ways. I have a lot of scary situations in the plane and that carries over to a big ballgame. Last fall I thought I was lost once, and I was low on fuel. I called Grissom Air Force base and they told me where I was. I thought I knew, but I lost my course. I sort of panicked. It was weird. It takes a lot of concentraton. You always have to be thinking of something in the plane. You always have to think ahead.

"I wasn't nervous the first time I flew [the first month of his freshman year]. But the second time I went up I was thinking, 'Man, maybe that was just luck.' That's the way it is. Everybody says you're not nervous on the first one. It was the same way in basketball. I wasn't even nervous my first game. I was just amazed at how loud it was. But by the third or fourth game, I was getting nervous.

"I think I'm more disciplined than a lot of guys because of flying. Sometimes it's tough to do both, though. Last spring, right before we went to Australia, I had a week to get 20 hours of flying in. I had to fly before practice, and fly right after practice. There were a couple of other times last year I had to fly right before practice. When you're in an airplane for two or three hours and come in here, you don't feel like practicing. Jet lag's a lot worse when you're the pilot.

"I'm shy, but I do have a temper. I could tell you some stories.

"I was at the drug store with my mom one time when I was a kid. I wanted this airplane, and she wouldn't get it for me. I just sat there and cried and acted the fool.

"And one time I had a Moped that was in the shop. It was a Thursday or something, and my mom said she wasn't going to get it out until next week. I got mad and hit the windshield in the car and cracked it. She was mad for a long time. I felt terrible."

12

•

In the Pink

Purdue would not have much time to enjoy the Michigan victory. Three days later they were in East Lansing to play Michigan State, a game that brought to life one of Keady's favorite battle cries: "Don't be human." That was one of his many exhortations to fight off human nature and mental fatigue. Another popular one, used often in practice, was "You're too young to be tired."

Michigan State was just 8-11 overall, 3-6 in the conference, and was coming off a 101-72 loss to Iowa. With the Michigan game just past, and another big game at Iowa four days off, it would be easy for this game to get lost in the shuffle.

And it almost did. Purdue burst to a 9-0 lead in the first three minutes, and led by 11 with 1:30 left in the half. But Michigan State scored the final five points to pull within six at the break.

Again, mental breakdowns were a factor. Michigan State's final two field goals had come on driving layups through the heart of Purdue's defense. Kip Jones muffed a layup in traffic when the ball slipped out of his hands. Stephens, forgetting the play that had been called on the last possession, pulled up for a jumper with 12 seconds left and fired an air ball. Mitchell, who hit just one of eight shots, had not run the baseline when the offense called for it.

Keady raged against the frailties at halftime, but the players didn't bounce back at the start of the second half. Three missed shots and two turnovers in the first three minutes allowed Michigan State to tie the game at 41, igniting the fans in Jenison Field House. Purdue clung to leads of one and two points for the next seven minutes, as Michigan State failed on several chances to take the lead, then appeared to put the Spartans away with a 10-2 burst that made it 65-56 with 6½ minutes left.

But just when it appeared the game had been tucked away, Michigan State took off on a 10-2 tear to pull within one point with four minutes left. Stephens, who had taken pills to soothe an upset stomach at halftime, then missed a three-pointer and the Spartans rebounded. Again, they had a chance to take the lead. But George Papadakos missed a hook shot in the lane, and Tony Jones rebounded. Scheffler then drew a foul after chasing down an offensive rebound and hit his first free throw. He missed the second, but the ball was deflected back out near midcourt, where Stephens ran it down and drew another foul. Stephens hit both free throws, opening a 70-66 lead with 2½ minutes remaining.

All seemed to be well again when Ed Wright threw the ball away and Purdue set up its control game. But the offense broke down and the shot clock expired with Tony Jones trapped in the lane, unable to get off a shot or find an open teammate to pass to. Moments later, Michigan State's Ken Redfield picked a rebound off the floor and layed it in, cutting the lead to two.

Stephens was fouled with 30 seconds left. Michigan State called timeout to let him think about it, and he missed the free throw. Mitchell forced a turnover on defense to get the ball back, and he drew a foul with 15 seconds left. But he, too, missed.

The Spartans had one last chance to tie the game, or take the lead with a three-pointer. But teams suffering through tough times usually manage to find ways to make things even tougher for themselves. This time, Ed Wright dribbled the length of the floor and rushed an off-balance 10-foot jumper from the right baseline. Stephens grabbed the rebound, and was fouled. He hit both foul shots this time, sealing the victory in the nick of time.

They had dodged a bullet, and were grateful. Keady was frustrated by the poor performance, but wasn't going to dwell on it. He knew an occasional letdown was inevitable, no matter how much he begged, kicked or screamed. The trick was to win the letdowns. Thanks to a few clutch plays and Michigan State's self-destructive tendencies, they had done just that.

Earlier in the day, a driving snowstorm had hit Lafayette, threatening to close the airport and leave the team in East Lansing for another evening. But shortly after the game, the coaches learned they would be able to fly back home as planned—the second close call of the evening. As they squeezed into their seats on the airplane and began working on their boxed lunches, the relief they felt was obvious.

Keady: "If I had a dollar for every time there's a loose ball and we can't come up with it, I'd be driving a Mercedes."

Lewis: "And you'd have a driver named Julio."

Keady: "I knew we were in trouble when we got off the bus tonight and Wortman (Bob, the head of Big Ten officials) met me," Keady said. "He said, 'Well, I saw the Michigan game Sunday and they only made one bad call the whole game.' So what was I going to say? He said they should have called double-dribble when that one guy went into the lane."

Brugos: "So what'd they think about Steve's shot that one time (against Michigan) when he turned in the lane and got tackled. Remember that, Steve, that time you turned left?"

Keady: "You turned left and got your hair cut."

Lewis: "Yeah, when Steve got up he was bald."

Reid: "You ought to shave your head bald, Steve."

Keady: "He does, I'm going to bust you!"

Kip Jones: "Just cut it like Billy's, Steve."

Lewis: "Don't do that. Somebody might come along and drill three holes in your head and take you bowling."

Scheffler: "Why can black guys get their hair cut that short and white guys can't?"

Mitchell: "Because all black guys wear it like that. See, if you cut yours short like that you'd look crazy because nobody else would have it like that. And you know how bad it looks when it's that short."

Keady: "Hey, if Tony gets his cut like that again I'm going to harelip him. It looks like crap. Hey Melvin, you need to get one of those haircuts where they put those thin marks in the side. How come you don't have those two little lines? What are those called?"

Mitchell: "Parts. Ryan's got a part."

Kip Jones: "Why don't you get an arrow and your number carved in it?"

Mitchell: "No. What about Mitchell Lee (a former Minnesota player who had been charged with rape, then found innocent). He had that champagne glass with bubbles coming out cut into his hair because he got acquitted. That was his way of celebrating."

Keady: (unwrapping a cigar) "Everette! Want a cigar?"

Stephens: (laughing) "No, I already got one."

Keady: "What happened to the one the other night you had? It was mine."

Stephens: "Was it? I thought it was for the way I played in the game."

Keady: "For tonight's game you can give it back."

As the plane left the runway and settled into a smooth flight home, Stephens and Lewis, sitting next to each other, and Mitchell, sitting one row behind them next to Scheffler, began harmonizing quietly on various soul hits.

"Hey, why don't you guys sing something by the Carpenters?" Kip Jones asked.

"Everette, you're keeping everybody awake!" Keady said, faking annoyance.

"You ain't lying!" Stephens said, laughing.

"Coach, you can sleep when you get old," Kip Jones said.

Yeah, and that's tonight," Keady said.

It was 1:20 a.m. when they arrived home, still safe and secure atop the Big Ten.

With eight games left to play, the Big Ten race was down to a three-team sprint. Purdue was 9-1, Michigan 9-2 and Iowa 7-3. Everyone else was playing for pride or a postseason tournament berth.

For Purdue, a win in Iowa City Monday night would narrow the field of contenders to two and set up a strong finishing kick to the wire. Four of its final seven games would be at home, and two of the three road games were against Northwestern and Wisconsin, two of the weaker teams.

Although the bottom teams can pose problems, one of the more impressive things about Keady's coaching record is that his teams rarely lose to teams with lesser talent. He was concerned, however, with his teams recent inconsistency and didn't want to continue testing fate, particularly on the home court of the 13th ranked team in the nation.

But Iowa coach Tom Davis was playing the role of devil's advocate. On the day of the game, he was quoted in the *Des Moines Register* as saying: "Purdue can relax a little for our game. When you look at the teams they've beaten and the places they've played, they can afford a loss or two now." Keady, naturally, didn't quite see it that way.

Carver-Hawkeye is the newest arena in the Big Ten, just four years old, and the most plush. Few locker rooms anywhere are as nice as Iowa's nationally-ranked women's team's, and the men's locker room is the lap of luxury. The front part is a miniature theatre for viewing game film, with two curved rows of cushioned seats, a large screen, an overhead projector and beverage dispensers. The dressing area is like that in a concert hall, with private dressing stalls for each player complete with mirrors framed by light bulbs and padded stools.

Even the visitor's locker room has some fancy trimmings, but it has one outstanding quality: its walls and carpeting are pink. Psychologists identify pink as a passive color, one that has a soothing effect on people. Theoretically, it would have a negative effect on a team trying to psych up for a game. At Iowa, where the visitor's football locker room also is decorated in pink, the game plan apparently is to try to get the upper hand on opposing players before they even slip into a jock strap.

There is no pink influence to be found around the playing area, though. With 15,500 fans packed in tightly, Carver-Hawkeye rivals Mackey's decibel level when the going is good. And for this game, featuring two nationally-ranked teams and ESPN's national television audience (because of the broadcast, the game would not start until 9:40 p.m., Indiana time), the fans were insipired. As the teams huddled before the tipoff, the band blared an eerie, rhythmic cadence, the cheerleaders pounded their megaphones on the floor and the fans stood and clapped, all in unison.

Iowa's game plan was surprising. It pressed fullcourt, as always, but then dropped back into a standard zone defense, daring Lewis and Stephens to shoot three-pointers. It didn't need to ask twice. The two combined to hit three of Purdue's first six field goals from behind the three-point line. But missed shots and turnovers began to mount, and Iowa came back to take the lead at 23-22.

From there, the game began to unravel. Kip Jones was called for traveling as he went up for a shot along the baseline. Iowa turned the ball over, but Jones lost the ball again driving the lane. B.J. Armstrong picked up the loose ball and headed downcourt, but hesitated on the dribble and traveled. Davis jumped up to protest, believing McCants should have been called for a foul while diving for the loose ball that Armstrong picked up, and was slapped with a technical foul. Lewis hit both foul shots, giving Purdue a 24-23 lead, and Purdue got the ball out of bounds as well. Lewis scored again 11 seconds later when he broke free from a double-team, cut to the lane, took a return pass, scored and drew a foul from Kent Hill. He hit the free throw again, completing a sudden five-point swing that boosted the lead to 27-23. The technical on Davis and the foul on Hill both were questionable calls, but Purdue had reaped the benefits. It held on to lead at the half, 36-34.

Iowa's defensive strategy began to pay off at the start of the second half, as its fullcourt pressure forced turnovers, and its halfcourt zone inflicted paralysis.

Purdue finally busted the zone in simple, dramatic and close-range fashion. Mitchell, running the baseline, made eye contact with Lewis, who was standing above the free throw circle, pointed skyward, ran to the basket from the left side, caught a lob pass and slammed it through to make it 38-36. A few minutes later, after Stephens' three-pointer had give Purdue a 45-40 lead, Mitchell and Lewis teamed up again. Running from the right side this time, Mitchell showed off every inch of his impressive vertical jump to catch a pass thrown slightly too high and jam it through the basket. Purdue led 47-40 now, with 14:20 left.

Berning, who had played just three minutes in the previous two games because of his back spasms, and practiced little in the past two weeks, dropped a three-pointer from the right corner three minutes later, making it 54-46, then added a rebound basket to give Purdue a 10-point lead.

The Hawkeyes never got closer than six points after that. Their fullcourt pressure defense continued to cause turnovers, but they had been forced to switch to a man-to-man defense in halfcourt play. That allowed Purdue to exploit Iowa's most glaring weakness, post defense.

The most explosive example came with 3:48 left. While Hill was shooting a free throw for Iowa, Stephens scurried around to his teammates and set up Mystifier, the same lob play that had worked against Michigan. Kip Jones would set a pick at the free throw line, Scheffler would clear his man out of the way in the lane and Lewis would lay the ball up above the rim. Ewer, ironically, had privately suggested the same play during a timeout a few minutes earlier.

It worked to perfection. Stephens' dunk gave Purdue a 70-57 lead, sealing the victory. Another team had been eliminated from the Big Ten race.

"Coach, that was a great play," Stallings said on the bench, turning to Keady.

"I didn't call it," Keady shrugged.

Again, they had not played exceptionally well, only well enough to win. They had been flustered by Iowa's fullcourt pressure, committing 16 turnovers. They had allowed 19 offensive rebounds. Mitchell had fouled out after just 20 minutes, scoring eight points. But they had made the plays when they had to, enough for a 73-66 win.

There were no fans waiting when the team arrived home shortly before 3 a.m., only a few friends and the Boilermaker Special. Inspiration, however, wasn't necessary, especially at this hour of the morning and this point of the season. Next up, in six days, was Indiana.

Ryan Berning

"I was born in Effingham, Illinois, then I moved to Indianapolis when I was about six months old.

"My parents divorced when I was five, so my mom had to get a job at Gringo's, this fast-food Mexican restaurant near Speedway. We moved from our house into an apartment then. I started playing organized ball in the fourth grade. I started every year through the seventh grade. In the eighth grade I started one game, then we moved to Lafayette.

"It was a scary situation. My brothers and I didn't go to school for two weeks when we first moved up here. We used to put it off and tell mom we'd do different things for her so we wouldn't have to go to school. We'd put stuff away, organize the apartment and do stuff for her, because she had to work right away.

"Finally my mom made us go. She said, 'O.K., you guys have stalled long enough.' Then my very first day, my first full day, I almost got into three fights. There were two guys who thought I was stealing their girlfriend. One guy just wanted to fight to see how tough I was. I mean, there ain't no way. You see how skinny I am now. There was no way I was going to fight them.

"The one kid's name was Butch. He was 15 or 16 in the eighth grade and could grow a full beard at the snap of a finger. I mean he was huge. He punched my locker and said, 'I heard you called me a faggot.' I said I didn't. He said, 'Well Mike said you called me a faggot.' I said, 'I ain't that stupid.' He goes, 'I hear you've been talking to my girl.' I said, 'No, I ain't that stupid; I wouldn't do anything like that.' The truth is, I wasn't talking to her.

"The other guy who wanted to fight me, I just asked his girlfriend how to get to my next class. People told him they saw us talking, but all I was doing was asking how to get to my next class. I didn't know my way around the school.

"One of those guys is dead now. He died about two years ago. His wife found out he was going to leave her for somebody else and served him rat poison. I don't know about the other two. Two of them quit school. I became pretty good friends with the other one. I didn't ever give him a hard time about it, though, because I was still a skinny kid. I didn't want to press my luck.

"They had a special tryout for me for the basketball team and I made it. Then I sat the bench. It was hard adjusting from playing to sitting. Here I'd been a starter in the seventh grade, and now I was the 12th man on a 13-man squad. All these guys had been playing, and they didn't like me too well, either. I guess the rumor got around that I was supposed to be pretty good or something. I never played that year, and I was ready to quit.

"But mom stuck behind me the whole time. If it wasn't for mom sticking behind me, I don't know. I probably would have quit. She was there at every one of my games. I even told her not to come, and she still came. I knew I wasn't going to play. I'd look up at her in the crowd and she'd give me a fist, like she was behind me. The most I played the whole year was a quarter-and-a-half, which was like eight minutes. Most of the games I didn't play at all. I was a Minute Man. We were the renegades. If we were blowing people out, we'd come in.

"After that year, I was bound and determined to do something about it. So there's this park, Tapawingo Park. I was there every night during the summer. I'd go down about 5 o'clock and leave about ten. I was the first one there and the last one to leave. I played there every night. Every night.

"At the park, they accepted me well, because I was down there so much. The guys I was playing with at school were involved with track and baseball, so it was mainly the older guys, the college kids. They all helped me. They called me the Golden Boy, because I had the golden touch.

"We had to change junior highs after my eighth grade year, so here I am changing schools again. I only knew half the people. I was an outcast again until the season started.

"But my freshman year, while the guys were playing football, my eighth grade coach, Alan Nail, worked with me. He took me out to this other gym, at a closed-down school; he had keys to the gym and was able to take me down there. He got me some ankle weights and we'd do a lot of ballhandling drills and stuff. He was quick. Every day he'd just push me harder and harder. He knew I could shoot, I just needed to work on my defense and ballhandling. We did it five days a week after school, until basketball practice started, for about two hours, dribbling, defense, footwork, stuff like that.

"I started my first game as freshman, and went on to be MVP. My sophomore year, I was about 6-5 and 150 pounds. I played half the junior varsity game, and then dressed for the varsity. But I started two games later that year on the varsity.

"The last time I saw my dad was when I was a junior in high school. The first night he was up, we played New Castle. I had 16 points, but I was a little nervous. I kept looking in the crowd to try to find him, but I couldn't find him. We lost by one point in overtime, but I missed a tip-in that could have won the game. The play was designed for this other guy; he shot it, and it came off the right side. I was right there, but I tipped it and it hit and rolled off.

"My dad spent the week with us. He stayed downstairs on the couch and mom slept upstairs. He was playing the mother's role, cooking and picking us up from school and stuff. My mom didn't like it too much, because she was wondering what it would have been like if he had stayed the whole time. She didn't feel very comfortable. But I liked having a father, because I had never really had a father. It was like a dream come true. But I haven't seen him since.

"He's been married and divorced three times since he left mom. I don't know where he's at now. When he left, we still stayed in contact until my senior year. He didn't send me a graduation card, and he didn't send me a birthday card, so there was a downfall there.

"A couple of times I've had dreams about him coming to the door. What would I do? He's my father. Just being a Christian, if I'm at the door, is God going to let me in or not? That's the way you've got to look at it. You've got to have faith. And you've got to keep the past behind you. I think I would. It would be hard not to. I understand people making mistakes. He just made too many mistakes when he was married to my mom.

"Purdue didn't start recruiting me until after the season. I had visited Miami of Ohio and Wisconsin, and also Butler and Illinois State before the season.

"I knew if Purdue wanted me I'd want to come here. I had always wanted to play in the Big Ten. Growing up in Indianapolis, I was an I.U. fan, like most people, because of Randy Wittman and everything. I came up to Lafayette and I still liked I.U. a little bit, but the more I got into Purdue basketball the more I liked it. I was certain that Coach Keady was where I wanted to go. I thought he got the most out of his players. It looked like he gave everybody a fair chance. Just coming and watching the games, you could see his players wanted to be out there playing hard.

"But a lot of people around town didn't think I could make it here. The Central Catholic coach then, he said something in *The Journal and Courier* that I'd make a good small forward at a smaller Division I school, but that I'd never make it in the Big Ten. My athletic director wanted me to go to Miami of Ohio; that's where he had gone. And all the different players around here thought I'd never play at Purdue. They said I was stupid for coming here, that I'd never play. But that was just more motivation. It just made me work harder.

"I've always wanted to succeed and prove people wrong. I think I'm done proving I can play now. My motivation is just wanting to succeed and just having fun. Going out and working hard every day, just making everyone else better. The guys on the team make it fun to be out here. You just want to prove yourself.

"I want to make my mom proud, too. That's part of it. We've always been real close. Mom only missed one of my high school games after my sophomore year, and she makes it to all the away games she can here. My mom and girlfriend, they're both helping me mature."

13

●

Sweet Revenge

The home game against Indiana was sure to play to a capacity crowd, plus anyone else who could be shoehorned in. But considering the number of people who *wanted* to be there, it was more like a private showing.

It represented the toughest ticket for any sporting event in the state, the only possible exception being the Indianapolis 500. The next toughest was when Purdue played at Assembly Hall, which represented slightly better odds for fans because it held about 3,000 more people. Mackey was sold out by season ticket sales alone, so the fan on the street had virtually no chance of getting a ticket for this game unless he was willing to pay a scalper's price of up to $150 apiece. The athletic department held tickets back for special occasions, of course, but it couldn't possibly satisfy the demand for *this* kind of special occasion.

The public's interest was so great for the game that crowd control became a prime issue. Four days before the game, George King circulated a stern memo through Mackey: "There will be no one admitted thru any door, upper or lower level, without a ticket. We all share this responsibility!! Don't embarrass anyone!! There will be a policeman on each door!!"

For the coaches, ticket management also became a matter of vital concern. Former players and recruits, two groups that couldn't be refused, showed up in force. Current players also wanted to buy extra tickets for their family, as many as ten apiece beyond the four complimentary ones allowed by NCAA rules.

In the days leading up to the game, the players, coaches and other athletic department employees could expect to hear from long-forgotten friends who, coincidentally, just happened to get in touch to catch up on the events of the past few months (or years, as the case may have been), inquire how the family was getting along, and oh, by the way, did they have any extra tickets for the Indiana game?

And everyone with a favor to collect, whether real or imagined, came calling. Earlier in the week, a young woman walked into the Sports Information Office looking for Mark Adams, an assistant, whom she had met briefly the previous summer.

"Mark told me any time I needed tickets to come in and see him, and I haven't asked him for any the whole year," she announced.

"I'm sorry, there are no tickets," the secretary, Jan Winger, said.

"Oh, come on," the woman said.

She didn't get them.

But there are some groups a university can't afford to refuse. Purdue-Indiana games now carry such magnitude within the state that tickets to see them become political tools to be used by the high and mighty to pry and repay favors. It is the ultimate way to impress another politician or important client. One state legislator called and asked for 33 tickets for her counterparts. She got them.

As the team began preparing for this twice-annual Armageddon, signs of its mounting popularity were everywhere. The latest issue of *Sports Illustrated* included a feature article on it, written after the win at Michigan. Balls were coming in by the gross to be autographed. Interview requests for the players were skyrocketing beyond control. Lewis, normally a cooperative subject, begged out of three requests for telephone interviews from out-of-state reporters one evening to keep a dinner date with a former AAU coach. At the same time, a local cable channel was filming a mini-documentary on Stephens, and various newspaper reporters were waiting after practice for Mitchell.

Experience had taught the players to be careful about what they said in interviews, because anything resembling a slight to the opponent was sure to wind up on a locker room bulletin board. The season before, after the game prior to the one Indiana would play at Purdue, Garrett had mentioned he didn't think Purdue wanted to win the Big Ten as badly as Indiana did. It wasn't meant as an insult, only as an indication of how badly he thought the Hoosiers wanted to win the league title. But it was too glaring an opportunity for Purdue's coaches to pass on. The quote was photocopied and enlarged—literally blown out of proportion—and tacked to the locker room bulletin board a couple of days before the game. The coaches didn't really think it would mean that much to the players, but figured it couldn't hurt. And it didn't. Purdue went on to win by 11, while Garrett scored two points and fouled out.

Stephens remembered that episode after talking with a reporter from the student newspaper at midweek. Asked how he viewed the rivalry as an out-of-state player, Stephens said he didn't have any special feeling for it as a freshman, but had grown to hate I.U. and everything about it, even the color red, over the years. He didn't mean it literally, though, and realized the impact a statement like that might have if published. He sent a request back to the student reporter to have the story toned down, and it was.

Actually, Purdue's players weren't directly motivated by the idea of playing Indiana much more than they were other Big Ten teams. Their trek toward a share of the Big Ten title the previous season, in which each game seemed more important than the last, had taught them that a game can only get so big, and after you've played in so many, they all start to run together. But *this* game sparked so much enthusiasm among the fans that the special feeling couldn't help rub off on them.

Just like the days leading up to the earlier game against Indiana, however, the challenge for Keady was getting his players to feel some of that enthusiasm during practice. Stallings and Weber were out of town scouting high school players Monday, Tuesday and Wednesday, leaving practice to Keady, Wood and Reiter. Keady also had brought in Jim Thrash, a former assistant coach at Fresno State and one of his closest friends. Thrash, who had left coaching to work for a commercial real estate firm in Albuquerque, would assume the role of special tutor, particularly for the defense, as Presley had done.

Practice that week was sluggish—and costly. On Friday, during a 10-4 Game, Kip Jones re-sprained his ankle. All in all, the week did not provide the kinds of workouts Keady wanted leading up to a big game, particularly this big game. The intensity still was lacking, particularly from the Black shirts. Kip Jones was hurt. And Reid, who had been so impressive early in the season, was still struggling, physically and mentally. Keady had told Reid's father early in the season his son had the makings of an all-Big Ten player. Now, Keady was worried Reid might become so discouraged that he would consider transferring.

"How do we ever win a game?" Keady wondered aloud as he pulled himself up to his customary position on the countertop in the weight room. "We seem so horrible all the time."

Saturday's practice began with a retake of the team picture at 2:30. The first picture, taken before practice started in October, had included Arnold, Stack and Fernung. Arnold and Stack were gone now, and Fernung had hurt his knee early in December and barely practiced since then. It also hadn't included Rea, who, in a unique way, had become an integral element of the team. This time, Rea posed. Fernung, unsure of his status on the team now, showed up just in case, but found there wasn't a uniform waiting for him. It was very much a different team now than the one that had posed back in October.

Still, the national ranking and Big Ten lead belied the coaches' feelings about the team's progress. It was giving up more than 73 points a game in league play, sixth among the conference teams. And it had outrebounded only three Big Ten opponents in the first 11 games, Northwestern, Wisconsin and Iowa.

Most troubling, the coaches didn't think the players displayed often enough the kind of pit bull intensity Keady sought in practice. The day before, Lewis and Stephens had asked Keady if he would waive the rule requiring a sprint for every offensive rebound allowed above 10 this week. They had allowed Iowa 19 offensive rebounds, but had outrebounded Iowa overall, and the players thought that should negate the punishment. Keady said he would think about it. But the very idea they had brought it up, the apparent quest to take the easy way out, troubled the coaches.

"I told Jim when we went home last night, you wonder how we've won any games this year," Keady said. "It's unbelievable. I was so goddamn depressed when I went home last night."

"I was, too," Stallings said. "I've been depressed since before the Iowa game, coach. I look out there in practice and it doesn't seem like there's any intensity. I told Woody last week, I said, 'Woody, we're going to get blown out at Iowa.' Then they go out and play their ass off."

Part of the answer to the riddle was that Keady's standards for intensity simply were higher than for the majority of coaches. Because he was always intense, every day, he had trouble comprehending why the players couldn't be that way, too. But the fact was, his players were more intense day in and day out than most college teams. Motivating his teams to play hard was the cornerstone of his coaching success, and other coaches often marveled at how he did it without making his players hate him at the same time.

So if this team wasn't quite as mentally tough as he wanted, it still gave up nothing to most of its opponents. Besides, Keady realized the personality of this team was a rather gentle one. He considered his players to be good kids, people he was proud of and enjoyed being around. They often drew compliments for their exemplary public behavior from restaurant waitresses, hotel managers and others who had had bad experiences with other college teams. "We've got to have one of the most polite teams in the country," Kip Jones once said. "Of course if we weren't, Coach Keady would kill us."

The flip side of that, however, was that they lacked a street fighter's mean streak. Translated to basketball, that meant they were mature enough to put forth a serious effort on a consistent basis, but lacked the kind of killer instinct coaches love. When they played a weak opponent, or took a comfortable lead against a strong one, they tended to relax rather than put them away for good. As their winning streaks grew longer, it became increasingly difficult to keep them practicing hard. The war against human nature always raged.

The players, on the whole, came from solid homes with strong support from at least one parent, and they were much closer to being spoiled than deprived. The only one who had grown up in a genuinely tough neighborhood was McCants, and he probably was the most serene, pleasant member of the team. On the whole, they were a team with a suburban, rather than inner city, personality. And since modern medicine had yet to come up with a method of transplanting personalities, Keady knew not much could be done to change it. All he could do was keep driving them, hoping his hard edge would keep them sharp. And in the long run, he thought it far better to have good kids who sometimes lacked intensity than troublemakers who were a little more hard-nosed.

Keady made one final impassioned speech to his players after the video session in the Union Saturday night. The week of practice had not been particularly good, and the fact the team was returning to the comforts of Mackey after three consecutive impressive road wins set up the unusual possibility of a letdown against Indiana once again.

"I want you to have great defensive fundamentals for when we get in NCAA play," Keady said. "I want you to be able to pass the basketball to people—the right people—and be fundamentally sound on defensive technique; and if you do, you'll be a national champion.

"But tomorrow, it's going to be very important you come out and fight their ass and be more competitive than they are, be ornerier than they are, and just take the game away from them.

"This game is a great, great sporting spectacle, guys. You're never going to be able to participate in anything this fun again, until you play again against Indiana there or here. So be ready. Enjoy it, don't be afraid of it. If you're afraid of it, it will destroy you. That's what they want to do, intimidate you.

"I want you to kick their ass, that's what I want you to do. Because it's a competitive game with a guy who tries to dominate the world of competitive basketball, and it isn't right. It's not fair to the other coaches that he doesn't have to go to the damn league meetings, it's not fair to the players that you don't get chosen for all-star teams [Knight, because of his power within amateur basketball, was often accused of manipulating the selection of offseason teams for the benefit of himself and his coaching friends], and there's only one way to handle it: be a man and kick their ass. And you walk away and say, 'Hey, I did the job because I'm a better person than he is.' If they beat you, you shake their hand tomorrow. If you beat them, you be humble. The guy is not right, and the only way to whip people like that is to play them straight up and kick their butts. So let's have some fun at it and be ready to go."

For any college team, a nationally-televised game is fun. For Purdue, no regular season game could possibly be more fun than a nationally-televised game against Indiana at Mackey Arena. The television lights alone cast a special glow. There were 54 of them, each 1,000 or 1,500 watts, which combined to make the arena four times brighter than normal.

That just about matched the feeling Purdue fans had for the game. Each year, playing Indiana provided them a shot at evening the score. The Hoosiers might have a larger fan following in the state, they might get more national publicity, and they might have won the national championships, but defeating them in Mackey could go a long way toward making it all more bearable.

And more often than not, the fans got their wish. Knight, despite having superior talent most years, had won just four of 14 games there. His 1975 and '76 teams, both of which finished the regular season undefeated, had won there by a combined total of four points. His '81 and '87 national championship teams had both lost there.

Because of its acoustics and the proximity of the fans, no arena in the Big Ten is louder than Mackey during a big game. The noise drenches the players like a rainshower, a shimmering din that still rings in their ears when they escape to the locker room at halftime. It also energizes them. In games like these, Lewis said, you never get tired.

Lewis and Mitchell had tried to explain the special atmosphere the night before the game in the Union to Rea, who was about to make his maiden voyage into a brave new world.

"When we beat Louisville [on national TV] last year, man, you couldn't hear," Lewis said. "Even when we came out to warm up, it was loud as hell. That mother is *loud*. And just don't let us get a run. Don't *let* us get a run."

The adrenalin began building for the players long before the tipoff. The players who shot around on their own before the team took the floor for the official warmups got a sneak preview of the game's heightened magnitude. Their every move was cheered, and they were glad to oblige. Rea, with a lift from Brugos and Scheffler, dunked for an *Indianapolis Star* photographer. Brugos dunked for a CBS cameraman.

"And I dunked for the *Wall Street Journal*," Berning said wryly, as the players headed to the training room to stretch.

There was a more serious item to contend with, however. Kip Jones was still limping on the sprained ankle he had aggravated in Friday's practice. A pain-killer was injected while his teammates stretched. But in a way, the injury eased a problem for the coaches. Mindful of how well things had gone in the second half at Indiana when Tony Jones started, they had been considering starting Tony Jones anyway, because it improved Purdue's defensive matchups.

Wood and Reiter cornered Kip Jones as soon as he entered the locker room with his teammates, explaining why he wasn't going to start and that it was only for this game. "I know, I know," Jones said, shrugging them off. "I'd do the same thing."

One of the biggest adjustments for the game, however, might have been the one facing Keady. He had allowed a camera crew from Channel 18, the Lafayette station which carried his Sunday show, into the team's inner sanctum to film the pregame, halftime and postgame activities. CBS also was there, to carry part of his pregame talk live. That meant he would have to watch his language in the locker room, even if his team was playing poorly.

The thought of what would happen at halftime if his team stunk up the place in the first half was intriguing. What would take precedence, Keady's intensity or his civility?

His players helped save him from finding out. Twelve seconds after the tipoff, Lewis plugged into the electricity flowing through Mackey by cutting underneath the basket and hitting an 18-footer from the right baseline. Garrett, the primary object of Purdue's attention for the afternoon, traveled on Indiana's first possession, and McCants came back with a turnaround jumper over him. Tony Jones then picked up a loose ball after Calloway lost control, and Mitchell was fouled in the lane by Garrett. He hit his first foul shot, then missed. But a lane violation against Indiana gave him a second chance, and he took advantage.

Barely a minute had passed, and it was 6-0. And Garrett had a foul.

Garrett finally scored for Indiana with a turnaround jumper, but McCants rebounded Mitchell's miss and scored, Mitchell blocked Smart's shot and rebounded it, and Stephens hit a jumper just inside the three-point line. It was 10-2, and the fans in Mackey, who had been armed with gold burlap "rowdy rags," were making a serious attempt at raising the roof.

If fate was to be kinder to Purdue this time than it had been in Bloomington, the first hint came a few minutes later. McCants took a pass in the lane, lost control, got the ball back and forced an off-balance shot that flew high into the air and fell through. Not only that, he drew Garrett's third foul in the process, with 15:39 still to play in the first half. The pieces were falling together perfectly for Purdue.

Todd Jadlow was immediately sent in for Garrett, and McCants' three-point play extended Purdue's lead to 16-8. But the Hoosiers gradually fought back, finally taking the lead on Smart's driving layup with 8:25 remaining that made it 27-26. Stephens' jumper returned the lead to Purdue, but Indiana took the lead again on consecutive field goals from Edwards, one a three-pointer, that made it 32-28.

The Hoosiers' lead held for five minutes, until Knight unintentionally shifted the momentum back to Purdue. Jadlow, who had been trading bumps and bruises with McCants since his entrance into the game, was called for a foul away from the ball in front of the Indiana bench. Knight protested vigorously and was quickly slapped with a technical foul—one of the sweetest sights imaginable for Purdue fans in Mackey Arena.

McCants hit the two free throws from the foul, then Lewis added two more for the technical. Purdue now led, 44-42. Mitchell mishandled a lob pass for a dunk on the ensuing inbounds play— he was looking directly into the glare of the TV lights, he said later—but Jadlow missed a free throw at the other end and Stephens came back with a three-pointer with 56 seconds left. Just like that, Purdue led 47-42.

Calloway hit a leaning jumper in the lane to quiet the crowd, then Purdue set up for the half's final shot. Tony Jones took it, but earlier than Keady wanted. With ten seconds left, he swished a jumper from just inside the three-point line. That left Indiana time to score again, which it did when Smart dropped a three-pointer over McCants at the buzzer.

Purdue's hopes got a major boost less than four minutes into the second half when Jadlow bumped McCants from behind and fouled out. The two had been engaged in hand-to-hand and word-for-word combat all day—"Shut up, Opie," McCants said at one point after Jadlow, who had the look of a country kid, had egged him on—and McCants had won. Garrett, who was waiting at the scorer's table to replace Jadlow anyway, would now have to play the final 16:13 with three fouls.

Mitchell's heart no doubt skipped a beat at the thought of what awaited him. It was the same situation he had thrived upon the second half in Bloomington. The foul-laden Garrett couldn't afford to challenge him inside with so much time remaining, and nobody else Indiana had was able to. Once again, the foul lane would be his personal horn of plenty.

He went to work immediately, scoring over Garrett to give Purdue a 60-53 lead. Edwards then missed, but Lewis, caught up in the mounting momentum, came back and rushed a three-pointer that bounced off the rim.

A television timeout followed.

"Guys, every day in practice we talk about putting people away, and you come back and take a shot like that with no rebounders and you let them back in the game!" Keady said in the huddle. "Now wise up! We keep talking about it, and all you do is keep doing it. If you put their ass on defense for awhile first, that shot's OK, but try to get it inside first."

"My fault, fellas," Lewis said.

Getting the ball inside, Purdue scored moments later as Mitchell slid around Eyl for a layup. The lead was now nine. But again the Hoosiers rallied, scoring nine unanswered points to tie the game with 12 minutes left. Garrett, however, picked up his fourth foul during that stretch, further weakening their inside defense.

With the final bell nearing, the game's intensity picked up another notch. It was like two heavyweights going toe-to-toe, trading punches in flurries and then sitting down for quick rests between rounds. Purdue slugged its way to a four-point lead. I.U. called timeout, then rallied to lead by one.

Finally, with Garrett out of the game for a brief rest, Purdue began landing some telling blows. McCants scored underneath with seven minutes remaining to regain the lead. Edwards then missed a three-pointer. Lewis rebounded, and later fed Mitchell on an inbounds play for another basket underneath to increase the lead to 78-75. Mitchell had scored eight of the team's last ten points.

Lewis, however, forced another three-pointer that missed, and Mitchell put up a rare miss inside, allowing Indiana to close within one again. But Stephens came back with a crucial three-pointer from the left baseline to make it 81-77. Calloway then missed, Mitchell rebounded and Keady called timeout.

If he had taped his earlier speech on shot selection, he could have simply replayed it here. The message was the same.

"We tell you and tell you and tell you, and practice and practice and practice, but you guys still force shots!" he shouted, barely audible above the celebrating crowd. "Now goddamnit, be patient!"

Lewis knew who the message was directed to.

"My fault, my fault," he said.

A minute later, after Edwards' jumper made it 83-79, Keady called for the control game. He wanted to slow the tempo, force his players to make careful decisions. Lewis, Stephens and Tony Jones spread out near the midcourt line and ran a weave among themselves, passing and cutting, to run down the clock. Finally, Lewis dribbled to his left, ran off a pick from Scheffler and fired a three-point attempt.

It was a questionable shot to take at such a crucial moment. Ten seconds still remained on the shot clock. And Keady had just yelled at him about his shot selection. And Garrett was flying at him, waving his arms.

He swished it.

The crowd exploded. Purdue now led 86-79, with 2 1/2 minutes left.

The Hoosiers made one last push. After cutting the lead to 90-85, Tony Jones threw the ball out of bounds against their fullcourt pressure defense with 50 seconds remaining. Indiana now had the ball, with enough time left to make up a five-point deficit.

But Edwards missed an 18-footer. Tony Jones grabbed the long rebound and threw it to Lewis, who quickly fed Mitchell breaking for the basket. Mitchell, remembering his missed dunk against Iowa earlier in the season, was careful to use two hands this time. He did, however, dunk it backwards. The final score was 95-85.

For Mitchell, it was a near carbon copy of the game in Bloomington, except this time his efforts went toward a victory. After scoring just three points in the first half, he finished with 24 points, and added nine rebounds. Both were game highs.

McCants also answered to an ineffective game in Bloomington, scoring 21 points, and was named the Player of the Game by CBS. Lewis, however, might have turned in the best performance, bad shots and all. He scored 22 points, passed out a career-high 14 assists and grabbed eight rebounds.

Stephens added 16 points to go with seven assists, and Tony Jones had turned in a solid 37 minutes—six points, four rebounds, four assists and good defense. Scheffler got in for 15 minutes, Berning for five, and Kip Jones four. Nobody else played.

The biggest statistics of all, however, might have been those belonging to Garrett: 18 minutes, 10 points.

And, there was a victory within the victory. Purdue had outrebounded Indiana 37-27, allowing just nine offensive rebounds. There would be no sprints to ask out of this week.

Keady made the rounds in the jubilant locker room, shaking hands with everyone and passing out congratulations. But most of all, he had a warning.

"It's a great, great victory, but it's just one W," he said. "Illinois is playing the best in the league, we've got to get ready, but let's go enjoy this one tonight.

"Together!"

"We attack!"

Temple had overcome a halftime deficit to beat North Carolina that afternoon, so Purdue would remain second in the national polls. But that was insignificant at the moment. It still led the Big Ten with an 11-1 record. Michigan, which would beat Michigan State the next day in Ann Arbor, would remain in second at 11-2. It was indeed a two-team race.

Kip Jones

"When I was younger I got harassed all the time by my friends. I wasn't with the people I wanted to be with, the jocks, when I was younger. I just didn't fit in with them. It seemed everybody grew up faster than I did. I was the ugly duckling. I got picked on a lot. I was real skinny. Maybe that's why I do it now; it's weird, because you should learn from it and shouldn't pick on other people. People used to call me Beanpole, and nicknames associated with being skinny.

"I just didn't fit in in grade school, and seventh and eighth grade, even my freshman year in high school. It seemed everybody else was stronger, and I was weak. That always bugged me. I didn't want to go over to the football stadium and lift weights with those guys because they were stronger. They'd make fun and stuff. I used to go lift weights by myself. I was always more coordinated than other people, I just wasn't as physically strong. Now I hang around with the same guys, and they seem weak.

"I thrived on playing against bigger people when I was growing up. A kid's got to have a head start in a sport to like it. To really like something, you've got to be a little bit better in something. That's the way I was. I was a little better from the start, so you want to play all the time then. When I was in seventh and eighth grade, I played against high school players and adults. I got beat on a lot, but I held my own.

"Then when I was in high school, I started going to the parks in Fort Wayne because there was better competition there. My fresh-up on my own. The thing about playing against black kids there, if you're no good you're going to get harassed. I was the only white kid at Weisser Park. They asked me to play. They thought they were just going to beat up on me, but I played really well the first time, and after that they never did say anything or care. They always knew who I was. They used to call me 'The White Shadow,' because I'd slip in and out on the weekends.

"I was scared to death the first time I went. I walked up and there was about 20 kids there shooting around. I walked up and heard one of them go, 'Hey, a white boy.' I went up to this one kid and asked him if he cared if I played there. I said, 'If you want me to leave, I'll leave.' He goes, 'I-I-I-I don't know.' It turned out this guy was retarded. It's funny, I go to the park now and he thinks I'm just a dunk machine. He gets crazy every time I get there and can't hardly talk.

"It was a lot different. When we fouled somebody in Decatur, we called the foul. But there, it was the other way around, the offensive guy would call it. So when I got the ball inside, I'd go up and get fouled and I wouldn't call it because I'd be expecting him to call it. Then everybody on my team would get on me because I wouldn't call the foul. I got known for doing that because I didn't play that way. But it made me play stronger.

"I expect to hear people make fun of my free throws. When I see a 50 percent free throw shooter on TV I think, 'God, what's his problem?' And I'm shooting 33, so I can't say anything. I'm a basketball player, I'm supposed to shoot my free throws. I think Coach Keady gets hassled more than I do about it. But it's got to come around. I've just got to get a streak to get going.

"I can sit down and tell sombody how to shoot a free throw, it's just a matter of doing it. I feel confident. I feel I'm going to hit them in a real pressure situation, but at other times I don't know. It's weird.

"Last year when I had two free throws against Illinois when the score was tied, I knew I was going to make it. The first one went in and rattled out and barely missed. I knew the second one was going in. It was an awesome feeling. There's nothing better. It was unbelievable. Everybody was going crazy.

"It was like I felt the energy from everybody else in the place coming down on me. After I made it I had my hands up in the air and I was looking up at the crowd; it made everybody so happy. It was awesome. It was like being an entertainer.

"The press in high school really built me up and gave me a false sense of security, I guess. I thought it would be a lot easier to do well in college. I haven't done as well in college as I expected me to, or as everyone else expected me to. Just because I played well in high school; I averaged 30 points, I got picked to play in McDonalds, I played well at Five Star. It's weird. In the Indiana all-star game I did well. Then I come here and I'm pretty much a role player. It was weird. I don't know how it ended up like that.

"I did well in pickup games when I first got here; I always do well in pickup games. But I had a hard time with the coaches standing there. I couldn't shoot early on from the outside. I was always nervous in practice the first couple of weeks. I was always short on my shots because I was nervous and that gave them the idea I can't shoot.

"I'm a better shooter from 15 to 20 feet than I am from 15 on in. That's weird. But in the lane it seems I have a hard time shooting well. But coach sees me shoot the inside shots and there's no way he's going to let me shoot farther out than that. So it's a touchy situation.

"Even this year, I hit my shots before practice started. Then the first couple weeks of practice I couldn't hit a shot again. If he put me at 15 feet and let me shoot it I'm sure I'd hit the shots. But with coach, you've got to make him believe it somehow by playing first. You've got to prove it, and if you screw up you compound it and make it worse.

"Coach doesn't worry about making you too tight. That's your problem. Like he says, he's not interested in feelings, he's interested in results. The players that excel on his teams are usually the players who are able to take criticism really well and not let it bug 'em and just go out and play and not worry about it.

"It was difficult for me at first, but I feel I've grown up a lot. I've grown up knowing the coaches are just trying to help me and aren't putting me down. You look at Troy, Todd, Everette and Melvin, and they all have the same attitudes. They all fit a mold a little bit. They try to do what the coaches want, but there's that free spirit they've got. They're the type who excel under coach.

"I learned after Iowa State that Coach Keady will never go through a losing season. He could have terrible players on the team and he won't go through a losing season. He would just work the team to death until they did finally start winning, and come down on them about attitude problems and stuff. If you're losing it's not because the other team's better than you, it's because you're screwing up. If you lose, he's going to make sure you end up winning.

"He seems so loyal to you, he makes the players have loyalty to the team. It seems like you're always helping the team whether you're playing or not.

"A lot of times, coach guesses about problems we're having. He'll just see something little then guess and goes on about it, then later you'll wonder why he did it. But in the long run you'll be able to figure it out. He's a unique guy in his coaching methods. He's got to be one of the best coaches in the nation.

"We're winning not because of our talent, we're winning for a reason. He has everybody in the right spot. He could take Illinois' team and take them to the Final Four in no time, if he had athletes like that. We don't have great athletes, the awesome athletes. It's also easy to get lost in his offense, too, like Doug [Lee] did.

"But you can't be pissed off. If you're pissed off you've got an attitude problem and he won't accept it. There's times when you are pissed off, but you can't show it and you can't do anything about it, so what's the use of getting pissed off?''

14

Answered Prayers

For the coaches, the glow of the victory faded quickly, even before
their heads hit their pillows that night. Stallings and Keady both
watched videotapes of the television replay Sunday evening at their
homes, and Weber and Wood watched it Monday morning in the
lounge. For analytical eyes feeding on mistakes, it offered a smorgas-
bord.

"Jesus Christ!" Weber shouted as the video exposed a defensive
lapse in the second half.

Keady walked into the room at that moment, coffee cup in hand.

"Horrible," he said. "We're just horrible on defense, I'm telling you.
I watched this son of a bitch last night until two in the morning..."

"And you vomited," Weber said.

"Oh, it's ridiculous," Keady said. "You know what we do best?
We're relaxed on offense. That's the thing we do best. We don't have
any goddamn idea how to play defense."

There was one thing impressive about the replay: the arena. The
added lights made it look like an entirely new facility, bringing out
the color of the crowd and the gold boundary on the floor. For home
viewers, it was the equivalent of trading in a black-and-white television set for a color set.

In its regular darkened state, Mackey Arena provides an excellent
setting for those in attendance. The floor is lit like a stage, offering a
clear view for the fans. And the darkness in the stands makes for a
perfect shooting background for the players. But more people watch
the games on television than in person, and for them the unlit back-

drop gives the appearance of an old, dreary facility. That was the image—of the team and even the university—beamed into homes across the midwest, and it no doubt made for an unfavorable first impression. Weber remembers watching televised games from Purdue while growing up in Milwaukee, and how Mackey's darkness influenced his image of the school. Now, as an assistant coach, he had to answer endless questions from recruits who were getting the same impression he had. Keady had approached the administration over the summer about having lights installed permanently—the cost was about $70,000—but was turned down.

Now, however, CBS was offering to leave the lights up, because it had decided to broadcast the showdown against Michigan in two weeks as well. They could be used for Thursday's game with Illinois if the coaches wanted.

They wanted.

"You know the first thing Loren Clyburn ever said to me, the very first thing?" Stallings said. "He said, 'Coach, why does your arena look so dark? Why is it so drab?' Here's one of the nicest kids I've ever talked to on the phone, and he asks why the arena's so dark."

"What about the lobs?" Keady asked, referring to the one Mitchell had lost in the lights against Indiana.

"Screw the lob plays," Stallings said, laughing. "Use 'em. If we can learn how to stop somebody, we won't need the damn lob plays."

"[CBS announcer] Jim Nance even called it 'beautiful Mackey Arena,'" Keady said. "I about fell over."

Something else was encouraging. The players were showing few signs of burnout. This is the time of the season many players and coaches, particularly those from losing teams, begin feeling the drudgery of all the practices and games. Even the previous season at Purdue had been emotionally draining, as each game along the uphill stretch drive toward the Big Ten title became more important than the one before it until the crash in Ann Arbor. To combat fatigue, Keady had reduced practices to two hours, excluding video and weightlifting, beginning in January. He also hoped the focus on the NCAA tournament rather than on the Big Ten title would help ease the pressure.

But he wasn't backing off too much. The coaches had decided in the locker room Sunday there would be no video session before practice on Monday, but had changed their minds after confronting the harsh reality of video replay. Weber called upstairs to Lorraine, and asked her to call the players and have them come in a half hour earlier for video.

"I tell you what, I want us more ready for Illinois than any team we play," Keady said. "Those bastards will *not* come in here and win. We may have to play all night, but we're going to beat 'em."

Accomplishing that was going to have to start with defense, the coaches figured. Keady had gone over defensive drills with Thrash, who left Monday morning, and committed them to paper.

"We're going to drill them like it's the Marines," Keady said. "And I've got all the drills right here."

"I think it's going to be very difficult for the players to change anything at this stage," Stallings said.

"They're going to do it," Keady said. "Don't worry about it."

Practice returned to normal that day. The lighting technicians and announcers were long gone, as were most of the fans who had been stopping by to watch the workouts leading up to the Indiana game. In fact, if the calendars hadn't argued to the contrary, the players would have sworn it was October, so basic was the practice schedule. The "Emphasis of the Day" was footwork and fundamentals. The managers barely needed to break out the balls.

The players spent most of the afternoon on defensive stance, footwork, containing the dribble, double-teaming, free throws, passing and other rudimentary elements of the game. All in all, it was an unusual position, literally and symbolically, in which to find the number two ranked team in the country, the first-place team in the Big Ten and probably the best team in Purdue's history. But then basics were what had gotten it to that point in the first place.

Tuesday's and Wednesday's practices were equally sharp and enthusiastic. The coaches demanded that they be that way, jumping on each mistake and applauding each success. The win over Indiana was nearly being treated as a loss, and with good reason. Until the previous season, Purdue teams had lost the game following a victory over Indiana five consecutive times, a clear indication of the emotional investment they put into the rivalry. The spell had been broken the year before with a victory over Ohio State, and nobody wanted a relapse, particularly now with the increasing opportunity to win the Big Ten title outright.

Keady began bearing down, even in subtle ways. During Wednesday's workout, he called for another 10-4 Game. Reid, whose enthusiasm had picked up noticeably after receiving a pep talk from Keady the day before, hit a three-pointer right away to give the Whites a 7-0 lead. Lewis answered with a three-pointer for the Blacks, but Reid dropped another three-pointer, despite a stout-hearted defensive effort by the Blacks, to end the game after just three shots.

"Way to be unconscious, Billy," Brugos said as the Whites headed for water and the Blacks to the end line for a sprint.

"Two-and-a-half in 30," Keady said. "No, wait. Make it 29." The standards were being raised.

Illinois was vastly improved from the first week of January, when Purdue won the Big Ten opener in Champaign. It led the league in defense, allowing 68 points per game. It also had won its previous four games and was accomplishing what Purdue's coaches were only dreaming of: blowouts. The week before, it had beaten Ohio State by 32 points and Wisconsin by 20.

But Purdue wasn't exactly slumping, a point it made immediately in the game. McCants, continuing the roll he had initiated against Indiana, scored eight quick points, dominated the boards and took a charge, leading the way to a 22-13 lead. Lewis then added an 18-footer and a three-pointer—both on assists from Reid, who was making a rare first-half appearance—to push the lead to 30-15.

The lead was still 13 at the half, but there were a few troubling statistics. Purdue had shot more free throws than any team in the league going into the game (28 more than runnerup Iowa) because of its emphasis on getting the ball inside. And its overall free throw percentage had crept up to 71. But Illinois had shot 16 free throws in the first half. Purdue shot eight, and hit only three. McCants, with 11 points, was just 1 of 5.

"What the hell's going on?" Keady asked in the locker room at halftime. "Get the ball in the hole, Mel! It's damn ridiculous. About this time of the year I think the moon comes out wrong for you and it affects your arm."

The players muffled giggles.

"I went to Mt. Carmel (when McCants was in high school) that time and you couldn't make a goddamn layup or free throw," Keady said. "Make the damn free throw! You've got a gift horse, look it in the mouth. You know what that means?"

McCants said he didn't.

"Well when somebody gives you a gift, don't take it without looking at the guy's mouth, you've got to check the animal out."

Keady turned back to the chalkboard, aware his translation of the parable was lacking something.

"That makes a lot of sense," he muttered.

Everyone cracked up. But Keady still wasn't amused.

"Christ, I've never seen anything like it!" he said. "How can free throws be so goddamn hard? Step up there and shoot 'em. Hell, it's a license to win. That's why we go inside, because we want you to shoot a lot of free throws."

The players returned to the floor with more admonishments of starting quickly ringing in their ears. And they responded, stretching the lead to 17 after the first five minutes. The Illini made two runs, cutting the lead to 10 each time, but both times Lewis hit three-pointers to turn them back. But shortly after the second one, with 5½ minutes left, Lewis grabbed a rebound, drove the length of the floor and, forcing the play, lost control of the ball. Lowell (Get off me, dog!) Hamilton followed with a jumper to reduce the margin to 11. At the next break in the action, a frustrated Keady jumped up and called Lewis over for a lecture on decision-making.

Lewis, realizing he was about to be scolded, jogged over, smiled and put his hands on Keady's shoulders. The crowd broke up. Keady, taken back by his senior's salesmanship, smiled, and simply asked a question: "What's going on, did the gamblers get to you or what?" Lewis laughed and said yes, as a matter of fact they had. Keady laughed, and the matter was dropped—further evidence of Lewis' knack for keeping out of trouble and of Keady's capability for being won over.

Although the outcome was still in doubt, the mood within Mackey had shifted from intense to lighthearted. During a timeout with 3:53 left, the cheerleaders paraded a large sign to midcourt and showed it off for the fans. It read: "Final Four." The NCAA tournament was still three weeks off.

The game ended 93-79. McCants starred once again, with 22 points and 11 rebounds. He even managed to hit three of four free throws in the second half despite the coach's tragic Greek analogy.

Lewis was typically steady, with 19 points, seven rebounds and seven assists. Mitchell added 18 points and Stephens 16 points and seven assists.

But the most encouraging thing about the game was the boost the bench had provided. Brugos, Reid, Barrett and Rea got their first game action in nearly a month, and all took advantage of it. Reid finished with two points and two assists in five minutes. Brugos hit a bucket and took a charge in two minutes. Barrett hit two free throws in one minute.

And Rea sent everyone home smiling. After Keady put Reid, Brugos and Barrett into the game with 49 seconds left, the fans began chanting "Marvin! Marvin! Marvin!" He got the call at 29 seconds. At 10 seconds, after Hamilton missed a three-pointer, he grabbed a long rebound and took off for the basket. The crowd buzzed with anticipation, but his layup from the left side was blocked out of bounds.

There were six seconds left now. "Get Marvin open!" Wood shouted. Rea took the inbounds pass, drove for the lane, stopped and tried an off-balance 15-footer. It missed, but he was fouled. There was one second left. The band was playing, the players were off both benches ready to head to the locker rooms and fans were standing in the aisles. The public address announcer asked everyone to stay off the floor.

Rea's first shot bounced off the back of the rim and out. The fans groaned. But Rea swished his second shot, as the crowd erupted and his teammates ran to the free throw line to congratulate him.

"Hey Marvin," Kip Jones shouted in the locker room. "Don't score any more points and you'll be the first one-point scorer in Purdue history!"

For that one point, Rea received his first invitation to the postgame press conference. On his way across the hall, he was beseiged by kids in search of autographs, some of them as tall as him.

"Damn, you score one point and everybody wants to talk," he said.

Rea walked into the media room a few moments later, eyed all the reporters, television cameras and microphones, and stopped dead in his tracks.

"Oh, man, they don't want me," he said. "No way, man."

He was nudged to the front and, after Lewis, Mitchell and Mc-Cants had taken their turns, stepped up to explain himself.

"On the first one it felt like I had a brick on my arm," he said. "But then I heard Coach Stallings yelling to relax, so I tried to relax."

Relaxing for the next game, two nights later, would be easy. The challenge, in fact, would be to not relax too much. It was against Northwestern, which had won just one game since its early-season upset of Indiana, and now sat in the Big Ten's cellar at 2-11.

Northwestern, because of its tradition of futility, doesn't consistently draw well at home, but the fans will turn out for the big games. The chance to beat the Big Ten leader certainly qualified as a big game, so, with generous help from Purdue fans—who bought up about half the seats—Welsh-Ryan Arena was filled to its capacity of 8,117.

But whatever they lack in numbers, Northwestern's fans are capable of making up for in volume. The members of the pep band, wearing striped rugby shirts and blue jeans, sit just around the corner from the visiting team's bench. They yell almost as much as they play, which on some nights makes them a more difficult obstacle for opposing teams than Northwestern's team.

Keady had been one of their favorite targets the previous season. He wore a gold sports coat for that game. The band members, deciding he looked like a Century 21 real estate salesman, chanted, "Sell us a house! Sell us a house!"

Then, in the first half, Keady discovered his zipper was stuck at half mast with a corner of his shirt tail sticking out. Reiter noticed it when Keady stood up once in front of the bench. "Coach! Coach! Your zipper's down!" he whispered loudly.

"I know!" Keady said. "Why do you think I'm holding this warm-up in front of me?"

Northwestern's band wasn't treated to any such revealing displays this time, but it did get to watch Purdue's players get caught with their pants down for 20 minutes. The Wildcats jumped to a 25-12 lead, and still led by nine at the half.

After the game, reporters would ask Keady about his halftime address to the team, assuming fire and brimstone. But that wasn't the case. Keady knew Northwestern had played as well as it could play. And he knew his players, having already defeated two tough teams that week, were due for a letdown. His first words upon entering the locker room after meeting with the assistants were, "OK, relax."

The game turned around immediately in the second half. Stephens hit a 17-footer, McCants hit a layup on a nice feed from Lewis and Kip Jones added a three-point play to slice the lead to two points within the first two minutes. Northwestern called timeout, but it didn't matter. Lewis hit a three-pointer to give Purdue its first lead of the game shortly after play resumed, then added another one on the next possession to make it 37-33 before four minutes had passed.

The Wildcats, their confidence already fragile from all their previous losses, never recovered. Purdue outscored them 45-18 in the half, and the final was 69-51. Something else of interest to Purdue had happened that afternoon: Michigan lost at Iowa, so Purdue ended the day at 12-1, and the Wolverines at 11-3. It was indeed a two-team race.

"You guys did a great job," Keady told the players in the locker room. "You won three games in one week again, that's twice you've done that and that's damn hard to do. You're off until Monday. You've done a great job this year, guys, I'm very proud of you.

"But hey. If we do that at Madison . . . They've got a hell of a lot more players. We can't let Wisconsin get started like that."

The win put Purdue two games up with four to go. The players—and coaches—were in a dreaming mood. Keady mailed in his ballot for the United Press International All-Big Ten team. He put four of his starters—Lewis, Stephens, Mitchell and McCants—on the first team, along with Michigan's Gary Grant. He put Kip Jones and Tony Jones on the third team, and voted for Lewis as the league's Most Valuable Player. Keady joked about his ballot, but then emotion often overruled logic when his team was involved.

"Hey, we're finally first in something," Keady shouted on the flight to Madison as he looked over the latest Big Ten statistics.

"What, coach?"

"Field goal percentage," Keady said.

"What are we in free throw percentage?" Reid asked.

"Fifth," Keady said.

"There's no excuse for that!" Kip Jones said, his grin betraying his attempt at disgust.

The team, naturally, was loose as it prepared to play Wisconsin. And the coaches, naturally, were a bit frightened. The Badgers were much like Northwestern, a lower division team that Purdue could only lose to by beating itself, but still dangerous enough to pose problems. The fact a Purdue team had not lost to Wisconsin, either at home or in Madison, since the 1976–77 season, when Lewis, Mitchell and Stephens were mere 11-year-old kids, added to the apprehension. Sooner or later, something had to give; the coaches hoped it wouldn't be this team's intensity.

Wisconsin also figured to have an emotional edge, since this game would be its last of the season at home. With a 4-11 conference record, 10-15 overall, an upset over the first-place team in the conference was the most meaningful thing it had left to play for in the season.

Keady, however, was bringing in another reinforcement: Sidney Moncrief, the star guard from the NBA's Milwaukee Bucks who had played at Arkansas when Keady was an assistant there. Arkansas had reached the Final Four in Moncrief's junior season, and came within one game of repeating the trip when he was a senior. Keady, who had helped recruit him, considered him one of the best players and people he had ever coached.

When he had contacted Moncrief about meeting his team a few months earlier, Keady had no idea what its status would be when it hit Madison. As it turned out, the timing could not have been better. With the dog days of the season upon them, the players could benefit from hearing a different voice, particularly one belonging to a respected NBA player. And while Keady had not fed Moncrief any lines, he couldn't have given a more appropriate lecture himself.

Moncrief talked of execution, patience, unselfishness and unity— the same sort of homespun advice Keady had been doling out all season.

Moncrief, who brought with him the kind of late-season pains typical of NBA players—he had stitches inside his mouth, a jammed finger, a jammed thumb, a shoulder that had been knocked out of its socket and chronically sore knees—also stayed for practice. His message and his presence—probably the latter more than the former— had a noticeable impact on the workout that followed.

Lewis seemed the most affected, showing even more vocal leadership than usual. He directed traffic, shouted encouragement and passed out praise throughout the session. He also tried to leave an impression of his own. Early on, after hitting a three-pointer in a fullcourt scrimmage, he immediately glanced over at Moncrief as he ran back on defense—just to make sure the old pro had noticed.

Wednesday night's upbeat workout, however, didn't completely soothe the coaches. The nagging feeling of impending doom continued to hover over their heads. The win streak was now eight, and the Big Ten lead unexpectedly comfortable. The spirit among the fans back home, meanwhile, had soared to a premature conclusion; T-shirts, sweatshirts and other souveniors declaring the team as the 1988 Big Ten champions had already hit the stores. If anything could jinx a team, that was it. Besides, the team seemed to have a knack for playing well only when it had to. How long before it flirted with disaster once too often and got punched in the kisser?

As Keady had lunch with his assistants at the hotel the afternoon of the game, the vibes weren't good. The assistants had received word Wisconsin's head coach, Steve Yoder, and his assistants had skipped Wednesday's practice in favor of recruiting, leaving it to a graduate assistant. That seemed to make the game all the more eerie.

"I can hardly stand it," said Stallings, who had jumped off the recruiting trail himself to rejoin the team Thursday afternoon. "I haven't even been at practice this week, and I'm a nervous wreck."

Keady faced up to the hint of trouble in his usual manner at the team meeting Thursday afternoon.

"I'm going to tell you right now, guys, if they beat our ass you know where we'll be when we get home tonight; we'll be on the goddamn practice floor," he said. "Because you're not going to let a team like that beat us. Like I've told you every time we come here, the only way they can beat us is if you let them.

Wisconsin Field House, built in 1930, is the second-oldest arena in the Big Ten and the third smallest. In 1969 it was still presentable enough to host the first two rounds of the NCAA tournament—Purdue, in fact, beat Miami of Ohio and Marquette in it on its way to the Final Four—but now it was an outdated, drafty recruiting obstacle. It was, on the other hand, a tough place for opponents to play in. The cold northern air blew in through the doors, swept through the outer lobby and chilled the playing area with nothing to block it. In past seasons, on particularly frigid days, Purdue's coaches recalled sitting on the bench and shivering.

After the players dressed in the locker room, with pipes hissing and clanking overhead, about half of them went out to shoot around on their own. Scheffler, meanwhile, sat on a folding chair in front of his locker and closed his eyes. A few moments later, Lewis spotted him. "Hey, look, Scheff's asleep!" he said, and the other players in the room picked up on the joke. Scheffler started to defend himself, then let it drop.

But five minutes into the game, despite Keady's repeated emphasis on a quick start, the starters were the ones who seemed to be dozing. They had hit just two of their first eight field goal attempts and committed three errors. Wisconsin was leading 8-5.

Keady substituted Scheffler and Tony Jones for Kip Jones and Mitchell at the first timeout. Lewis missed twice more, but Wisconsin kept things close by missing two more shots of its own. Finally, Scheffler drew a foul and hit one of two free throws. Less than a minute later, he grabbed McCants' missed shot and scored, tying the game at 8. Mitchell's back-to-back field goals, a 17-footer and dunk on a lob from Stephens, made it 12-8. Wisconsin missed, and Scheffler rebounded. Kip Jones missed, and Scheffler rebounded and scored. It was 14-8.

Wisconsin was still within four points with five minutes left, but Lewis and Stephens hit back-to-back three-pointers to ignite a 10-2 run that opened a 28-16 halftime lead.

Keady appreciated the lead, but not the listless, sloppy manner with which it had been achieved. His team had hit just 41 percent of its field goals and committed ten turnovers. Only by the grace of Wisconsin's mounting futility—the Badgers hit just 8 of 31 shots—was that good enough for a 12-point lead.

"We talked about coming out strong at the start of the game and it had no effect on you," Keady said in the locker room. "Somebody's got to give us some leadership."

"Have some fun at it, guys, let's go!" Keady said. "Are we going to be uptight down the stretch and screw this thing up? Play basketball!"

They played. McCants scored on a goaltending call to open the half. Wisconsin missed, and Lewis hit a three-pointer from a foot behind the line. Wisconsin turned the ball over, and Lewis dropped another three-pointer. Barely two minutes had passed in the half, and it was suddenly 36-16. Game, set, mismatch.

Scheffler, however, wasn't through. He scored ten more points during a three minute, 20-second stretch later in the game, hitting a short jumper in the lane, a dunk, a layup, a dunk and two free throws.

He finished with 15 points and ten rebounds—both career highs—in 22 wide-awake minutes.

Scheffler's performance earned him another invitation to the postgame press conference. His ruggedly efficient game always grabbed the attention of reporters who had not yet seen him play. And his unique personality always left lasting impression.

"It was kind of like a football game there early, wasn't it?" one reporter asked. "You were kind of cleaning house, weren't you?"

"So much as being like a football game, yes, and that was the more enjoyable part of the game," Scheffler said, still in his sweats. "It was somewhat frustrating...I'm glad the referees let the banging go on inside as much as they did. That makes it an enjoyable basketball game."

"Gene Keady talked about your confidence level when you came to Purdue compared to now. Has there been a great change?"

"Definitely. Earlier on I used to worry about...I'd get so worked up I'd hyperventilate in the game. I'd be in like 30 seconds and pulling on my jersey. It wasn't because I was tired or anything, it was because I was nervous."

"You said earlier you needed this kind of game tonight after the last three weeks. Mission accomplished?"

"I hope so. I don't know what the rebound total was, but...."

"You had ten."

"It was ten?" Scheffler slapped his hand on the table in front of him and let out a devilish laugh. "All right! I had a little deal going for ten rebounds with my roommate, Scott Bowen. He has to call the girl of my choosing now."

"And do what?"

"He has never been on a date yet! And if there are any good-looking girls you know of, call my roommate! His name is Scott Bowen. I mean, he's not a geek or anything, he's just really shy and bashful and we've been trying to set him up with a girl. He has to call anyone I choose."

The reporters were half laughing, half puzzled. They had never encountered a postgame interview quite like this one.

"Is he your only roommate?" someone asked.

"Yes," Scheffler said. "Now Barney Rubble down the hall, and Len, they made a deal about rebounds and points for pizza. But that's against NCAA regulations, so..."

More laughter.

"If you want to get technical; there's so many rules," Scheffler said, grinning.

"Do you know your own strength, do you know how physically dominating you can be?"

"No, I find it very flustrating sometimes, so much as knowing when to push and how to push and things like that. I feel very inhibited so much as myself, I still haven't learned the game, when you can push and how you can push...I always get called for holding. I mean, I'll push with this arm, but I don't see why they call me...I was thinking about this earlier if you know what I mean...."

"You're tough to hide on the court; they can see you. Did they stop pushing back tonight once you got in a physical game?"

"No! No, [Danny] Jones and 43 [Patrick Tompkins], they were still giving some shots all the way down the line. It was still a very physical game. I wish almost that they...instead of just trying to call... they [the refs] should make it really no touch or really let the touching go, because it seems like all of a sudden they'll...and all of a sudden they'll pick out little things, which makes it very flustrating and very inconsistent and it's harder to play a very physical game then."

"OK, thank you."

"Thank you," Scheffler said.

From the relative tranquility of the Great White North, the team flew back into a hotbed. There would be one day of brief preparation, and then the biggest game of the year to date: Michigan, and a chance to clinch the Big Ten championship outright.

CBS again would be on hand to televise it nationally. Sportswriters from around the country, many of whom were making their first trip to West Lafayette, also were coming in. Purdue, ranked number two, was 25-2 overall, 14-1 in the conference. Michigan, ranked 10th, was 23-5 and 12-3.

For Purdue, the game offered a tantalizing opportunity for poetic justice: winning the conference championship at the expense of the team that had ripped its heart out the season before.

The circumstances, however, would hardly be ideal. Michigan would be playing with one more day's rest, having trounced Northwestern in Ann Arbor Wednesday night. Purdue had arrived in West Lafayette at 12:15 a.m. Friday morning, which meant a short night's sleep for everyone. Keady was up at seven, shoveling snow off his walk and preparing to be in his office by nine. At ten, he would leave for Chicago to take part in a publicity-drumming press conference sponsored by CBS and the NCAA at Ditka's, a restaurant partly owned by Chicago Bears' coach Mike Ditka.

Keady returned just as the players were gathering in the lounge to watch video that afternoon, but had to skip that to tape a segment for his Sunday TV show.

Again, the atmosphere wasn't conducive to preparing for a big game. It was at moments like this that Keady's cooperative spirit threatened to get the best of him. Virtually all media requests were being approved. The result was a half dozen or so sportswriters and nearly as many sportscasters waiting on the floor to talk with Keady and a few of the players. CBS had set up a chair and portable lights at the edge of the court, barely out of bounds.

With Keady attending to media commitments, and Weber and Stallings out recruiting again, the video session in the lounge was left to Wood and Reiter. Mitchell also had to be excused because of a class commitment; he said a teacher had forbid him to miss two of the three help sessions available, and this was his last chance.

Reiter's stray dog theory took effect again as the video from the first half of the previous night's game rolled. The coaches tried to keep the players' attention, but they were having trouble maintaining a serious atmosphere with such a one-sided game on the screen and such an exciting game on the horizon. As was often the case, Kip Jones and Billy Reid were at the heart of the mischief.

"Man, these guys are so sad," Jones said as the Badgers began to crumble.

A few seconds later, Jones threw a bad pass.

"Nice pass, Kip," Reid said, looking up from the basketball he was signing. "Pretty sad, I'd say."

"Shut up, Reid," Jones said.

Moments later, Jones missed a free throw.

"Nice free throw, Kip," Reid said.

"Man, I'd love to just punch that guy," Jones said with a grin, smacking his fist into his hand.

Wood and Reiter dealt with the matter the most effective way possible, which was to report it to Keady when the players took to the practice floor. Keady immediately whistled the team to midcourt for a quick lecture.

He started calmly.

"The higher you go in Division I basketball, the more distractions you're going to have," he said.

Then he kicked into gear.

"So you better be pretty goddamn mature to handle it and not have your head up your ass, Billy and Kip! We can't be goddamn airheads and win a national championship. So you better both do what the coaches tell you and shut up or get your ass in the dressing room. You understand that? Because it's tough enough with the media dogging everybody's ass. They're trying to do their job and we're trying to do ours. But if you can't handle it, we're going to get beat. You've got to worry about basketball and nothing else."

"I just want to say something, too," added Lewis, a polished veteran of the media game. "Like coach said, man, you can't let this distract you. We've got to have our eye on one thing. All this here don't mean shit if we don't win."

"It ends," Keady said. "They all vanish as soon as we get beat.

"I don't know what the problem was, but if one of my coaches is upset, I'm upset. They have one thing in mind, to get you guys the best possible success they can possibly get you. Academically, character-wise or basketball-wise, we pull for you. If somebody gets after your ass, we've got to get with it. We love you guys here and we love you off the court, but by God you'd better have your heads on right or you're going to get your ass kicked."

Thusly warned, the players began practice, and Keady returned to deal with the distractions. He conducted a quick interview with an Indianapolis TV station, then stopped to autograph a ball. He then greeted Ed Janka, a Nike representative who worked as the firm's contact with its coaching clients and then moved on to talk with Tom Heinsohn and Verne Lundquist, who would be broadcasting the game for CBS. All the while, he kept an eye on practice. Thanks largely to his jump start, it was running smoothly.

The atmosphere for this game was an instant replay of the one against Indiana a week earlier, although the fans' motivation was more pragmatic than emotional. Again, Mackey was lit up and bathed in black and gold. Again, Keady let the television cameras into the locker room.

Keady wrote four points of emphasis on the board, all of them relating to fundamentals and execution. Then he added one final thought. In the bottom left-hand corner of the chalkboard, in large numbers, he wrote "104-68"—the score of the previous year's game in Ann Arbor.

"You seniors have come a long way, but you're always going to be judged by how you do at the end of the season, aren't you?" he told the players. "It's a damn shame, and I'll always be proud of you, but that's the way it is and I'm going to do something about it. Today, let's start doing something about it and go out and beat a quality team on our court in a game that means something."

After the players left for the initial warmup, the coaches sat for a few minutes in the locker room, mulling over the unique opportunity ahead of the team—clinching the Big Ten title with one week still left in the season. In October, November and December, they would have laughed at such a notion.

"We've never made it easy on ourselves," Keady said, walking out of the bathroom at the back of the locker room. "Can we do it just once?"

The first couple of minutes, keeping with recent trends, didn't offer much hope. Michigan jumped to a 4-0 lead.

A slow start like the ones at Northwestern and Wisconsin would be disastrous in this game, given the caliber of the opponent. Stephens, however, got things started with a three-pointer off a pick by Kip Jones. Mills missed, Stephens rebounded and Mitchell got a fastbreak layup from Lewis. McCants then stole a pass off the fullcourt press, and Mitchell hit Stephens, running off Kip Jones' pick, with a lob pass—just as in the game in Ann Arbor—for a wide-open layup. Purdue led 7-4.

At the next break in the action, with 16:31 left, Scheffler replaced McCants, who complained of stomach cramps. It was at then, coincidentally, that Purdue broke loose, outscoring Michigan 22-8 over the next eight minutes for a 31-16 lead. McCants returned in the midst of the run to score nine of Purdue's final 11 points.

Michigan fought back, though, pulling to 33-24 and getting two chances to score again. But Stephens made a spectacular block of

Gary Grant's baseline jumper, and Kip Jones drew a foul on a rebound of the miss that followed.

By this time in the season, Jones' trials at the free throw line had become legendary among Purdue fans. Every time he stepped to the line, the crowd began buzzing, as if watching a trapeze artist prepare for a dangerous somersault.

Jones' first shot bounced twice off the rim and fell through. The crowd broke into a hearty cheer; Jones stepped away from the line and broke into a huge grin. But he missed the second attempt, and Mills' jumper moments later cut the lead to eight.

Lewis' jumper and McCants' two free throws returned the lead to 12, then Mills scored again in the lane to make it 42-32 with 43 seconds left. Keady called for one shot. The play to be run was Boilermaker. But Tony Jones, dribbling in outside the three- point line, was called for a five-second count for not advancing the ball with ten seconds left.

Another broken play at the end of the half. Keady, remembering the Indiana game when Jones had to rush a shot at the end of the half that set up Smart's three-pointer, was livid. "Goddamn, Tony, what's wrong with him?" Keady shouted in the coaches' locker room. He kicked one of the plastic chairs set up for the post-game press conference and sent it flying ten feet toward Weber's feet. "We work on that all the time, how can that happen?"

"Coach, nobody helped him," Weber said. "He's supposed to be the three-man on the play, he shouldn't even have the ball..."

Keady cut him off. "Oh, bullshit! He's got his head up his ass!"

Keady quickly calmed down, and began going over the usual halftime checkpoints. The assistant coaches pointed out Lewis and Stephens had been out of position on the play, leaving Jones little choice but to stand and dribble the ball. When he met with the players, Keady discussed the matter only briefly, and closed the subject by taking the blame himself.

The halftime lead slipped to six early in the second half, then ballooned to 12. Michigan, however, whittled the lead down to two, 65-63 with 2:55 left. The game, and perhaps Purdue's outright Big Ten Championship, was slipping away.

Finally, with 2:36 left, McCants was fouled by Hughes away from the ball. His first free throw bounced off the front of the rim, the back, and in. His second swished. It was 67-63.

The game was now an instant replay of the one in Ann Arbor, with Purdue trying to nurse a small lead to the finish line. And again, poise pulled it through. Grant rushed a three-pointer over Stephens, and Mitchell tipped the rebound to Tony Jones. Robinson then fouled Lewis trying to steal the ball from behind. Lewis hit both shots, making it 69-63. Grant scored over Stephens to cut the lead to four. But then, the clincher.

With the shot clock running out, Stephens had nowhere to go with the ball but to McCants, who was standing on the left baseline about 15 feet from the basket. McCants was out of his range, but turned to shoot to beat the clock. Rice foolishly fouled him, giving him two free throws.

After a Michigan timeout, McCants swished the first free throw. He missed the second, but Mitchell, standing in the farthest spot from the basket along the lane, came off Lewis' pick of Robinson, grabbed the rebound, scored and was fouled. The free throw "stunts" that had been run throughout the season had finally paid off, in a big way.

It was a play remarkably reminiscient of one in 1984 that had been crucial to Keady's first Big Ten championship. Then, in the season's final regular season game at Minnesota, Purdue needed a win to tie Illinois for the league title. Purdue was hanging on for dear life in the final minute when Steve Reid shot an air ball on a free throw attempt. But Ricky Hall swooped around from the outside of the lane, picked up the ball before anyone else could react, and dribbled it back outside to seal the victory.

Mitchell hit the free throw to complete the three-point play, increasing Purdue's lead to 73-65 with 1:09 left. Grant then forced a three-pointer over Stephens that missed the rim, McCants rebounded, and Lewis was fouled. He hit both shots. Victory was assured. The crowd went wild, celebrating Purdue's first solo flight atop the Big Ten since 1969 with chants of "Big Ten champs! Big Ten champs!"

Scheffler ended the game appropriately. Rebounding a Barrett miss in front of the basket with 12 seconds left, he crouched, paused, gathered himself, then jumped and dunked the ball with three defenders hanging on him, and was fouled. It was a shot symbolic of Purdue's entire season to that point—a slow start, a determined effort and a successful climax. He hit the free throw to complete the three-point play—his only points of the game—and finish off an 80-67 win.

Overall, Purdue's patient, penetrating offense had paid off again. Michigan got off 19 more field goal attempts, but hit only five more. Purdue shot 31 free throws, Michigan four. For the season, Purdue had now shot 759 free throws and its opponents 461. Purdue outrebounded Michigan 41-25, and held it to just nine offensive rebounds. No sprints this time.

While the players and assistant coaches scurried to the locker room to celebrate, Keady stayed on the floor to be interviewed by CBS. Before reaching the other side of the court he was met by Pat, who planted a kiss on the corner of his mouth. As Keady did the interview, the camera slowly zoomed in on his face, focusing tightly on the red lipstick imprint for the nation to see.

After a quick interview, Keady rushed to the locker room to join the team. This was exactly the moment that made it all worthwhile for him as a coach. All the hassles were forgotten: the occasional disciplinary problem, the constant struggle to keep the players intense, the perpetual obligations to the fans and media. Nothing compared to the thrill of walking into a locker room and celebrating a conference championship with a team that had fulfilled its potential. The feeling was the same for the players. The preseason conditioning, the meetings, the grueling practices, the high-volume lectures...it seemed a small price to pay for this moment.

"Way to go, guys! Way to go!" Keady shouted at the top of his lungs, pumping his fist as he entered the room. The players, who had been celebrating on their own in rather routine fashion, all shouted back and instinctively rushed to meet him in the middle of the room.

"Coach! What's that? What's that?" Lewis asked, pointing at Keady's mouth.

"You've got lipstick all over you!" Mitchell said, in mock horror.

The players laughed and began chiding their coach, the way fifth graders tease a classmate who just got kissed by a girl on the playground.

"It's from my honey, my wife," Keady said, raising his arm.

"Together!"

"We attack!"

"Way to go!" Keady screamed again, resuming the celebration.

He pulled out his handkerchief and wiped off the kiss seen 'round the world and began working the room, exchanging bear hugs and handshakes with the players and assistant coaches.

"Hey, guys!" he shouted again, getting the players' attention.

"Let's swim and lift weights at 4 tomorrow. And it'd be kind of nice to be here early and watch the girls beat Ohio State. [Purdue's women's team was to play the next afternoon in a game crucial to their NCAA tournament hopes.]

"Congratulations! Big Ten champs!!"

There was one other thing. As the game clock ticked off the final seconds of the victory, Weber had turned to Keady with a thought about the upcoming Ohio State game—the one Keady had been saying wouldn't matter, if Purdue beat Michigan.

"Coach, we can't lose at Ohio State. We've got to get the number one seed," Weber said.

"So," Keady told the reporters afterwards, "we just changed our mind about that game."

Melvin McCants

"I have one brother and one sister. I'm the oldest. We lived in an apartment across the street from where they used to film 'Hill Street Blues.' They'd come and stay for a week or two and take outside shots to use. I walked right in front of the cameras one day when they were filming. I was coming home from school, and I didn't have any idea they were filming. All I heard was, 'Cut!' Somebody said, 'We got to start over, because somebody got in the way.'

"My mom was kind of strict. We had to be in at a certain time, way earlier than other kids. When I was a junior or senior in high school, I still had to be in by ten or 11 o'clock, all year. Even on weekends. I didn't hang out with other kids or nothing in high school. I just stayed home and watched TV, or sat out on my porch. I didn't really go nowhere.

"We fell out one time. I left home for a couple of days. This was my freshman year in high school. I was mad because she didn't give me no freedom. She treated me like a little baby. I had to come in a certain time, and all my friends would still be outside.

"That night I left, I didn't go nowhere, I just stayed out by my grandmother's house. I sat out on her porch. My mother thought I was high; she thought I had been smoking something because I was fussing at her and arguing. I used to drink a lot with guys from school, and we used to get high a little bit. But once I got in high school I quit because I never seen them again."

"I was never asked to join a gang, but I knew a lot of gang members. We had the Latin Kings, the Blackstone Rangers, and the Black

Rangers. A lot of people who were in gangs told me not to get involved, that it wasn't for me. They knew I was playing basketball and kind of had a big future ahead of me, so they told me not to get involved in that stuff.

"I've seen people get shot before. I've seen a lot of fights. I've seen crap games get held up, and that was kind of scary. Some of the friends I hang out with, they used to carry guns. That was kind of scary, too. But they were real good friends.

"Even still when I go home, people there look out for me. They don't let nobody else mess with me. I just walk through that area. I'm not afraid, because I know most of the people around there.

"I used to hate basketball. I hated basketball so bad. I loved baseball. People were always wanting me to play basketball, but I just wanted to throw a baseball with somebody.

"I was a lot better baseball player than basketball player. That was my game. I still think today I'm probably better at baseball than basketball. I haven't played baseball in awhile, but I still think I can play it better than basketball. I played every position. You name it, I played it. I was pretty good. They used to call me Dave Kingman [who played for the Chicago Cubs at the time].

"One of my best friends told me he wanted me to play with him on this team when I was in the sixth grade. That's when I started playing basketball. I wasn't no good, though. I didn't start progressing in basketball until my sophomore year in high school. I was taller than everybody. Every grade I was in, I was the tallest guy. I used to be real short and fat. I used to just eat and eat. Then I just shot up all of a sudden.

"Sometimes I hate it being tall, because you can't buy the clothes you see other people wearing, or the shoes, or you can't fit into a car. I wore number 50 in high school. I changed because it was getting too small for me. My freshman year here they gave me 45, but I didn't like that at all. So then I got 35. The big numbers make you look big. I don't want to look big.

"The only thing I don't like about college basketball is I don't like the attention. People are always stopping you and making you late for class. They're talking to you about this or that. Sometimes they ask the stupidest questions, like, 'Do you know Troy Lewis?' Or they ask if I play basketball. But I've kind of gotten used to that.

"I don't like to go out, though, like to the mall. I hear people saying my name. They walk by and they say, 'Hey, that's Melvin McCants.' I think, 'I got to get out of here,' because there's people just staring at me. I didn't like it in Lafayette at first. When I took my trip, I didn't go anywhere. I didn't like it at all, really. It was quiet. There weren't any buildings or anything. It took me awhile to get used to it. I didn't get used to it until my sophomore year.

"When I first came down here my freshman year before classes started, I stayed in Tony Branch's [a former assistant coach] apartment for a week. He was gone, though. I kept a knife under my pillow. I was scared. I had never stayed alone before. And I kept a light on, too.

"I think I'm kind of lucky to be here now. I know a lot of people would like to have an opportunity to be in my shoes. Every time I go home, a lot of people say they see me on TV, or ask me to autograph something. A lot of people there hope I make it big.

"It's tough keeping up with classes, because you've got to work your butt off to pass. When things aren't going well in class, it rubs off on your game. There have been times here when things aren't going well in a class, and I come here for a practice or a game and I just don't perform well. But I don't let it bother me no more. I've experienced it so many times I'm just used to it. Now I know what to do to prevent it. But fans, they don't know. They just think you're a terrible player.

"It's still not easy, because when we go on the road you're always missing class. That really hurts me, because I'm not really a quick learner. It takes awhile for me to learn something.

"My family's all expecting big things from me, and I don't want to let them down. So I'm just going to keep trying to do the best I can. I know I can do it if I just try. Getting that degree, that's more important than anything. My family is second, and basketball is third. Everything else comes after that."

15

Flat in Columbus

The players who dared attend the girls' game the next afternoon found out quickly the price of being Big Ten champions. A few of them tried to watch the first half of the game from the stands, but were beseiged by autograph seekers. They watched the second half from the safety of the back of the tunnel, where fans weren't allowed to go.

But all the hassles in the world were worth the opportunity that awaited them that afternoon at the swimming pool. The previous year, Keady had promised the players they could throw him in if they won the Big Ten. The win at Michigan State Thursday night set up the opportunity, but the loss at Michigan on Saturday ruined it. Big Ten champs or not, Keady was in no mood for a dip the day after losing by 36 points.

This time, there were no obstacles. The title was all theirs, and they were coming off a win. The coaches, anticipating what was on the players' minds, wore old sweats that they didn't mind getting wet.

The swimming session started innocently enough. But after a few minutes, Stephens, Mitchell, Lewis and the two Jones' gathered at the far side of the pool from where the coaches were sitting, obviously discussing some fiendish plot.

They started with Weber, picking him up by his feet and arms and swinging him into the deep end. Reiter went next, then Wood. They headed for Stallings, who was in a glass-enclosed office just off the pool area, but he begged them off.

"Hey, don't guys, I'm talking with a recruit," he said. He didn't tell them it was a signed recruit, Clyburn, but it worked. The players went instead after the prize catch, Keady, who went peacefully. They cheered wildly.

Drunk with their newfound—and very temporary—power, they went on a rampage. They turned back to Stallings, who had hung up the phone and was stripping off his clothes. The senior managers, Howat and Lyon, were next. Then Rudd. There wasn't a dry body in the house by the time Keady ordered them back in the water for the relay races.

But overall, the glow of the championship just won put everyone in a brighter mood. Tuesday morning, when Keady walked into the lounge for a video session, the players had written their own version of a practice schedule on the board:

Defense: Do what you want to do!

Offense: I got mines! Up to you to get yours!

3 p.m: Free throws, three laps, form shoot

3:15: Three-point shooting

3:20: Dunk contest. Competitive, losers run

3:30: Water

3:40: Stretch legs

4:00: Alley drills for coaches

4:10: Zone work. Shoot until you make. Losers get $5 lunch, winners get dinner at Sorrento's.

4:20: Defensive technique (underclassmen only)

4:30: Review Detroit tape; Mitchell will bring

4:50: Wild Goose—coaches only, players watch

The Detroit tape was a reference to one of the more memorable inside jokes from the previous season. At the video session after the team's game at the University of Detroit in December, Keady called for it to be reviewed. But it wasn't anywhere to be found. Reiter, who was in charge of such things and had made his first road trip with the team for the game, took the brunt of the blame for it. But Mitchell, who had played exceptionally well in the game—24 points and 11 rebounds in 31 minutes—was the primary suspect. The coaches hadn't seen the humor in it at the time, but it was part of the team's folklore by now.

A fun-loving spirit, as displayed by the mock practice schedule, was one of the things Keady valued most about the team. No matter how demanding he got with the players, he wanted them to enjoy the game. Any amount of joking around was all right with him, as long as it came at the appropriate times.

He talked about that at his weekly press luncheon later that day.

"They're really fun to be around," he said. "That's hard for a coach to say, because a lot of times you don't want to admit as a coach you let your kids have fun. We always want everybody to think we've got discipline and we've got control over them. If you think you've got control over a 19-year-old, you're crazy as hell. I don't think that. They've got a sense of humor. They can take a good ass-chewing and come back like I've never said anything to them and not take it personal. And they can take a compliment and not let it go to their heads.

"Besides, they know it's temporary and probably won't last long anyway," he added, chuckling. "They'll be back to the real world in about 30 seconds."

Keady was in a fun-loving mood himself on the trip to Columbus. A larger airplane had been chartered so that about 20 local alums could accompany the team. It was a treat for the fans and a profitable venture for the university, but a minor inconvenience for the players, who were much more cramped than in the airplane normally used for road trips.

But it was a short flight and a beautiful day, sunny and unseasonably warm. After landing in Columbus, everyone transferred to the bus waiting to take them to the hotel. Keady sat in the front seat and greeted everyone as they boarded. While he wasn't any less interested in this game than any of the others, he did seem to be less worried about it.

Everyone was in good spirits at the next morning's shootaround. Keady even shot for awhile with the players, giving away his 1950s roots by launching one-handed set shots.

"Wanna play H-O-R-S-E, coach?" Kip Jones asked, referring to the traditional shooting game in which players match shots and get a letter each time they fail to hit the same shot as their opponent. Keady accepted. Jones, as much as he struggled from the free throw line, was a good jump shooter from long range because he was forced to follow through to reach the basket. He began dropping jumpers from behind the three-point line. Keady began missing.

"Why don't you hit those in a game, you dumb shit?" Keady said, as Jones' teammates cheered him on. "You hit three-pointers and you miss layups."

Jones hit again, and again, quickly defeating his coach.

"I'll tell you one thing, your ass is in trouble if you miss a layup tonight," Keady said.

Jones grinned. "Go again, coach?"

"Hell, yes!" Keady said.

Jones was leading the second game, too, but it was cut off before its completion to stay with the practice schedule.

The free throw contest produced some surprises as well. Lewis and Brugos were eliminated early, leaving Stephens, Mitchell, Barrett and Ewer in the finals.

Stephens stepped to the line.

"Yeah, Bardo!" Lewis yelled from the sideine.

It worked every time. Stephens convulsed in laughter, and missed.

That left Mitchell, Barrett and Ewer.

"Hey, we've got all white guys left," Kip Jones said. "Oh, sorry Todd."

Mitchell went on to win it.

The game didn't figure to be a smooth ride into the sunset. The setting was similar to the one at Michigan the year before. It was Ohio State's final home appearance of the season. And with a 15-11 record, the Buckeyes still held out hope of attracting a bid to the NCAA tournament. A win over the second-ranked team in the country would help their cause greatly, although they probably would have to win at Michigan in their final regular season game as well. To add to the excitement for the home fans, ESPN was there to televise it nationally. All that would make a tough place to win even tougher. Ohio State had been awfully difficult to beat at home throughout the season, beating Michigan, Illinois and Iowa.

"I don't want you out there playing all tentative and uptight," Keady told the players before the game. "Hell, play loose, you don't have anything to lose. If we get beat the next three weeks, tell everybody to stick it up their ass and we'll go enjoy the spring. That's ridiculous to get uptight about that stuff. But at the same time you've got a chance to be the national champion, and that's what we want to be. That's what we've worked for all these months.

"It's not going to be easy, so you've got to play your butts off for 40 minutes."

From the very beginning, however, something was missing from Purdue's game. Kip Jones made an alert play to grab Mitchell's opening tip, but Stephens ran the wrong direction in initiating the offense. Lewis wound up firing a 22-footer that missed. At the other end Tony White grabbed an offensive rebound and scored for Ohio State.

Stephens didn't execute properly on the next two possessions, either, although Purdue scored on both. Still, the Buckeyes were obviously more intent. They jumped to an 11-5 lead, and missed a shot that would have opened the lead further.

Purdue scored the next ten points to grab a 15-11 lead. Despite allowing eight offensive rebounds and hitting just four free throws, they led 32-28 at the half. But the coaches were not happy with the lackluster performance. The relaxed mood of the past week vanished.

Lewis made a concentrated effort to get things started in the second half. He stole the ball on Ohio State's opening possession, and later converted a three-point play to push the lead to five. Ohio State came back to grab the lead on Jay Burson's jumper with 13 minutes left, but Lewis answered with a three-pointer. After an Ohio State error, Stephens drove the baseline and, in an awesome display of his raw athletic talent, dunked on 6-11 Grady Mateen and drew a foul. His free throw made it 47-42. All was well again.

But only for a minute. Francis drove through Purdue's trapping defense for a layup, then Mitchell missed inside and fouled going for the rebound with 11:53 left.

A television timeout was called.

"Steve, who you got?!" Stallings shouted at Scheffler, straining to be heard over Ohio State's band as he prepared to diagram the defensive alignment.

"I've been having a number of guys," Scheffler said. "The tall guy, Carter, and . . ."

"Just one answer, Steve!" Stallings said. "There's only one answer!"

Identifying someone as "the tall guy" didn't exactly narrow the field much in a college basketball game. But it, like all of Scheffler's answers, was totally honest. He had guarded three people in the game so far, and now he was trying to remember their names, particularly the one he had guarded most recently. Tony Jones whispered it in his ear.

"Carter," Scheffler said.

When the huddle broke a few moments later, Kip Jones offered some advice for Scheffler. "Get that tall guy, Steve," he said, smiling.

Ohio State promptly ran off nine consecutive points, capped by a jumper by the tall guy, Mateen, that made it 51-47. Keady called another timeout to break the momentum, and the fans exploded.

Purdue made repeated charges for the lead, but continually tripped itself up. Mitchell, the winner of that morning's free throw contest, had two free throws to tie the score with 7:45 left, but, for the second time in the game, missed both. But he wasn't alone in his futility. McCants missed the front end of a one-and-one at 7:05. A minute later, Kip Jones did the same. Forty seconds later, Scheffler missed his first of two shots, then hit the second, ending a streak of five straight misses, and seven potential squandered points.

That proved to be too great an obstacle to overcome. Purdue pulled to within one point with 4:48 left, but Mitchell later fouled out, much to the delight of the Ohio State fans, and the Buckeyes went on the win 71-60.

Keady's plan not to get too upset over a loss if it happened was the farthest thing from his mind as he headed into the locker room. All he knew was, his team had played poorly and had lost to an opponent with less talent; worse than that, its hopes for a number one seed and momentum heading into the tournament were in danger.

He kicked a large plastic dispenser full of water, twice, on his way into the locker room, skidding it a few feet across the floor. He picked up a roll of adhesive tape from the trainer's table and flung it across the room, then walked back into the corner by the toilet stalls. It was another loss, one that shouldn't have happened, logically, and he hated the very thought of it. He paused a few seconds, then walked back into the main room, leaned against a trainer's table and sighed. "Well, they got what they wanted, so they're happy," he said quietly, referring to the victory's meaning for the Buckeyes.

Keady stared at the floor, saying nothing. The assistant coaches, scattered around the room, did the same. The only noise was the public address announcer's voice echoing through the arena, reciting Ohio State's individual scoring totals. "Tony White, nine points.

Grady Mateen, ten points. Jay Burson had 12." After each listing, the fans, most of whom hadn't left, cheered.

Keady collected his thoughts for 15 seconds, then walked through the door leading to where the players were sitting, with their heads bowed. He picked up a piece of chalk and wrote three words on the board: "Finish the job." He then put the chalk down and turned to the players.

"Huddle up," he said quietly.

The players silently stood and raised their arms.

"I want to tell you one thing, guys," he said. "It takes men to play this game. You better get your heads up and walk out of here, compliment them and get your ass ready to play Minnesota. That's a joke, what we did tonight. You have never proven to me you can finish the job in the big time. Nor have I proven it to myself yet. And I'm part of you.

"Together."

"We attack."

The players returned to their lockers and began undressing in silence. For Keady, the next stop was the postgame press conference, at the opposite corner of the arena. As he walked along the court's baseline, and then the sideline, he was escorted by shouts from Ohio State fans. "Good luck, coach." "Nice game, coach." And, from one man, "Hey, Gene, you going to lose in the first round again?"

Keady ignored all the greetings, walked into the cubbyhole that served as an interview room, and met the press.

"Well, I don't have a whole lot to say, other than Ohio State played a great game tonight," he said calmly. "They did what they had to do to get in the NCAA, and that was good for them. Hopefully that's good for our league. We just didn't play well enough to beat them. We didn't do the things we have to do on the road. So we have a little bit of a situation where hopefully we can beat Minnesota and get a number one seed. But that remains to be seen. I think their emotion was the difference in the game. They've played extremely well at home, and you've got to hand it to them. Questions, please."

That done, Keady made his way back to the locker room. But shortly before reaching the door, a young man wearing a Cleveland Browns' hat, standing 15 feet to his left, yelled for his attention.

"Hey, Gene, LSU this year?"

"Huh?" Keady replied, uncertain if the man was trying to make a good-natured joke about Purdue's previous bad luck in tournament draws (in 1986 it had had to play LSU on LSU's home floor), or was simply being rude.

"You going to play LSU?" the man said.

"What's that supposed to mean?" Keady asked. "They're probably not even going to be in the tournament this year. You trying to be a smartass, or what?"

Wood, who had been standing nearby, walked over to the man. "Hey, buddy, we don't need to hear that," he said. "You won the game. Why don't you just keep your mouth shut?"

Stallings, much angrier, walked up to the man and stuck a finger in his face. "You better shut your mouth, or I'll knock your ass from here to next week!" he shouted. Then Keady joined the group. "What are you, some kind of smartass?" he said, his temper flaring.

By now, security personnel were being summoned in case the encounter progressed beyond words. "Leave him alone, he's an idiot," Weber shouted, standing off to the side.

The man shrugged and walked away. "What's your problem, guys?" he said innocently.

As soon as it was over, Keady was smiling about the incident. "Don't worry about him, coach, he's a Browns' fan," a man wearing a striped Ohio State sweater yelled down from the balcony overhead. "Yeah, but Larry Clisby's a Browns fan, and he's a nice guy," Keady answered, laughing.

Keady's mood hadn't changed, however. A few minutes later, he summoned his assistants into the locker room for another meeting. He was livid over the way his team had played, particularly Stephens and Mitchell. Stephens had scored eight points, hit 3 of 11 field goal attempts, committed six turnovers, and been guilty of several more mental mistakes. Mitchell's return to his home state was even less productive. The next morning, it would be announced he, along with Lewis, had been named first team all-Big Ten by the league's coaches. But tonight, he showed none of that form. He had scored two points, hitting one of eight field goal attempts and none of his four free throws, and grabbed just three rebounds in 33 minutes before fouling out.

Weber, Stallings, Wood and Reiter listened to Keady rant and rave about the way the team had just played. They agreed with him, but they reminded him of all the good things the team still had going for it and how this outburst could influence the players' psyches. It was no time to let things turn sour.

The ride home was awkward because of the fans who had accompanied the team. It wasn't a good time for the players to mingle. But the fans, trying to show their support, kept passing out compliments and good wishes.

Keady, in particular, was in no mood to be consoled. Bob Schwartz, a local booster and one of Keady's best friends, moved across the aisle to sit next to him for a minute.

"Coach, don't feel bad," Schwartz said.

"To hell with you, I *want* to feel bad," Keady said. "I *do* feel bad. We just got our ass kicked when we shouldn't have."

"Well, I've got a big surprise for you," Schwartz said.

"I don't need a goddamn surprise; I need a W," Keady said. "I need Everette to play good." It was the kind of thing Keady would only say to a friend, and Schwartz didn't take it personally.

"OK, be that way," he said, moving back to his seat.

Mitchell, meanwhile, was particularly despondent. "If I had peed a drop, we would have won," he told Wood.

When they arrived in West Lafayette, at 2 a.m., Keady asked the alumni to unload first so that he could talk with the players one more time. The players turned around in their seats toward the back of the plane, where Keady stood in the aisle. He spoke calmly, quietly.

"Honesty without love is brutality," he said. "We've always been honest with you guys and we've always loved you. You guys are the Big Ten champions. You need to walk out of here with your heads up and learn from it and admit that things aren't always going to go like we want them to go in life.

"I'm going to tell you one of the things I'm disappointed in right now is, if the White squad doesn't start getting with it, we're not going to beat anybody in the tournament. We're not going to get better if we don't have the second group pushing us. It's up to you guys to develop the first group. That's the only thing I'd say I'm slightly disappointed in, because we need you guys who don't play a lot to push the people who are starting. Without competition, you never get better in life.

"You guys who got some nickle-dime injuries, shake it off, forget about it and be men. If you've got something serious, the doctors aren't going to let you play. I don't want any young man hurt for a ballgame, that's ridiculous. But if you're feeling sorry for yourself right now, that's bullshit. Because you've got a lot to be proud of. The coaching staff loves you. You've got a great opportunity now to do something. The only thing I'm disappointed in is the fact I thought we could be 17-1. But we're not. But we can still be 16-2. We can still get Minnesota and use it as a springboard. I'm going to tell you one thing right now, if we let Minnesota play with us, then we might have some problems.

"All that counts is that you care. Hell, I can want to be 17-1, I can want you to make your free throws, but if you don't want to, we're not going to do it. We've got guys on that White squad lollygagging around, not getting any better, because you don't push yourself. That's all bullshit. We had a staff meeting the other day about scholarships, worrying about who might not get to play if we get this guy or that guy. That's ridiculous. You've got to prove to us that you deserve to play. That's life. We spend half our time worrying about you guys, and I'm not sure you worry about us. I'm talking about the last six or seven people.

"Now get home and get to bed, and we'll see you at two o'clock tomorrow."

The coaches' meeting the following morning, like most of the recent ones, didn't include Weber and Stallings. But they were on their way home. Weber had been scheduled to fly to Texas and Stallings was planning stops in Dayton and Cincinnati, but Keady ordered them off the recruiting trail for a few days. The emphasis was going to be on the current players for awhile, rather than potential future ones. The team was hitting the home stretch, and Keady wanted everyone running in the same direction.

The loss still weighed heavily on Keady's mind. Negatives abounded. The team, as Wood pointed out, had just lost on national television to an opponent that had successfully defended it with a triangle-and-two. Michigan State had used the same defense effectively as well. Surely they would see it again. Stephens again had not been able to consistently execute fast breaks. And Keady was most discouraged by the fact some of the players, particularly Mitchell and Stephens, had not seemed mentally prepared to play.

"Boy, if you don't have some kid that's a hard-nosed leader, you've got to be an asshole all the time to motivate them," Keady said. "Just like Mitchell. We'd been nice to Mitchell for three games now, hadn't we? He has to have his ass kicked. That's a shame, how human nature . . .like Kip letting White get those tip-ins."

"It's their personalities, Coach," Reiter said. "That's the guys we've got. We've got to stay on 'em."

"Yep," Keady said, turning to make out the practice schedule. "It's a lovely profession, isn't it?"

Overall, however, the coaches remained upbeat. They believed they hadn't really been beaten all season in the Big Ten, but rather had beaten themselves in the losses to Indiana and Ohio State. A bad pass and a missed free throw in Bloomington, and a few missed free throws and lack of concentration in Columbus. . .if not for those self-inflicted wounds, they would be undefeated in league play.

Keady gathered the team in the lounge before practice Thursday to pass along a story about the warmup suit he was wearing then, and had worn much of the season during practice. It was one he had received the past season—black, trimmed in gold, with "NCAA 1987" stitched over the heart.

"You all thought I wore this warmup because I liked it, right?" Keady said. "I hate this goddamn warmup, for two reasons. Because first of all it was made in Iowa City. I don't hate Iowa, I hate it because they're our competitors and I want to beat them.

"The second reason I hate it is because of this [NCAA 1987] on there. When I wake up in the morning, it reminds me of Florida. And I'm motivated by it. When we beat two teams in the NCAA, I'm going to burn this son of a bitch. That's what I did to motivate myself during the year. I wore it because I hated it. It reminds me every time of what? That I want to be the best. And I want you to be the best. It reminds me of what I have to do as a coach to get you prepared, and that's why I wear it. And I'm going to wear it until we do well and get over the hump, you understand? It motivates me.

"You all thought I wore it because it's a nice warmup, right? You're wrong. There's a lot of things about me you don't know. I think that's what you've got to understand about people. Sometimes you know people, and sometimes you don't. I thought I knew Kip Jones. I didn't know that asshole could shoot three-pointers. He kicked my ass yesterday, and that was a surprise to me. I liked that, because he competed. I like Tony Jones, because he's bullheaded. That mother will be successful in life, and I love him for it. But he's got to do some things to get over being bullheaded; when he works on his defense, for example. And there's some other things I like about you guys that you don't even know. Don't ever underestimate a person or team when you're playing them, because there's things you don't know about them.

"It's important for you to understand that this basketball team is going to be a small part of your life. But if you can do something these next three weeks, it can be the most important part of your life as far as you doing something very special—and you're very close to that."

It also was a memorable day for Berning, who hadn't played in more than two weeks because of his back. That morning, he had received permission to participate in half-court drills again, ending his exile on the sidelines. He also received something else: a telegram from his father, sent from Memphis, Tennessee.

It read:

"Congratulations on the championship game and a great season. I am very proud of you. Keep up the good work. Love, Dad.

"P.S. Be careful of your back. Hope to see you soon."

It was the first contact Berning had had from his father since his junior year in high school. The telegram stirred some of the jumbled feelings inside him, but the chance to resume practice made it a good day, regardless.

The practice was one of the best of the season. Keady ordered chairs set up on the corners of the floor for the players to run around when they jogged their three laps; no cutting corners today. Ropes were strung across the entrances to the playing area, closing the workout to the public, although a CBS camera crew was on hand to film a feature on the team.

The fresh outlook was most evident in Brugos, who was suddenly becoming one of the most vocal and enthusiastic players on the team.

The turning point for Brugos had started a few weeks earlier, under strange circumstances. He had been a few minutes late for a video session one day because he misunderstood the starting time. When he arrived, the lounge was dark and Keady already was going through the tape with the players. The assistant coaches decided to take on the role of diplomats. Keady hadn't noticed Brugos' absence, so they allowed him to slip in quietly. They knew Keady would be forced to discipline Brugos if he knew about it, and they thought it would be better for everyone involved if the issue was ignored this time. Some of the other players were aware of it, too, and agreed.

Besides, it gave Wood an opportunity to apply some pressure. Wood told Brugos he wouldn't report his tardiness to the boss if he would start working harder in practice. Brugos, inspired by an intense desire not to run the stairs after practice, agreed. Wood stayed on him consistently, and lo and behold, Brugos began trying more consistently. He still had his lapses, such as in the days leading up to the Ohio State game, but not as often. And when he did try, he had success.

Keady's plea to the White shirts on the airplane gave him another boost. Brugos had laid in bed staring wide-eyed at the ceiling. Keady's words had hit him hard. Could it be the White shirts' fault if the team didn't do well in the tournament? For Brugos' analytical mind, it was an interesting concept. The reasons for a team's success or failure had to start somewhere, and who was to say it wasn't with the reserves? "That snapped me out of it, it really did," he recalled later.

He decided then and there to assume leadership of the White team, as Arnold had done in December.

"C'mon, fellas, we don't need that losing feeling any more," Brugos said, as the players gathered around Keady at the chalkboard the next day in practice.

He then proceeded to play as hard as he could, making sharp cuts to get open, crashing the boards, blocking shots and scoring almost at will. The flighty astronaut had become a model sub. He took a pass from Reid in the lane, turned, and exploded to the basket, scoring over McCants.

"Good job, John Brugos! Good series, John Brugos! Way to go!" Stallings shouted.

Moments later, Stephens hit a three-pointer over Reid. Brugos, ignoring their difference in jersey color, congratulated Stephens. "Way to shoot the ball, man!" Brugos hit Reid with a deft pass underneath the basket for a reverse layup. It went on like that, for the rest of the two-hour session. The rest of the White shirts picked up their play as well. Reid was hitting like he had the first week of practice, and working hard on defense. Barrett, as always, was aggressive and vocal. The

Black shirts, their intensity pricked by the loss and the White shirts' effort, were sharp, too. Perhaps the loss at Ohio State would turn out to be the best thing that could have happened to the team.

Todd Mitchell

"I try to play hard. Every time I play well I think, 'Hopefully I can get on a roll now.' But it's not easy to do. Sometimes you get down because you don't get the ball as much as you like. Early in the year I wasn't playing well because I wasn't shooting free throws well. There's just things you've got to overcome.

"A lot of times I don't feel...I'm not a Troy Lewis, a stationary jump shooter. I feel like I can dribble the ball and penetrate and shoot it that way. My quickness allows me to penetrate and shoot the ball, but in coach's offense that's not what he wants.

"I don't feel like I'm hunting shots, I feel that's where I can best shoot the ball. That affects me sometimes, because when I shoot the ball, I'm thinking, 'He's going to get upset.'

"When he said that about my dad after the Ohio State game, that made me mad a little bit. Coach has done that before, but I think he knows the kind of strong person I am, and I'm not going to get all pissed off at him and cuss him out and everything. I don't think there's anybody else on the team he can say that to but me.

"I think he gets on me a lot more than anybody else on the team, but he knows I understand what he says isn't personal. It motivates the other guys to play well.

"I think my dad and him are a lot alike. He knows how dad would feel as far as wanting the best for his son. Of course you want your son to score more, because you think he's a good player. If your dad thinks you're a better player than what you are, of course he's going to tell you to do more. I'm sure coach realizes that.

"I think to myself, 'What's the best for me, personally?' Sometimes what my dad says or what the coach says isn't the best for me. So I have to decide what the best for Todd is. Sometimes that's the way you have to go about it. Because this is Todd's last semester. After this, there has to be a life for me. The coaches, they're still going to have their jobs. They're still going to be in West Lafayette, telling another team that same thing. But I'm going to have to be doing something else.

"Coach might say, 'Todd, you're going to have to pass up some shots.' But I have confidence in myself that if I have the shot and I think I'm open I can make it. Usually if you pass up a shot it's very unlikely the ball's going to come around to where you can get that same shot again.

"I'm not saying I have the right to shoot it, but I think I've been here long enough that I think I've earned the right to shoot the ball. I don't think I've got the right, I think I've earned the right. There's times my dad says I should shoot the ball more, but there's times in the games when I don't. You have to hold up. There's also certain times in the game when I think I should shoot it.

"Coach sees that and says we're just thinking about our pro careers. But that's really not the case. I finally went to him and said, 'Coach, Troy and I and Everette are getting upset about that. Every time we try to do something on the court you say we're just thinking about our pro career, but we're really not. Some things we do now, we've been doing for three years. You never said anything about it before, but now all of a sudden since we're seniors we're thinking about our pro career. I don't think that's fair to any of us. We want to get to Kansas City just as badly as you do, and we're doing everything we can to get there. We don't even discuss that too much.'

"I think he really understood where I was coming from. He said, 'Okay, I can buy that.' I don't think he'll say too much about it anymore.

"That's the thing, you can always talk to him. If he thinks you're right, he'll listen to you. He's never above listening to what you have to say. He can chew your ass out, but later on that day he can joke about it and laugh about it. That's one of the unique things about him. He can chew your ass all day, but then you never really hold a grudge against him. We used to say a few years back, 'He can chew your ass and make you like it.' We've talked about that many times. Some coaches can do that and you just hate them. Hate them.

"You can't really describe it, it's just something he can do. He can holler at you, but he's really trying to teach you. He'll be really pissed, but right at the end when he's done hollering at you, he'll give you some word of encouragement. Right after he's told you how terrible you are, right at the end he'll say something positive. That's one of the best things he does. During a game he'll say, 'Kip, you're not blocking off, you didn't see the ball, you're not doing this...' But right after that he'll say, 'Come on, you're ten times the player he is.' He can be so negative, but that one positive thing at the end sticks in your mind.

"I think that's why coach treats me like he might his own son, because he knows I'm accustomed to his style, because he's like my dad. I used to work for my dad's construction company back home. Sometimes I think the longer I stay down here the better. Oh, man, he'll work your butt off. He doesn't like the men to work in the heat of the day. So he starts them at six. He worked my ass off—bricklaying, building scaffolds, pulling blocks all over the place, mixing mortar, driving tractors. The thing about it was, he always told me, 'You can't sit down, you always got to be moving, you've got to work twice as hard as everyone else, because you're my son and I can't let you be out here on easy street.' So I had to work twice as hard as everyone else.

"I worked for him the summer before my eighth, ninth and tenth grade years in school, for the regular union wages. But when I got off work I didn't want to do anything; I was too tired. I'd get off work at three or 3:30 and guys would come over wanting to play ball around five and I was dead tired. I didn't recuperate until eight or nine o'clock.

"I'd like to have my own business someday, but I wouldn't want to go about it the way he did. He did it the hard way. He started the business about the time I was born, and built it up himself. It almost went under once, but he got a loan from the bank and rebuilt it.

"But after all this time he's working just as hard as he did when he started. It's not supposed to be like that. As much as he's done, as much success as he's had, he's still working the weekends, still working until six or seven at night.

"When I used to work for him in the summer, I used to think, 'There's no way. There's no way I won't graduate. I'm keeping my butt in school. So I won't have to do work this tough.'

"You really hate to see that last home game come. I remember my freshman year when that game came, and we had to have it to make the tournament. Bullock and Reid and Atkinson came out and played their hearts out to win that game. You play so many games here and you're going to miss the place. There's so many memories and the fans have been so great.

"I enjoy the away games, too, because this is the last year you'll ever have great crowds like that, every time. That's why I really want to go out and play hard. Even if you do make the NBA, the crowd won't be like they are in college. It's a totally different atmosphere there. You've got to go behind your back and between your legs and dunk it before you get the crowd in the game.

"It's gone really fast. I can remember being a freshman like it was yesterday. But I've put in my hours. I can remember times I wanted to leave and times I was really happy. But overall, the time I've spent here I've enjoyed."

16

●

Grand Finale

With the glory of the Big Ten championship behind them and the anticipation of the NCAA tournament ahead of them, the celebrity status of the players was reaching new heights as they prepared for the final home game. Balls and other paraphernalia to be autographed flooded in, piling up in Weber's and Stalling's office and spilling out into the hallway. Requests for interviews from the media and personal appearances were almost as frequent.

The players were often amazed, even mystified, by the amount of attention they received from the public. What was it about them that inspired so many people to dress up in black and gold, paste bumper stickers all over their cars, and drive 200 miles just to see them play?

Earlier in the season, Lewis had received a letter from a local woman telling him she and her husband had just named their newborn son after him. Mitchell had a fan club in Toledo, whose members wore sweatshirts that read "Don't mess with Mitch." Stephens received fan mail from all over the midwest, including some from fans of other Big Ten schools expressing their admiration.

Their fame was a double-edged sword, however. On one hand, they received plenty of extra benefits. There was always someone offering to take them to dinner, just to share their company. It was much easier to meet women; sometimes it was effortless. Lewis and Mitchell, for example, had had roses, with a note attached, left under their windshield wipers, telephone numbers drawn in the dirt on their car and messages left on their answering machine from interested females.

But the attention wasn't always pleasant. Brugos recalled one painful slight in the form of a letter that arrived at Mackey one day earlier in the season. It was addressed to him, with a child's handwriting on the envelope. He opened it eagerly, thrilled that someone had noticed him and cared enough to write.

It read, "Dear John: Could you please send me a summer camp brochure so I can grow up to be as good as Todd? Thank you."

Not only was he warming the bench, now he was being asked to play secretary. He threw the letter away.

Fame definitely had its flip-side for the players. Signing all the balls and souvenirs that poured in became tedious after awhile. So did, for the more prominent players, satisfying all the interview requests from the media. And they never seemed to get a break from signing autographs. After a big win at home, when they were anxious to meet with their families, they usually walked into a sea of pen-wielding fans. They were under orders from the coaching staff to comply with the requests, and most of the time they didn't mind. But it amazed them how much their signatures meant to people.

"It's always the parents who are the worst," Mitchell said one day in the lounge when the players were discussing the phenomenon. "They go, 'Here, you've got to get in his face, like this. Here, let me do it for you.' The kids are always OK."

"I always sign theirs last," Kip Jones said. "If I see a little girl just sitting there off to the side, I'll reach out and grab her paper and sign hers first. I hate it when people start grabbing."

Most of the players were more receptive to making public appearances. They were usually booked by the coaching staff, in response to requests from various organizations. The coaches viewed the team as a public trust, and felt the players should be responsive to the people who supported them so well. They also thought the basic experience of standing up before a group and speaking was a valuable one.

Lewis frequently spoke out against drug use. It was a pet project for him, because he had witnessed firsthand the damage it could cause. His father had suffered from alcoholism. He was never abusive, he just drank too much. Finally one day he got so sick he had to go into the hospital. He never drank again after that. Lewis also had seen too many kids on the playgrounds in Anderson ruin promising basketball careers because of drug abuse.

Sometimes his talks opened his own eyes as much as those of the kids he talked with. He recalled one visit to a local elementary school in particular.

"When I was done I asked for questions, and they start telling me about their parents and stuff," he said. "One kid said, 'My father drinks all the time.' I didn't know what to tell him. This one kid said, 'My mother uses drugs.' I was telling them not to even hang around people who do it. When he said that, I was like, 'Oh, well.'"

One of the most unique public relations assignments of the season fell to Mitchell, courtesy of Wood, a few days before the game against Minnesota. He would go to Klondike Elementary, a nearby grade school, and read to two groups of fourth graders as part of their reading awareness program. It wasn't exactly the sort of thing Mitchell had envisioned as a kid when daydreaming about becoming a college basketball player. But he had found that, at least at Purdue, college basketball was more than defending Glen Rice and dunking on Pervis Ellison.

So there he was, sitting in a chair in the middle of a grade school classroom, with about 25 fourth graders spread out before him on the floor in a semi-circle. Mitchell was going to read to them from a book selected for him by the school: *The Goof That Won the Pennant*.

"I know when I was your age, your parents used to want you to read, but nobody really wants to do it," he said. "You want to stay outside, or watch TV. But I think that's one of the biggest things you can do at your age, learn how to read and get enjoyment out of it. Because as you get older, especially as you get in college, if you're not used to it, then you'll be in a little bit of trouble. That's one of the things hopefully today I can help you guys understand, how important reading is.

"So, we'll get started.

"'The gathering of the Blazers for the first practice of the season was more like the gathering of the circus than a baseball team. Roger, for example, came completely equipped with a professional glove, his own bat, his own helmet and even his own batting glove. Joe Ferguson came with both of his....'"

Mitchell read for ten minutes, showing the pictures in the book to the students as he went along. Then he took questions.

"How tall are you?"

"How long have you been playing basketball?"

"Do you like basketball?"

"What does it take to get into a school like Purdue?"

"How does it feel to be that tall and do a jump ball?"

"Is Coach Keady a nice coach?"

"Are you going to play pro ball?"

And, there was a comment in reference to one of the book's characters, who had a strange throwing motion.

"When you said Brian threw it like that, it sounded like Kip Jones shooting his free throws," one boy said.

The kids stopped by to shake Mitchell's hand and gawk at him on their way out the door. A new class would be brought in soon. Meanwhile, the teachers gathered around him by the door.

"Because of you, my class got to go out to play today, so they are forever grateful," said one woman, who had sent her classes out for recess so she could watch Mitchell read. "I said, 'Get your coats on and go out, so I can go downstairs.'"

"You should shake his hand, so you can tell your kids," another teacher said.

"I cleaned up the Pepsi he spilled. Now if my husband did that, I wouldn't do it. I'd say, 'Clean it up yourself.'"

"Would you shake my hand, please? I want to show my husband the hand that shook Todd Mitchell's hand."

"Nice to meet you. And I'll be rooting for you all the way. All the way."

The next class was brought in. Mitchell was introduced again. He stressed the importance of reading once more, and began the story.

" 'The gathering of the Blazers for the first practice of the season. . . .'"

As he left the school, the students lined the hallway to get one last look at the real-life college basketball star. They applauded and cheered loudly.

"Look, he ducked to get through the door!" one boy said in amazement, as Mitchell left the building.

Saturday's basketball game with Minnesota seemed almost incidental amid the coronation, reunion and going-away party that would take place Saturday. It would be the seniors' final game in Mackey Arena, where they had lost just eight games in their four-year career, only four in the past three seasons. Stephens' mother, Mattie, would sing the national anthem before the game, as he had requested in Ann Arbor. The Big Ten trophy would be awarded after the game. Keady was going to take the seniors and their parents out to dinner after the game. And, it would serve as one huge pep rally for the team heading into tournament play.

For Keady, the ceremonies began Friday afternoon after practice.

Told George King wanted to see him in the lounge, he walked in to find his parents and sister. It was the surprise Schwartz had hinted at on the plane ride home from Columbus. He and a few other local boosters who were close friends of Keady had flown them all out from Sacramento for the game. It would be a rare treat. They had seen Keady coach a few times in his career, but never in a game at Purdue.

If Keady had any idea what was going on, he never let on. "What is this?" he shouted as he walked into the lounge. "God dang! They told me George King wanted to see me! Dang! How'd this happen? Schwartzy, you did this, didn't you?!"

Somewhere between all the hoopla, however, they were going to have to play the game. It would begin at noon, a radical departure from the late shows they had been putting on throughout most of the season, but not unprecedented. In the past few seasons, they had started games at virtually every hour of the day, adjusting for time zone differences, from 10 a.m. (in Alaska) to 10:30 p.m.

Keady went through the standard pregame points on the board in the locker room, then wrote one final message: "Good luck seniors."

"We've come a long way together, guys," he said. "And we've got a long way to go. I want to be with you jerks another month. And I want to be able to work with you for another month in a basketball way. So let's get started now, whadda you say?"

They huddled, left to warm up, then returned for the final pregame locker room session. Keady was well into a discourse on shot selection and rebounding when Bill Combs, the team doctor, bounded into the room.

"Hey, that's for Everette's mother," he said, holding the door open. Off in the distance, the cheers of the crowd, responding to Mattie Stephens' *a cappella* performance of the national anthem, could be heard.

Keady stopped. The players, caught off guard by the interruption, sat silently, looking at Combs, then at Keady.

"Excuse me, coach," Combs said.

"That's all right," Keady said. "If it's for Everette's mother, it's all right."

Keady continued, then called for the huddle.

"Guys, last year, we talked about the three things we wanted to do," he said. "Improve, you've done that. Compete, you've done that. And have fun. Let's go have some fun today.

"Together!"

"We attack!"

After the final warmups, Lewis, Mitchell and Stephens were introduced to the crowd. They took flowers, hugs and kisses to their parents at midcourt. Then Keady's parents and sister were introduced. He stopped to shake hands with the fathers and kiss the mothers of the seniors, then greeted his father and sister. He then walked into the bleachers on the other side of the court to present flowers to his mother, while the crowd cheered wildly.

Keady appeared choked up when he returned to the players. "OK, let's get after these guys!" he said, ready for action.

"Wait," Lewis said. "They haven't introduced the starting lineups yet."

Caught up in the emotion, Keady had forgotten.

Finally, after a long, narrow wooden sign declaring Purdue's latest Big Ten championship was paraded before the fans, they got around to the tipoff. But all that had just transpired wasn't ideal pregame preparation, and it showed. With Richard Coffey, Minnesota's muscular forward, controlling the boards at both ends, the Gophers then went to work trying to crash the party.

They jumped to a 12-4 lead in the first seven minutes, as Purdue hit just one of its first eight shots and let Minnesota grab the first seven rebounds. It threatened to get worse from there. Kip Jones missed two free throws. Scheffler rebounded Minnesota's missed shot, but threw the outlet pass away. Minnesota missed again, but Mitchell missed an off-balance shot underneath.

Finally, there was a breakthrough. Scheffler rebounded another Gopher miss. Lewis took the outlet pass, dribbled downcourt, and hit Mitchell on the run with a crisp, one-handed bounce pass from 25 feet away. Mitchell dunked the ball viciously, drawing both a foul and a standing ovation. With four straight missed free throws behind him from the Ohio State game, he stepped to the line. The crowd hushed. He paused, crouched, fired—and missed the front rim completely. The crowd groaned. Both teams then returned to their benches for a television timeout. Mitchell grabbed a towel and sat down in a heap.

"We're going to have the rebirth of the free throw," Keady said, forcing a grin. "We're starting over, babe. You're all right."

"Hey, you've got the jitters out, now let's play," Wood said.

"Hey, let me tell you something, guys," Keady said. "They've had their ass kicked all year, and they don't care who you are. They're going to play loose and they're going to play hard, and that's what you've got to start doing."

Gradually, they did. Scheffler grabbed another rebound, then freed Mitchell with a pick. Mitchell hit from 15 feet. Minnesota missed again, and Berning rebounded. Mitchell drew a foul, and swished both free throws. Purdue was within two. Kim Zurcher hit two free throws to extend Minnesota's lead, but McCants scored in the lane. Minnesota missed again, and Lewis, whose offensive output so far consisted of a traveling violation, an assist and three missed three-pointers, nailed a three-pointer from the top of the key to give Purdue its first lead, 15-14.

By halftime, with a boost from consecutive three-pointers by Stephens in the final minute, it led 37-32.

Figuring the worst was behind them, and with the climax of the season still ahead, the coaches decided to emphasize positives. "We've got to get them feeling good about themselves again," Weber said. So Keady, ignoring the poor start, put on his rose-colored glasses for the players. The ball movement had been good. Scheffler, with six rebounds, was going to the boards well. And Mitchell had shaken off his dry spell at the foul line.

"I really liked the fact you hit two free throws after a tremendous air ball," Keady said. "That's character, buddy."

Purdue put the game away quickly in the second half. Lewis hit two three-pointers and McCants hit twice inside the lane to boost the lead to 11 in the opening 2 1/2 minutes. Minnesota was still within 12 with six minutes left, but Purdue scored 19 of the final 23 points for a 93-66 win.

The celebrating began early. During a timeout with 5:45 left, the cheerleaders paraded a large, yellow sign declaring "Kansas City, Here We Come!" Then, while the fans continued to cheer, they formed a pyramid. One cheerleader climbed on top, holding another sign that read, "Final Four." There was no mistaking everyone's dream.

One play stood out in the second half. Four weeks earlier, Lewis, he of the one-dunk college career, had pledged he would get another one in the final game. The day before, after practice, he had repeated the prediction. And with 6:47 left, it came true. Mitchell deflected the ball from Willie Burton at the top of the key. Lewis scooped it up and took off for the basket. "Take it," Mitchell shouted, running interference on Burton to give Lewis a clear path. Lewis dribbled in and, with one hand, dunked the ball cleanly. The crowd erupted. Lewis ran back on defense shaking his fist and dancing a little jig. It wasn't much of a dunk, but it was a dunk. For Lewis, it was the ultimate "get yours!"

The ragged beginning aside, it was a near-perfect ending to the season, and a near-perfect launching pad for the tournament. Lewis, despite hitting just 3 of 10 three-pointers, finished with 17 points and 12 assists. Stephens had 16 points and five assists. McCants, hitting 7 of 8 field goals, also had 16 points. Mitchell, rebounding from a dismal performance at Ohio State, had 15 points, six rebounds, four assists, two steals and a blocked shot. Scheffler, in just 19 minutes, had 10 points and 11 rebounds, breaking his career high set at Wisconsin. Berning, out of exile, had hit all four shots he took, a three-pointer, a two-pointer and two free throws. And the bench as a whole had hit 7 of 8 field goals and 9 of 10 free throws.

At the final buzzer, the players stayed on the floor as Mark Rudner from the Big Ten office presented the Big Ten trophy. The players paraded it around the court once, showing it off to the fans. Keady, who had just won his 100th conference game in eight seasons, then spoke to the crowd, praising the three seniors and the rest of the team.

"No matter what happens down the stretch, whatever we do from now on is frosting on the cake, but we want to go to Kansas City," he said. "We want to win six more games."

The fans roared again.

Then Lewis spoke: "I remember my freshman year the first day of training. It was so hard, I was thinking, 'Dang, did I come to the right place?' And I did!

"It feels good right now," he added, "but I know Monday when practice comes, we're the worst team in the country again."

Then Mitchell: "The Big Ten was great. But we've still got one more stop: Kansas City!"

And Stephens: "They always save the best for last," he said, getting a laugh from the crowd.

"The one thing I've grown to love more than anybody except my parents and God is Coach Keady. The more you know Coach and how he is and how he teaches you to be competitors, not only for basketball but for life . . . I really want to win the national title, not only for me and not only for the fans, but for him."

With that, it was time to cut down the net. Lewis went first, cutting off the bottom two inches, all the way around, for himself. Mitchell took the next two inches. Stephens snipped just a few strands.

"I just didn't want to be up there for a long time," he would explain later. "I'll wait until we get to Kansas City. I didn't want to be celebrating too much. We won the Big Ten, but we've still got a ways to go."

One by one, the players took their turns cutting the spoils of their sweat. As Scheffler went, his teammates shook the ladder. Rea didn't bother with the ladder, taking a lift from Scheffler and McCants instead. Then, it was back to the locker room.

"Way to go, Berning!" Keady shouted. "Good to have you back. Way to go, men! Hey, Everette, I'm not sure I deserve to have my name in the same sentence as God; you must have been a little shook up there.

"OK, let's huddle. Great job, guys, I'm very proud of you. That's what we needed, 27-3, gentlemen. That's not too shabby!

"Together!"

"We attack!"

There was one more thing. Weber asked everyone to come in 15 minutes early the next day. There were balls to sign.

Billy Reid

"It was hard playing for my dad. We were both too stubborn for each other. We didn't get along at all my junior and senior year.

"I got benched my senior year. It was in the first quarter and I missed a shot. I was mad; I didn't make a scene or anything, but I saw it was going to go long and started running back on defense. The ball came right back to where I shot from, and I could have got it. So he benched me for the rest of the game.

"My dad and I didn't really talk that much. He tried to keep it separated between home and school, but it spilled over. We were both not on good terms, really. We didn't hate each other or anything, but we didn't really like each other that much. Now we're fine.

"My older brothers [Steve, who played at Purdue, and Mike, who played at Colorado] and I used to really go at it. We'd play baseball games with a deck of cards, or *Sports Illustrated* board games. We'd take that so seriously, it was stupid. We'd break chairs. All three of us would just get out of hand about losing a game. We used to stay up until four in the morning sometimes. One time when I was a sophomore I had lost two games in a row, and was about ready to lose another one. So I took the card table and flipped it over into a lamp and broke the lamp. I got my butt kicked for that.

"When we were younger, we'd play nerf basketball. We'd play two-on-one, Steve against me and Mike. It was a really good nerf place because the ceiling was eight feet high and it was a big area. We played constantly. We'd get physical; well, I couldn't get physical with them then, but they got physical with me. We'd throw each other around. We must have put ten holes in the wall. My dad always said he's going to come to Steve's and Mike's houses, and mine when I get one, and come and screw a nerf hoop into the wall and make all kinds of noise and put holes in the wall. I bet he would, too.

"What we'd do, Mike would be out in the corner, and Steve would play in the middle of us. Mike would throw an alley-oop to me, and what would usually happen was Steve would just come plow me over. I'd try to dunk it and he'd knock me down and I'd start crying. I was in about third or fourth grade then. They'd hurt me all the time.

"We played a game called Super Booger, too. This was when we lived in Lawrence. We set pillows up around the fireplace, and I'd have four downs to get to the pillows. They'd get on their knees and I'd have a nerf football. They didn't tell me this then, but their only purpose—they didn't care if I scored or not—their only purpose was to see what kind of flips they could make me do. One would tackle me high and one would tackle me low and they'd get me in the air.

"And whenever I'd get hurt, they had this glass with half root beer and half water and they'd give that to me and tell me it would cure me; and I believed it. It was sickening. They picked on me a lot.

"I was always trying to get as good as Steve and Mike. I was always trying to do what they did. When my brother was in high school, I'd try to imitate that in grade school. And I think that got me a lot better. I just watched how they played. They learned it from my dad and I learned it from them. All the fundamental stuff.

"We had a really good intramural program in grade school. Our team averaged 32 points and I averaged 28 in the fifth grade. Steve coached us one time. We had a game against the fifth grade and sixth grade all-stars. It's weird, but—you know how you get chills when something great happens?—I got as big a thrill out of that as anything I've done. Steve was our coach. We were really outmanned, but Steve just had us dribble off picks all the time and shoot. We ended up beating the sixth graders. The whole school was there. During lunch the first graders and second graders went out to recess together, so the second graders picked on the first graders. The third and fourth graders went out together and the fourth picked on the third. And the sixth picked on the fifth. So the first and third graders were cheering for us, and the second and fourth for the sixth graders.

"It was packed, and it seems like it was loud as heck. We won something like 32-28, and I had like 28. It was great. We had this one guy on our team, Ernest Hernandez; he was real strong, and got a lot of rebounds. We used to get in fights all the time, he and I, but I remember hugging him after the game after we won.

"I got in a lot of fights with kids in school. I remember one time I got in a fight with my best friend, Tiger. We were playing football and Mike was playing quarterback for both of us. We used to hit each other really hard. I remember after I beat him, he threw his helmet and hit my dog—it was just a Schnauzer—right on the back, so I went after him. But I stopped that after awhile.

"It's been hard, not playing this year. It's hard to keep yourself motivated. The last couple of weeks and the start of this semester, I just wasn't into it at all. I was feeling sorry for myself, saying, 'It ain't worth all this,' but that was stupid. I didn't really care if I was messing up. And I've always cared about how I played. I'll pull myself together. The thing I've got to look at is building confidence in coach's eyes next year. And getting the Black team better. You've got to work hard to get them better.

"My time will come. If I don't start or play a lot next year it's my own fault. I've been in the program for a year and we've got some young guys coming in. If they beat me out, it's my own damn fault. I'm going to work real hard over the summer and get stronger and play a lot, hopefully."

17

Back to the Drawing Board

Sunday was D-Day. Draw Day. Purdue finished 27-3, was ranked second in the country by the wire services, and first by *Sports Illustrated*, prior to the loss at Ohio State. Only Temple had fewer losses. Logically, it seemed that would be good enough for a number one seed.

But Keady and his assistants had been conditioned to expect strange things when the NCAA Selection Committee announced the pairings for the tournament. In 1984, fresh off its Big Ten co-championship, Purdue was seeded third, received a bye, and sent to play at Memphis State. It wound up playing none other than Memphis State, the sixth seed, which had won its first-round game. The Tigers were an unusually difficult opponent to face so early in the tournament; they were 25-6, and had future NBA players Keith Lee and William Bedford in their lineup. They were even tougher to beat on their homecourt, as Purdue found out firsthand in a 66-48 loss.

In 1985, Purdue was sent to Notre Dame to play Auburn. Nothing unfair about that. It lost by one point when James Bullock's turn-around jumper at the buzzer rolled around the rim and out. The following year, after finishing the regular season 22-9, it was sent to LSU—to play LSU. Keady was incensed at having to give up a home-court advantage twice in three years. Fred Schaus, a former Purdue coach who was a member of the NCAA's Selection Committee, reported back that the committee simply had forgotten about its game at Memphis State. With McCants, then a freshman starter, severely hobbled by a sprained ankle, LSU won in double overtime and went on to reach the Final Four.

Purdue's luck didn't improve in 1987. It finished 25-5 and tied for the Big Ten title. Indiana finished with the same record and the same share of the title. In their two head-to-head confrontations, each team had won by 11 points on its home court. But the two teams that had seemed the very definition of equality during the regular season were handed vastly different tournament fates. Indiana was seeded first and sent to play in Indianapolis, a virtual homecourt edge. Purdue was seeded third and sent to Syracuse, New York. The debacle in Ann Arbor apparently had left a lasting impression on the members of the Selection Committee.

Purdue's tournament experience seemed haunted from the start that year. The team stayed at an older landmark hotel downtown at the suggestion of trainer Denny Miller. What Miller, nor anyone else at Purdue, didn't know was that the hotel also was hosting a huge St. Patrick's Day celebration. Every time Purdue's players and coaches left or returned to the hotel, they had to fight their way through wall-to-wall revelers. Getting an elevator was a stroke of luck; getting peace and quiet was a stroke of magic. It was hardly the stress-free environment appropriate for playing in a tournament.

It wasn't much better in the Carrier Dome. Purdue's first-round opponent, Northeastern, at 27-6, seemed to deserve a higher seed than 14th. At any rate, it provided a tough first test, refusing to go down without a fight—literally. Doug Lee played the best game of his career, with 29 points and 13 rebounds, to lead a 104-95 victory. But in the final moments, with the game slipping away, a seldom-used Northeastern reserve named Ernie Hall entered the game. Hall harassed McCants verbally, then, while running downcourt, elbowed him in the throat. McCants, to the amazement of everyone familiar with his gentle demeanor, turned and swung a roundhouse right at Hall that missed. A few tense moments followed, but no brawl erupted. McCants was ejected. Hall stayed in the game to pick up four fouls in less than a minute.

Lee was told after the season by one of Northeastern's players that Hall had been sent into the game by the coach, Karl Fogel, to start a fight, a last-ditch attempt to get one of Purdue's starters out of the game and shift the momentum. Hall certainly was well-trained for his role. He had a criminal record, and had been kicked off the team the season prior to that after pulling a knife on the football coach's son at a campus party. He was reinstated when Fogel took over as head coach that season. The following summer, he was murdered after a playground game in Washington, D.C. Hall, reports stated, had been goading a player on the opposing team during the game. Afterwards, the player's older brother pulled a knife and stabbed Hall, killing him almost instantly with one blow.

Following its rude introduction to the tournament, Purdue's season came to a crashing halt in the second round against Florida. It trailed by just two points at halftime despite not playing well. But the downward trend that had begun at Michigan in the final regular season game turned to a nosedive. The Boilermakers gave up 54 second half points (after allowing Michigan 56 and Northeastern 54 in the second half) and lost 85-66. Once again, it wasn't the sort of game James Naismith had in mind when he nailed up the first peach basket. Vernon Maxwell, a multi-talented guard who would admit to cocaine use the following season, spit in Arnold's face. It was a symbolic ending to Purdue's season.

The game plan for watching the draw also would be different this year. In the past, everyone had gathered in the same room, media included, and watched it on live television. Then, when the injustice flashed on the screen, reporters were on hand to record the anguish flashing on everyone's face.

This time, the coaches, along with Pat Keady, would watch the draw from a lounge in the football building. The players would watch in their lounge, with paper taped over the door window to blot out unwanted witnesses. The newspaper, radio and television reporters from Lafayette and Indianapolis would be waiting for them in the arena afterwards.

A clue to Purdue's fate in the draw came immediately as the pairings show began. Notre Dame was assigned to the East Regional, which meant it wouldn't be playing on its homecourt in South Bend.

"Guess who's going to be in South Bend?" Keady said, not needing an answer.

Half a minute later, he knew for sure.

"Now we will take you through the midwest brackets in South Bend, Indiana," the voice from the television said. "These games will be played Thursday and Saturday. The number one seed there, as expected, the Purdue Boilermakers...."

Weber let out a high-pitched shriek of joy.

"Oh, baby!" Reiter shouted.

"We got it," Keady said.

"That is good. That is very good," Weber added, shaking hands with Reiter.

They hardly could have devised a better draw for themselves. They were playing a mere three-hour bus trip from home, at Notre Dame's Athletic and Convocation Center, where their fans could follow them en masse. And they would play Fairleigh-Dickinson, which was rated by some computer services as the weakest team in the 64-team field. The second-round opponent would be either Memphis State or Baylor, a reasonable prospect considering the strength of the overall field. It was as if the NCAA had gone out of its way to avoid a repeat of its previous errors in judgment. This time, no team was awarded a homecourt advantage.

While presumably one of the weaker teams in the tournament, Fairleigh Dickinson was more dangerous than implied by the nickname occasionally imposed by its eastern rivals: "Fairly Ridiculous." It was 23-6 and had four senior starters. Three years earlier, as freshmen, those same players had made up the nucleus of a team that had nearly upset Michigan in the first round of the tournament. For Purdue, it was an opponent much like Ohio State. It didn't have to be at the top of its game to win, but it had to be reasonably close.

"You've got to understand that if we played these guys ten times, nine times we'd beat 'em, right?" Keady told the players. "But the one time they could beat you could be now. So you've got to be ready for that."

Everyone seemed ready. Monday's and Tuesday's practices were crisp and enthusiastic. Early Tuesday evening, the team left for South Bend. Keady was flying to Chicago to participate in another panel discussion of the tournament, and would catch up with the team later that night. Weber was making a quick recruiting stop. So Stallings, Wood, Reiter, the players and the rest of the traveling party boarded a bus outside Mackey Arena for the drive north. A crowd of about 300 fans, the cheerleaders, and members of the pep band came out in 35-degree weather to send them off.

There would be one more miniature pep rally. About an hour later, as the bus headed into Logansport, about 75 more fans were waiting by the roadside, cheering, waving gold towels and handkerchiefs, holding signs and honking their car horns. The coaches asked the bus driver to stop. Stallings stuck his head out the door to offer a quick thanks, and the bus pulled away. About half of the players were asleep, and didn't notice the reception.

As much as the coaches wanted to limit distractions, some were unavoidable at tournament time. The practice at the game site on Wednesday was open to the public, which required that it be more of a shooting exhibition than anything. And Keady and selected players, in this case the three seniors, were required to attend a press conference the day before each game for at least half an hour. There were the inevitable questions about past tournament losses, which gave Keady a chance to reiterate his new theme for the season.

"I tell you one thing, you're not going to ruin my damn summer if we get beat," he said. "We're going to walk out of here with our heads up. We want to win the national tournament in the worst way. But if we don't do it, we're going to walk out of here and say we tried our best. If we can do that, we'll sleep well. I sleep great every night. So it's been a tremendous year. Whatever we do from here on in is frosting on the cake."

The real workout that day would take place at the gymnasium at Bethel College, a small local Christian school. The gym was not much bigger than the playing court itself, and was covered by an arching wooden roof. The session was to be closed to the public, but more than 30 students and administrators managed to get in to watch, many of them standing in the doorways.

They had to be impressed by what they saw. The players were ready from the beginning, running quickly to Keady and shouting encouragement when he whistled them to midcourt to get things started.

"I'm glad to see you guys do that, because the 'Emphasis of the Day' is enthusiasm," he said. "And if you don't show enthusiasm, like in taking a charge or going from one drill to another, you know what we're going to do?"

"Get a drink?" Mitchell asked.

"No," Keady said, a devilish gleam in his eye. "Run!"

The entire session was upbeat. During a break for free throws, Kip Jones hit 9 of 10 shots.

"Way to go, Kipper!" Keady shouted, running over to rebound the last three for him.

They ran through fullcourt drills and a controlled scrimmage.

Brugos continued to sparkle, hustling, yelling and dominating the inside play. He seemed a reborn player. Earlier in the week, he had worn a t-shirt with the word "TEAM" printed in large letters and the word "I" printed in smaller letters beneath it, an expression of the cliché about the team being more important than the individual. "I'm trying to conform," he shrugged. So far, it was working.

Half an hour before the workout's scheduled completion, Keady had seen all he needed to see.

"Hold it," he shouted. "That's it, practice is over. Huddle up. Good job, men."

All that was left was to finish the free throw contest begun earlier in the day at the ACC. Barrett, who was becoming a regular in the contest finals, and Reid, were the only ones left. That delighted Stallings. Earlier in the day, when Reid had left his sweat pants behind at the ACC, Stallings tied two tight knots in one leg before giving them to Howat to return to Reid. Now, he would have another chance to torment his favorite subject.

"This will be over quickly, everybody," Stallings announced. "Two shots, no more. Don't worry, Reid's going to choke."

Reid rolled his first shot in off the rim. Barrett swished his. Reid swished. Barrett then hit twice in a row to speed the process.

"He can't hit two in a row, there's no way!" Stallings shouted as Reid stepped to the line. Reid missed his first shot off the front of the rim. The ball bounced back at his feet. He stomped on it with his right foot, and let out an exasperated scream. Some things hadn't changed.

The assistant coaches were so confident of the team's superiority over Fairleigh Dickinson that they decided to play the game close to the vest and not tip their hand to future tournament opponents. They would play nothing but "Blue" man-to-man defense and their basic motion offense, with an occasional "Yellow" fullcourt trapping defense after made free throws. And for the benefit of the scouts on hand, they put on some camouflage. They told Stephens to mix up his hand signals in the halfcourt defense, to make it look like he was calling for different formations. But everyone was to ignore him.

"No matter what we say or do, we're playing Blue," Stallings said. "Have some fun with it."

Scheffler raised his hand.

"Now don't start philosophizing with me, Steve," Stallings warned.

"No, what if Coach Keady calls something?" Scheffler asked. "What do we do then?"

It was a logical question. If Keady suddenly stood up during the game and yelled at them to play a matchup zone, were they to continue playing man-to-man? Would the coach be part of the scam, too?

He wouldn't.

Even in South Bend, just a few hours from Lafayette, the players met up with further evidence of the school's occasional identity crisis. The gift shop at the Marriott sold souvenirs for Indiana University and Notre Dame, but not Purdue. The hotel's meeting rooms were named after state colleges. The players watched video in the Indiana room. There also was a Notre Dame room and even a Bethel and St. Mary's room. There wasn't a Purdue room in sight.

And that night at dinner, at a restaurant across the street from the hotel, a woman stuck her head in the room where the players were eating.

"Are you boys from Purdue?" she asked. "Good luck, tomorrow, OK? We're Indiana fans, but we'll be pulling for you. We'll be watching. Bye."

The players, who didn't feel much need for charity considering the widespread and fervent support they were getting from Purdue fans, mumbled thank yous. As the woman walked away, Lewis, faking anger, plucked a roll out of the basket in front of him and cocked his arm toward the doorway.

The dinner also revealed hints of tension within Kip Jones. He had struggled in the previous two outings, scoring two points at Ohio State and five against Minnesota. In both games, he had played fewer minutes as a starter than Scheffler had off the bench. By now, his starting position was locked up, but the threat to his playing time and the arrival of the tournament combined to keep him on edge all week.

His outlet was to step up his role as an agitator, taking verbal jabs at his teammates—particularly the seniors, whom he thought needed to be humbled on occasion anyway. Such habits tended to distance Jones a bit from the other players, as was evident at that evening's meal. Jones sat at the end of the table, away from his teammates, and said little except to lob an occasional mild insult. Meanwhile, Pat

Keady pulled out a camera and began snapping pictures of the players.

"Smile, Kip," she said.

Jones turned her way and smiled.

"Say free throw," she said.

The other players laughed.

The flash didn't go off.

"You broke the camera," she said.

The players laughed some more.

"We wouldn't do it if we didn't love you, Kip," she said.

It was all intended as harmless fun, but Jones was too uptight at the moment to appreciate it. Normally gregarious around his teammates, he said little the rest of the meal. Brugos, sensing his feelings, lingered at the table after the other players had filtered back to the hotel to keep him company.

The beauty of games, however, was that they tended to dissolve everyone's personal troubles. And there would be no difficulty focusing on this one. Not only was it the tournament, it had the aura of a home game. Purdue fans filled most of the 10,760 seats in the ACC. When tickets had gone on sale for the regional the previous year, Notre Dame fans had swept them up in anticipation of getting to watch the Irish play there. After Notre Dame was sent east, most of those people sold their seats to Purdue fans. It made for a familiar setting for Purdue's players: a round, intimate arena dominated by gold and black. For added measure, it was St. Patrick's Day. Keady, Irishman to the core, wore green socks for luck.

Purdue was assigned to the locker room normally used by Notre Dame. It was an ironic twist. As far as Phelps was concerned, the Boilermakers weren't even welcome in the visiting dressing room during the regular season. Now they were housed in Notre Dame's locker room.

"Come on, now, let's go out and beat these cats by *two* points, man," Lewis said with sarcastic enthusiasm as the players huddled after stretching.

His teammates laughed. "OK, it's a serious game; this is the start of going down the road to Kansas," Stephens said.

"I don't want this to be the last time we stretch before a game," Mitchell said.

"Let's play hard, fellas," Stephens added.

Kip Jones would have something to say as well. After all the pre-game talk, the warmups and the introduction of the starting lineups, the players huddled one last time among themselves on the court before the opening tip.

"Hey, I know I've been an asshole all week," Jones said. "But I love you guys. Let's go kick their ass."

They did just that. Fourteen seconds after the tipoff, Lewis swished a three-pointer. Sixteen seconds after that, Mitchell was fouled and sank two free throws, making it 5-0. Purdue pressed fullcourt, and forced Fairleigh Dickinson to call timeout when nobody could get open.

Fairleigh Dickinson was never really in it after that. It pulled to within 11-9, but Purdue gradually stretched its lead to 13 at the half.

The second half went just as smoothly, as Purdue completely dominated the inside play. It pushed the lead to 18 less than five minutes into the period, and coasted from there. Keady's only challenge was to keep order, as the play grew increasingly sloppy. With the lead at 66-47, Kip Jones, who had been defending and rebounding well throughout the game, made two consecutive passing errors, and then fumbled an inbounds pass under Fairleigh Dickinson's goal that was converted to a basket.

"You're forcing passes, babe," Keady said after making a whole-sale substitution at the next break. "Why do you think you have to make things happen? Just relax."

A few minutes later, Jones, back in the game, missed an open layup.

"Kip, there's no point getting down on yourself, we're up 20," Keady said at the next timeout. "Heck, you're playing good." Keady then smiled. "How many rebounds you have, two?"

By now, the Purdue following was busy celebrating. The cheer-leaders help up a sign reading "Final Four." The band members sitting at the end of the court next to the bench began chanting "We want Marvin!" Rea, sitting at the end of the bench, faked a move to the scorer's table and got a big laugh.

Keady, however, wasn't done coaching. When Berning's man snuck behind him to grab a lob pass and dunk it, Keady jumped up angrily and sent Ewer into the game. A few seconds later, Reid forced a bad shot, his second of the game. Keady jumped up again and called for Barrett. Rea didn't get in until five seconds were left, when play was stopped on a goaltend of Ewer's shot, but everyone went home happy. The final score was 94-79.

McCants again had been unstoppable inside, improving his career high to 26 points while hitting 11 of 15 shots. Lewis added 19, and Mitchell 16. Kip Jones finished with six points and nine rebounds, tying his career high. Stephens struggled offensively, hitting just 1 of 5 field goal attempts, but did have seven rebounds and eight assists.

The first step had been easy. What would be almost as difficult, and in one case more time-consuming, would be the drug test that followed. The NCAA was becoming increasingly diligent in its efforts to fight corruption. Before the tournament, it required players to sign an affidavit stating they had no connection with an agent. And the previous year, it had instituted a policy of having selected players provide urine specimens after tournament games.

The primary intent was to help prevent the use of performance-enhancing stimulants more than common substance abuse. In fact, the test didn't even check for the presence of marijuana because of the complications that could arise if a non-user was exposed to secondary smoke. The athletes were warned to clear any medication through their trainers in the days leading up to the tournament. Even the soft drinks served in the locker rooms were caffeine-free.

The tests were not administered before the games because players theoretically could take a drug after the test and before tipoff. But the problem with doing it after the game was that the athletes who had played were dehydrated, and had trouble providing a sample.

The process was formal and methodic. The selected players—the five who had played the most minutes and one other random choice—were escorted to a separate room, where a battery of men and women wearing sport shirts reading "NCAA drug testing team" awaited them. Each player sat down and wrote his name, uniform number, class and position on triplicate forms, one yellow, one green and one pink.

"OK, we want you to open this packet and take out the plastic cup," the NCAA official said. "We're going to code this cup now. And then we'll take you back to the bathroom. Get as much as you can. We'd like to have it up to about here on the cup, because we're going to need two specimens, OK? As soon as you're finished, bring your specimen back here and we'll continue."

Upon the successful completion of the mission, the official

dipped two litmus strips in the urine and checked them against a color chart. The athlete was then excused; further tests of the sample were conducted later.

McCants, Stephens, Tony Jones, and Barrett were lucky. They came through quickly. Lewis and Mitchell, who had to go to the postgame press conference first, were brought in later. Mitchell also finished in reasonable time, but Lewis came up dry. The team bus left without him, as he sat and waited for nature's call. He gulped soft drinks, watched television and even had time to play cards with a Memphis State player, who had come in after the second game. Finally, about four hours after Purdue's victory, Lewis did his duty and called it a day. It had been a strange afternoon for one of college basketball's most outspoken anti-drug crusaders.

18 •

Another World

The second-round game was only two days away, but the players were grateful not to have a long wait. They had already been holed up in their ninth-floor hotel rooms for three days, and were starting to get stir crazy. Keady had let them out on their own just once, on Thursday night, to get something to eat. Other than that, they were eating, practicing, playing or watching video together as a team all but a couple of hours a day.

Some of the players had brought textbooks with them, but studying was difficult. What free time there was came in bits and pieces, a half hour here and an hour there, making it difficult to board a train of thought. And there was always a distraction to contend with. A hotel floor housing 13 college basketball players doesn't much resemble a library.

As for studying for Saturday's opponent, Memphis State, it would be more complicated than preparing for Fairleigh Dickinson had been. The ninth-seeded Tigers were 20-11 after beating Baylor in the opening round. That they had made it this far was impressive. In December, their two best players, Marvin Alexander and Sylvester Gray, had been declared ineligible for dealing with an agent. But they had shaken that off and finished the season strong. They were a quick, athletic team, the kind that could give anyone fits if they got on a roll.

Despite the messy episode with Alexander and Gray, Memphis State's program was well on its way toward regaining respectability. Its previous coach, Dana Kirk, had been fired for violating numerous

NCAA guidelines, and faced federal charges as well. Under Kirk, the program was a case study of the problems facing all of college basketball. It was highly successful and profitable, but highly unethical as well. Mitchell had met one former Tiger who bragged that the players there had continuously received new cars, and never had to go to class.

But Kirk's replacement, Larry Finch, seemed to have things moving along a more straight and narrow pathway. He had directed the Tigers to a 26-8 record the season before in his first year as head coach, and had barely skipped a beat this season despite the loss of two key players.

Keady, for one, was happy to have the chance to play Memphis State again. Purdue's tournament loss to the Tigers on their home-court in 1984 had been unpleasant beyond the fact it was beaten so soundly. Keady recalled one fan sitting behind the bench who spent most of the evening heckling the team, shouting things such as, "Man, if this is the best the Big Ten has to offer, it must be horrible." Afterwards, as Keady was walking off the court, another Memphis State fan, apparently not satisfied with the mere joy of his team's 18-point victory, had walked up to him and cursed at him.

Revenge was only an added attraction for Keady, however. A bigger point was to advance past the second round of the tournament, something none of his previous teams had been able to do. The only other time Purdue had won its opening-round NCAA game was in 1983. In round two, it lost to a much more talented Arkansas team by 10, as Keady went up against his former mentor, Eddie Sutton.

It was obvious, with Purdue's number one seeding in this tournament, a loss to the number nine seed would go a long way toward overshadowing the Big Ten championship and everything else that had been accomplished. But Keady didn't want his players thinking about that.

"There's no reason to be tentative, guys," he told them before Friday's practice at the ACC. "If you're worried about getting over the hump, hell, we've been over the hump for four years.

"You can't be saying we have to win this game. We don't have to win shit. Just play good, and it will take care of itself. There's no pressure on you to do anything. You've already proven you're a great basketball team. You've just got to go out and hopefully get into another world."

Friday's practice was closed to the public, so the team wouldn't have to go to another site to get its serious work done. The only real distraction of the day was the press conference before practice, which Keady and the three seniors attended. There, Keady was asked about a blossoming rumor that he would leave Purdue at the end of the season to take over the program at the University of Texas, where Bob Weltlich was on his way out. Dick Vitale had mentioned Keady as a top candidate for the job on television, and the rumor had spread quickly from there.

Keady answered questions about the rumor at the press gathering, joking that he didn't mind it if it helped him get a raise. It was the first the players had heard of it, though, and the line of questioning took them by surprise.

"Are you leaving us or something, coach?" Lewis said, turning to Keady, when he was asked if the rumor would be a distraction for the team.

"I might, if you don't start playing defense," Keady said.

Saturday's game brought a new wave of enthusiasm from Purdue fans. Some of the tickets that had been held by fans of the losing teams in the first round had become available, but not nearly enough to satisfy the demand. Because it was a weekend game, a lot more people were able to go. Some of the Purdue employees who had received tickets for Thursday's game were turned down for Saturday, to make room for other higher-ranking colleagues. The player requests grew as well. Lewis had 20 set aside for purchase by friends and relatives.

As the team bus pulled into the arena parking lot, desperate fans with stuffed wallets and empty hearts lined the way. One man carried a large orange sign with black letters reading "I need tickets." Another man leaning against a tree nearby seemed more resigned to his plight. He held a small sign reading, simply, "Help."

Purdue fans waving pom-poms cheered the bus as it made its way to the arena's back door. There, a television crew from an Indianapolis station was waiting, filming the players as they unloaded. Privacy was hard to come by at tournament time.

But finally, it was time to play again.

"Remember, they are scared shitless of you guys," Weber said when the players returned to the locker room after the initial warm man year I'd have my mom drop me off, and then after that I'd drive up. "It's like playing on our court, because we're going to have three-quarters of the place filled. And they don't want to be here."

Just as he had against Fairleigh Dickinson, Lewis hit the game's first shot, from 17 feet left of the basket. When McCants hit a turn-around jumper the next trip down, it looked as if another blowout was coming. But the Tigers didn't play scared, and Purdue cooled off quickly, hitting just two of its next 15 shots. After taking the lead at 6-4, Memphis State held on to it for the next 14 minutes.

Gradually, Purdue's defense began to take root. Switching back and forth between man-to-man, box-and-one and matchup zone—a far cry from its singleminded approach against Fairleigh Dickinson—it began forcing the Tigers into bad shots. Stephens' layup on a low lob pass from Lewis tied the game at 27, then Lewis drilled a three-pointer to recapture the lead with 3:16 remaining.

Kip Jones took over from there, putting together one of his best stretches of play all season. He hit the front end of a one-and-one at 2:45—earning a standing ovation—then made a delicate one-handed tip of McCants' missed shot the next trip down. With 30 seconds left, he took off on a dead sprint and picked off a pass near midcourt. He was fouled as he drove for the layup, and hit one of the two free throws to give Purdue a 38-33 halftime lead.

Purdue started the second half with a bang, too, only this time it pointed the gun at itself. It set up in a fullcourt press as Memphis State inbounded the ball to start play. But Stephens lined up as if the teams would be shooting at the same basket they had in the first half. That left Elliot Perry, the Tigers' standout freshman guard, wide open for an uncontested layup.

The embarrassing mistake seemed to give Stephens a much-needed jolt. After hitting just 1 of 5 shots the first half, he rebounded his own missed shot and scored on Purdue's next possession. After Memphis State missed, he hit a 17-footer. And when Kip Jones hit Mitchell with a lob pass for a dunk that made it 44-35, Memphis State was forced to call a quick timeout.

The three baskets had more than made up for the one huge goof, so Stephens was off the hook when he joined the huddle.

"What were you doing?" Keady asked him, forcing a smile. "We're always at the basket in front of our bench the second half!"

"That'll be on the highlights, Bud," said Weber, also smiling.

Lewis stood up, put his hands behind his head and flapped them at Stephens, imitating donkey ears. He definitely had been "donkeyed" (in the team's lingo, this meant being made to look like a fool). As the huddle broke, Kip Jones shouted a reminder: "We're going *that* way," he said, pointing to Purdue's basket.

In hindsight, the mistake might have been the best thing that could have happened. It certainly seemed to loosen everyone up. Mitchell rebounded Memphis State's miss when play resumed, then Lewis dropped a three-pointer. Stephens rebounded the Tigers' next miss, and Lewis hit Mitchell for a layup, completing an 11-0 spurt that boosted Purdue's lead to 49-35 less than three minutes into the half.

Memphis State never recovered. The killing blow came midway through the half, with Purdue leading by 12. Tony Jones made a superb defensive play in stopping a two-on-one fast break with a blocked shot, executing it just the way it had been taught in practice drills. Finch, already frustrated because he thought the play near the basket was getting too physical, jumped off his bench to protest, and was slapped with a technical foul. Lewis hit one of the two technical free throws, then Tony Jones passed to Mitchell for a layup on the ensuing possession.

Tony Jones then picked off a steal and hit Kip for a dunk, and after Kip rebounded a missed Memphis State shot, Mitchell added two more free throws to make it 69-50 with 9:48 left. It was over. The final was 100-73, Brugos providing triple figures with a sweet move and left-handed jump hook. Keady pumped his fist in celebration as the buzzer sounded. It was the biggest win of the season; probably the biggest of his career. And a little bit of payback, too.

Everyone had played well the second half. Lewis finished with 22 and McCants with 20. Mitchell scored 14 points in the period to finish with 15. Stephens scored seven of his nine. Kip Jones finished with six points and a game-high eight rebounds.

And Tony Jones and Scheffler had been outstanding. Jones had ten points, six assists, four rebounds and three steals in 24 minutes. Scheffler had 13 points and six rebounds in 17 minutes. The depth that had been the team's Achilles heel the previous season was now one of its strengths.

"And then there were 16." Stallings shouted as everyone huddled in the locker room, identifying the number of teams that would be left in the tournament at the end of the weekend.

"Good job, guys," Keady said. "That's one more step up the mountain.

"Together!"

"We attack!"

The players stayed for the first half of the days' second game, between Kansas State and DePaul, then boarded the bus to return home. Keady, who had heard about the reception awaiting the team in Logansport on the way to South Bend, predicted there would be 5,000 people waiting there to greet the team on the way back.

He was off just a bit. It had been announced on the radio after the game that the team would stay for all of the second game. So when the bus rolled through Logansport, much earlier than the townfolk were expecting, there were two fans waiting for the team, a man and a woman who stood alongside the road in front of their van and cheered.

"Well, there's the 5,000 fans," Keady said, laughing.

When the team arrived at Mackey at 8 p.m., it was packed—with fans attending the high school state tournament game being played there. The players didn't mind sneaking in unnoticed, however.

"We're right on the verge of doing something that's very, very difficult to do if we keep our heads right," Keady told them before unloading. "Don't be talking to the press about anything that you'll learn to regret. Just keep going like you have been. You're doing great. The coaching staff is very, very proud of you. Take care of yourself tonight, there's no reason to celebrate anything yet."

19

The End

Round three of the tournament, to be played in the Silverdome in Pontiac, Michigan, wouldn't start until 10 p.m. Friday. Keady decided the players needed rest more than they needed work at the moment, so Sunday they lifted weights and swam (sort of) and Monday they shot 100 free throws and 100 jumpers. That was it.

Earnest preparations resumed on Tuesday. The opponent would be an old friend. Kansas State, the same school—but definitely not the same team—that Purdue had trounced 101-72 on December 20, had defeated DePaul after Purdue's win in South Bend.

The assistant coaches, who had stayed to scout that game, also had viewed hours of video on the Wildcats by the time Tuesday's practice arrived. Obtaining video during the tournament can be difficult, because it is considered disloyal for teams to send out tapes of fellow conference members. Still, it is a common practice, and Purdue's assistants were able to get a few on a hush-hush basis. They also bought eight more at a discounted price of $735 from a video taping service, Hoop One, which tapes games off satellite. They would be able to watch video to their hearts content.

All the analysis had left the coaches with mixed feelings. They thought Kansas State was a vastly improved team from the one that visited Mackey in December. That loss, in fact, had been a turning point for the Wildcats. They went on to adjust their starting lineup and abandon their fastbreaking style for a more deliberate pace, a move that paid off handsomely. They finished the regular season 22-8 and placed second in the Big Eight, defeating national power and conference champ Oklahoma and instate rival Kansas twice. They had grown into a patient, poised and intelligent team, one that reflected the experience of a team with four seniors in its starting lineup.

But Kansas State wasn't as physically intimidating as Memphis State or several Big Ten teams. They relied most heavily on Mitch Richmond, an unorthodox 6-5 senior who was the Big Eight's best player behind Kansas' Danny Manning. Richmond was a legitimate three-point threat, and a dangerous penetrator with a vast array of head fakes and spinning moves. William Scott and Steve Henson also were fine shooters. But Kansas State's inside game did not pose much of a threat, particularly on offense.

The coaches were confident. And therefore nervous.

"This is the first time in my coaching career I really felt we should beat somebody," Keady said, exaggerating his points. "It's the worst feeling I ever had."

Keady received some unusual phone calls during the week. One was from Glynn Blackwell, the Illinois guard, who called Keady to ask for a ticket for the games in Pontiac. Blackwell had called Mitchell first, but Mitchell had none available and told him to try Keady. Blackwell did, and got the ticket.

An even more bizarre call came early one morning from a man who identified himself as a Purdue alum in Indianapolis. Since Indiana had lost its first game of the tournament and was finished for the season, he suggested that Purdue hire Knight as a consultant. Knight's tournament experience would be helpful, he thought, and it would be a nice gesture as well. He said he had 15 businessmen willing to finance the operation, but needed an answer quickly to try to set it up.

Lorraine thought it was a practical joke at first, then realized the man was serious. She took the message. Wood, however, told her not to bother passing it on.

"Tell him Coach Keady has all the consulting he needs," Wood said. "And tell him he can send the financing to Weber, Stallings, Reiter and Wood if he likes."

Keady's mail was slightly more predictable, as letters from well-wishers flowed in. Among them were notes from two prominent football coaches. Iowa's Hayden Fry wrote to say he regretted the two had never had a chance to meet and encouraged Keady to "get after their ass." Notre Dame's Lou Holtz also sent his regards.

One letter, however, stood out. It was from a man in Houston who identified himself as a Purdue alum. Keady read it to the players before they watched video on Wednesday.

"Dear Gene: Congratulations on a very fine season. Here's wishing you and the Boilermakers success toward the NCAA championship in Kansas City. My wife and I have been to eleven successive Final Fours and have tickets and reservations for this one. We've met you and Pat at several recent Final Fours and enjoyed visiting with you. I've followed your three seniors since high school and know why you are so proud of them.

"This year, however, it does not look like I will be able to go to Kansas City. My son, Darrell, also a Purdue grad, is fighting for his life with cancer. He loves Purdue and Boilermaker sports and is still following basketball the best he can. He and his wife of eighteen months planned to meet us in Kansas City for the Final Four. We are at his home in Houston, Texas on a day-to-day basis trying the eighth different cancer treatment and hoping for a miracle. He's shown remarkable courage and fight in the effort. He'll also be pulling for you and the Boilermakers."

It was a rare letter: one that offered good wishes without asking for anything in return. Keady had already decided to send the man an autographed ball, which the players signed on the spot.

"A lot of the things you do, you don't even realize you're helping people," Keady said. "The very fact you've got an opportunity to do something special for a lot of people is even more important than us winning. If we can do something like that, it's important that we keep this thing going. We know we want to win for ourselves, as a selfish thing, but as far as helping people, we can do some good there, too."

The coaches primary concern for the week was convincing the players to forget how easily they had beaten Kansas State in December. The coaches considered the Wildcats one of the most improved teams in the nation (they had led the Big Eight in three-point shooting and free throws, and were second in defense) and knew they would be a much different team than the one that had stumbled in Mackey earlier.

"You can't be satisfied," Keady said. "You can't be thinking you've been through something we've never been through before. That's ridiculous, because you've got yourself in a great, great situation. There's 16 teams left; everybody can coach, everybody can play.

"And get this implanted in your brain. This Kansas State team is not the same one we played in December. They changed their offense and they have a different attitude toward everything. You've got to understand that that game has to be erased. You're playing a completely different team. You cannot rely on what we did last time."

After solid practices on Tuesday and Wednesday, the team flew to Pontiac early Thursday morning. The ideal plan would have been to fly up Wednesday night after practice, but because several athletic department employees were flying with the team—the university had chartered a commercial jet this time—it became important to save a night's hotel bill.

The players checked into their hotel and ate breakfast, then began preparing for practice. Wood had arranged for them to work out at nearby Oakland Community College from 12:30 to 1:45, after which they would bus to the Silverdome for an hour-long shooting practice that was open to the public.

It had been a few weeks since Berning had been hurt, but he made up for lost time early in the workout by colliding with Mitchell and cutting open his lip. He later would require one stitch to close it. After a brisk workout that featured emphasis on the fullcourt press— they were going to run a customized version for Kansas State's sake, trapping the point guard, Henson, but nobody else—and last-second game situations it was time to go to the Silverdome.

Wood had called ahead to make arrangements, and had been told the ride would take no more than five minutes. And it probably would have, if the bus driver assigned to the team had known the way. But as he made his way along back streets and through residential neighborhoods, the assistants began exchanging nervous glances. Keady, checking his watch, was stewing, but said little.

Finally, the driver admitted he was lost and stopped at a convenience store. Wood jumped out and asked for directions. It turned out they were just three traffic lights away, but they were widely-spaced lights. After a few more agonizing minutes, the bus pulled into the Silverdome parking lot and up to the nearest gate. The players hurried off and walked through the revolving door, but it turned out they were on the wrong side of the building. They piled back on the bus and were driven to the other side, and tried again. It still wasn't the proper gate, but it was close enough. The players entered the sunken stadium from the top and walked down the aisles to the playing floor—18 minutes late.

Keady was seething, but kept it inside. There was no point adding to the tension now. Besides, it was more important for them to shoot at the dome's baskets than for him to shoot from the hip. The Silverdome is a massive structure with an inflatable roof that holds 80,000 people for football. But it is home to the Detroit Pistons of the NBA as well as the Detroit Lions of the NFL. For basketball games, the floor is moved to a corner of the stadium floor and a curtain drawn across the middle to close off the area. It's hardly intimate, but it is practical as far as satisfying the huge ticket demand for NCAA tournament games.

Another mixup delayed the team's return to the hotel. Keady stayed after practice for a press conference, so the team was supposed to leave without him. But nobody got the word. Keady wound up beating the team bus back to the hotel, after it had waited for him for 45 minutes.

Still, all the hassles didn't seem to bother the players. That evening at dinner, Tony Jones and Rea kept busy sneaking silverware and salt shakers into teammates' pockets and seeing how long it would take for them to notice. Later, before the video session at the hotel, Lewis and Mitchell performed an impromptu standup routine of Keady's mannerisms and expressions while waiting for him to arrive. The players and assistant coaches were howling when he walked in the room.

The next day was an exercise in biding time. There was an hour-long shootaround in the morning, lunch and another video session. Once more, Keady reminded the players of their mission.

"Be ready for a close game," he said. "Because in order to be a national champion, you've got to win the close ones, you've got to be a little bit lucky, and you've got to hit your free throws. You can't be uptight about it. You've got to step up there and say, 'Hey, I'm glad I got this free throw, I want it. I'm going to make this son of a bitch and we're going to walk out of here with a W and we're going to come back Sunday and kick somebody's behind and then we're going to go to Kansas City and have some fun.' That's the way you've got to think about it."

Finally, shortly before 9, after a quick dinner and more waiting, it was time to leave for the game. The bus driver from the previous day had been taken off the job. The replacement knew the way, so things were looking up already. Of the 31,309 fans in the Silverdome that night, about 20,000 were Purdue fans. It was like a mass coronation for a new national power, and a coming-out party for its supporters. Never before had more Purdue basketball fans gathered in one place for a game. But the stadium was so huge that it absorbed much of the noise, creating an almost eerie atmosphere. Rather than a blast, their cheers sounded more like a distant echo.

As Keady went over the usual pregame instructions, the players began to get restless, shifting their weight, rubbing their hands and taking an occasional deep breath. This was the moment when the tension was the greatest, because there was no outlet for it.

"This is what all young boys, from the time they're seven years old, work for, guys," he said. "How many times in your life are you going to get to play in front of 30,000 people and have a chance to go to the Final Four? Not very often. So let's take advantage of it and go out and have some fun at it and work our butts off to get to Kansas City. But we're a long way from there, guys. A long way. We've got to go out and play 40 minutes of basketball and be very smart and be intent on defense and play in a frenzy."

Keady talked awhile longer, then called for the huddle. The players stood and gathered in the middle of the room. They were like racehorses now, pawing the ground in the starting gate. They clapped their hands, slapped each other's backs, and exchanged high fives. Brugos and Scheffler hugged each other.

"Inside," Kip Jones said. "Inside game."

"Show 'em what we're about," Lewis said.

"All right, let's go now, men," Keady said. "We've been waiting for this game ever since we got back from Australia. Now let's go out and get after these guys and don't let them up!

"Together!"

"We attack!"

After warmups, another quick meeting in the locker room and pregame introductions, it was showtime.

"We're playing at home!" Weber shouted before the starters took the floor. "This is our homecourt!"

The way the game started, it was indeed as if Purdue owned the place. Kansas State started in 3-2 zone, but McCants took a pass inside on the first possession and hit a turnaround jumper. Kansas State missed twice on its first possession, McCants rebounded, and Stephens dropped a three-pointer. Kansas State turned the ball over on a traveling call, and Stephens came back and nailed another three-pointer from almost the same spot. Kansas State missed, and Mitchell hit a jumper in the lane.

The game was barely two minutes old, and Purdue led 10-0. Kansas State called timeout.

"Don't relax now!" Keady said in the huddle. "Let's get after these guys and get them out of here! Dominate the first five minutes and get them out of here!"

Purdue had a chance to move in that direction when Kansas State missed two more shots on its next possession. But Stephens tried another three-pointer, and missed.

Scott broke through for the Wildcats with a three-pointer with 17:20 left. He added another one over Lewis' outstretched hand a minute later, closing the gap to 12-8. From there, Purdue's lead was like a balloon, expanding and contracting, but never breaking. It led by four, by seven, by one, by six, by three.

Then, it put together another rally to close the half. Stephens hit his third three-pointer. Tony Jones, now guarding Richmond, drew a charging foul, and McCants hit another turnaround in the lane. Richmond missed again. Stephens shot an air ball on another three-point attempt, but it fell into Mitchell's hands. He jammed it through the basket, giving Purdue a 42-32 lead.

The lead was nine when Kip Jones rebounded a Kansas State miss moments later, setting up the last play of the half. But Stephens briefly lost control of his dribble as everyone else began their cuts, throwing the play out of sync from the beginning. With nobody open, Stephens went up for a three-pointer from the top of the key, but was guarded too closely. He quickly dumped the ball off to McCants, who turned and fired a 12-footer in the lane that bounced in and out.

Another half-ending play had broken down. Still, it had been a good start. The only real problem to attend to was Scheffler, who scored one point, grabbed one rebound and committed two fouls in nine minutes. Scheffler had been visibly tense, a throwback to his freshman season when he sometimes hyperventilated in games. His legs were shaking, and felt heavy. He later would blame himself for going overboard in mentally preparing for the game that afternoon, concentrating beyond readiness into nervousness.

"Scheffler, you need to start playing more aggressive," Keady said upon rejoining the players. "You're letting Meyer just shove the shit out of you. You start getting back in the ballgame."

"It's just a game, Steve," Wood said. "Lot of people, funny atmosphere. . . ."

"It's a basketball game!" Keady said. "Would you be uptight if we were playing in summer camp in June? Well, that's what you've got to act like. Go out and get what we've worked for. We have worked too hard to get uptight."

"You are better than any of their big people," Weber said. "I mean, there's no comparison."

"It's true," Reiter said.

Scheffler nodded.

Keady calmly went over other points. They had given up nine offensive rebounds, but only commmitted two turnovers. Lewis and Stephens had hit 6 of 10 three-pointers, but they still needed to get the ball inside. McCants was still shooting well; he had hit 4 of 7 shots.

"OK, let's go!" Keady said. The players stood up, clapping enthusiastically.

"Get a spurt on 'em," Wood shouted. "Right now!"

"We're playing to go to the Final Four, now suck it up," Keady said. "Defense will win it for you.

"Together!"

"We attack!"

But something happened at the start of the second half, something that was puzzling to players and coaches alike.

Meyer started it off by driving the baseline around Lewis and hitting a layup, making it 43-36. Mitchell hit one of two free throws to bump the lead to eight, but then came the collapse. Kansas State ran off 10 straight points, capped by consecutive three-pointers by Scott, to take a 46-44 lead just three minutes into the half. During that stretch, McCants lost the ball out of bounds, Mitchell threw the ball away, Stephens charged, Lewis missed a three-pointer and McCants missed in the lane. It was just as stunning as their 10-0 run to open the game had been.

Keady called timeout.

"We said you've got to come out to play, goddamnit!" he shouted. "Just settle down, guys, you're all right."

Tony Jones quickly tied the game with a 15-footer. A minute later Purdue regained the lead on Mitchell's rebound basket, and then again on McCants half hook in the lane. But the Wildcats gradually took control. Scott hit another three-pointer to open a two-point lead. Three minutes later, Richmond added another one to stretch the margin to three.

"Get the ball!" Keady shouted at the next timeout. "They're outfighting your ass all over the place! That's ridiculous to let those guys kick your ass on the boards. Relax, Mel; let's go, babe. Just settle down, guys, and play some basketball now. They're just outbattling you."

"Hey, it's a long way from being over!" Weber said. "We've had a little bit of a bad spell, and they've had a good spell. Our time is coming."

Not right away, however. With McCants missing consecutive jumpers, Kansas State added two more field goals to open a 61-54 lead.

Lewis' three-pointer brought Purdue within four, but then came the most ominous play of the game. With Purdue's defense rejuvenated by Lewis' basket, it stepped up the pressure. But Richmond, under pressure from Mitchell and shot clock, launched a three-pointer from slightly to the right of the top of the key, throwing it more than shooting it. It *banked* in. McCants then took a pass in the lane and turned to the basket, but collided with Henson. No call. Kansas State recovered the loose ball.

Kansas State's strategy was to shorten the game as much as possible, run the clock on every possession and therefore limit Purdue's opportunities. With the shot clock down to seven seconds, Richmond went one-on-one with Mitchell, faking a jumper from the top of the key, spinning and firing a leaning, off-balance 15-footer. It swished. The lead was nine, with 6:49 left. Twenty thousand Purdue fans gasped.

Kansas State had come from nine points down to nine ahead in a little more than 13 minutes, and now was threatening to turn the game into a rout, just as Purdue had in the first half. But now it was Purdue's turn to rally. Lewis' two free throws, McCants' blocked shot and Stephens' three-point play closed the gap to 66-62 two minutes later. Four points down, 4 1/2 minutes to go. The game, the season, had come down to a 10-4 Game.

"We're going to make our run, now!" Keady said at the television timeout that followed.

"We have all kinds of time," Stallings said. "We don't have to rush any shots."

"Hey, we've got to rebound down there!" Weber shouted. "They keep missing shots and they keep getting it back. Everybody has to rebound!"

"Everybody box out!" Mitchell screamed. "Everybody!"

"Let's go, this is it," Keady said. "We don't have anything to wait on, guys. Let's go!"

What followed, however, was a study in missed opportunities. Stephens blocked Henson's shot on the next possession, then took the outlet pass from Lewis. Mitchell was sprinting downcourt on his right, and Kip Jones on his left, but two Kansas State defenders were waiting for them. Overanxious, Stephens tried to force the play and lost control of the ball. Kansas State came back with a three-on-one break and scored on a layup from Scott, stretching the lead to six. It was a four-point turnaround.

A minute later, the lead still at four, Mitchell drew a foul underneath and was awarded two free throws to close the gap. He was shooting 72 percent for the season, and he had hit all 10 of his free throw attempts against Kansas State in December. But he missed both this time, bouncing each one off the right side of the rim. Kansas State rebounded, and called timeout.

"My fault, fellas; my bad," he said as he returned to the bench.

"Come on, Todd, get your head up, babe!" Keady shouted. "You'll still have a chance this game, believe me. We've got to get the fire back in our eyes. Let's go!"

A minute later, Stephens got them back in it with a three-pointer that trimmed Kansas State's lead to 69-67. And later when Bledsoe, a 52 percent foul shooter, missed the front end of a one-and-one, they had a chance to tie the game, or take the lead with a three-pointer.

Stephens faked a three-pointer, then passed to Lewis, who dribbled to his right and fed Mitchell on the baseline. The ball was deflected out of bounds, to Purdue.

There were 44 seconds left. The shot clock was turned off now. Purdue called a timeout. The play was set up to inbound the ball and run the offense, taking the first good shot. If they didn't score or hit a two-pointer, they would foul Bledsoe again. If they hit a three-pointer, they would drop back into man-to-man.

As it turned out, they didn't get a shot off at all. Stephens took the ball at the top of the key and moved to his right. Mitchell cut across the lane and posted up. Stephens faked to him, then passed. But Mitchell had turned to cut the other way after the fake, and the ball bounced to Bledsoe. Mitchell fouled him immediately, with 27 seconds left.

Bledsoe hit the first free throw, and missed the second. Purdue still could tie with a three-pointer. McCants screened for Stephens at the top of the key, but as Stephens dribbled off it to his left, the ball grazed his knee and slipped away. Stephens, a look of sheer terror in his eyes, lunged for it. So did Lewis, who was running up from the baseline. They were both too late. They collided as the ball bounced out of bounds and into Wood's hands. Later, Wood would recall that the thought flashed in his mind to quickly slap the ball back inbounds and hope nobody noticed.

Purdue was in a truly desperate situation, now. It had no timeouts, and trailed by three with 19 seconds left. Lewis fouled Henson on the inbounds pass. Henson, the nation's best free throw shooter at over 90 percent, hit both of his attempts, stretching the lead to five. Mitchell missed a three-pointer, but Tony Jones grabbed the long rebound and passed out to Stephens, who hit another three-pointer, his fifth of the game, from 22 feet. The lead was two.

But time was running out. Tony Jones fouled Richmond on the inbounds pass, with three seconds left. Richmond hit, then missed. Kip Jones rebounded and quickly passed to Stephens, who rushed upcourt. But his 40 footer was released just after the buzzer, and bounced off the backboard.

It was over: The game, the season, and, for three seniors, a college basketball career. They had overcome the obstacles of injury, ineligibility and uncertainty to form one of the nation's top teams, a

29-game winner that glided through the Big Ten with rare and surprising dominance. But now it was over, as if they had been awak-
ened too soon from a good dream.

The players filed into the locker room in absolute and stunned silence. They had shown confidence publicly all season. But since the
growing pains of December, they had all shared the same private gut
feeling as well: that the season would end in Kansas City, not Pontiac.

For 15 seconds, nobody said a word. Then Weber spoke up.

"You had a hell of a year, guys," he said, his voice breaking.

Keady was the last to arrive in the room. "Well, guys, we had our
chance," he said. "You played a great game tonight, really."

He paused, searching for the right words.

"We had one of those opportunities and we didn't take advantage
of it," he said. "But you had a tremendous season. I can't say anything
except I'm very proud of all of you. I hope you have a great, great future in whatever you do. Seniors, you did a great job leading us. I
couldn't be prouder of you three guys. It's one of those situations
where we just couldn't operate and execute when we needed to. They
wanted it worse than we did and they got after us. That happens.
That's not going to let you get yourself down, I know that. So get yourself up here, let's huddle up."

It would be the last time that season.

"I'm not sure what we're going to do tonight as far as going back,
but stay here close so we can tell you," Keady said. "Let's go. You had
a great season, and I'm very proud of you.

"Together."

"We attack."

Only about half the players got out the words, in a soft, barely audible mumble. Then they all sat back down, still dazed by what had
just happened.

"Man," Stephens said in his high-pitched whisper. "I just wasn't
ready for it to end."

Keady left the room and walked down the hallway to his right,
into the tile bathroom and shower area used by NFL teams. He took a
small drink of water, dropped the paper cup on the floor and sat
down on a bench. In eight years at Purdue, he had whipped the odds
and built a legitimate national power. Over those years, he had compiled the best record of any Big Ten coach. He had won three Big Ten
titles in the last five years, and had recently been named the league's

Coach of the Year for the second time. But his first thoughts after a loss always were to blame himself.

"I can't coach," he said softly. "I can't coach the big one."

Stallings, standing nearby, started to console him, started to explain the loss had been far too complicated to blame on any one individual, including the coach.

"That's bullshit, Kevin!" Keady said. "It happens every goddamn time I get in a tournament. I haven't won the national yet."

Back in the locker room, Wood sat on the floor, holding his head between his knees. He began to sob, then got up and moved into the hallway to compose himself.

The cold reality of losing in the NCAA touarment is that ten minutes after one of the biggest disappointments of your life, you have to go discuss it with the media. Two golf carts were waiting at the end of the hallway, one for Keady and one for the three seniors, to take them to the press tent at the other end of the stadium. They rode through a small pack of still-celebrating Kansas State fans, underneath the portable grandstand and around to the back of the press tent.

"My hat's off to Kansas State, they did a tremendous job competing," Keady told the reporters. "Their coaching staff did a tremendous job getting them back from a season that could have been a poor one. We had a great season, we just played a team that was better than us tonight. They played great. They're a very fine basketball team."

Sitting at the head table with him, Stephens forced a small smile. Mitchell stared ahead blankly. Lewis clasped his hands in front of his face and closed his eyes. Among the players, he was easily the most devastated. It was high school all over again.

The questioning finished, Keady walked out of the tent through a back door. A man was waiting for him with a basketball in one hand and a pen in the other, silently requesting his signature. There was no escaping the autograph hounds. But Keady ignored him, stepped back onto the golf cart, and rode back to courtside to tape his postgame radio show.

The seniors walked back to the locker room. Lewis, inconsolable, broke off from the other two and took the long route.

Keady had one more chore to perform before leaving: taping his Sunday television show in the locker room. The players, meanwhile, boarded the bus and rode back to the hotel. There was silence, except for Scheffler, Brugos and Kip Jones, who discussed the meaning of it all. At least they had a Big Ten championship to show for themselves, they figured. What about teams like Michigan and Illinois, good teams who didn't win anything beyond a lot of games. Did their players feel their seasons had been wasted?

A lot of Purdue fans obviously didn't think that about their team's season. Several hundred of them were waiting for the players at the hotel, filling the lobby and spilling into the parking lot and back hallways. They sang the school song and clapped in rhythm as they formed an aisle for the players to pass through.

The assistant coaches, who had driven separately to scout the Kansas-Vanderbilt game earlier in the evening, were waiting for them outside their rooms. "Hey, Bud, can I shake your hand," Stallings said to Lewis. Lewis reached back without looking up. "You had a great season. You had a great career," Stallings said.

Weber reached up and grabbed McCants by the shoulders. "Hey, big guy," he said. "You carried us on your shoulders these last three weeks, don't be down on yourself. You missed a few shots tonight, but that's when somebody else has to come through. You were great. We wouldn't have been here without you."

Wood stopped Brugos, his special project the last several weeks, and whispered something in his ear.

"I just feel so bad for coach, man," Brugos said. "I wanted us to win it for him."

Wood said to turn the moment into something positive, as motivation for next season.

"Oh, yeah," Brugos said. "I've already been thinking about that. It's a big motivation."

Each of the seniors, winners of 96 games over the past four seasons, approached Weber individually a few minutes later and told him they were glad they had chosen Purdue.

"I had a great four years, and I loved it here," Stephens said. "I feel so good about it."

Fifteen minutes later, Keady returned to his suite. The assistant coaches walked down to meet him. He had, they told him, just completed his best coaching job yet, even better than in the '84 season.

"The thing that's frustrating about coaching is, why can't I feel that way?" Keady wondered. "Why can't I feel like I did a good job? It feels like it's my fault we lost. Like it's my fault we didn't say the right things to get them to do the right things."

"You know why we win?" Wood said. "Because you always look at yourself first."

"Coach, this whole tournament thing can happen when you least expect it," Reiter said. "In two years, next year, you can come in and win three games, four games, who knows? It happens."

There was a mountain of what-ifs to discuss. What could they have said differently at halftime to prevent the letdown at the start of the second half? What could they have done differently defensively? What if Mitchell hadn't missed so much practice time the second semester because of his class conflict? The chart kept by the student managers showed he had shot 700 fewer free throws in practice than most of his teammates. Would that have made a difference in the game? Scheffler, so nervous the first half, had been used just one minute in the second, which threw off the normal substitution pattern. Maybe that had been a mistake.

Ultimately, they had no answers. Kansas State had defended them the best way possible, with a triangle-and-two. And it had hit all the crucial shots it needed, including 8 of 10 three-pointers. They had played well, really, just not quite well enough.

"Coach, you said all along if you lose you lose, and you just have to tell them to kiss your ass. That's how you have to do it," Weber said.

"We don't have to answer to anybody," Stallings added. "We played hard all year and we played good, and. . . ."

"Mitch Richmond hits a three-pointer off the board, what are you supposed to do?" Weber broke in. "They gave us chances, we just didn't have anybody come through."

"Somebody's going to say we choked, but you don't win 29 games choking," Wood said. "It happens. We had a great year."

"There's no doubt we'll all be sick when we wake up in the morning, it's just a feeling you have when you hate losing," Keady said. "But what gets me is, you've got to rise above it. And we didn't rise above it. What causes you to do that? I've never found an equation. Just once, I'd like to finish the season feeling good about myself."

"You should!" the assistants said in unison.

"I can't help it if I feel that way!" Keady said. "I've got the wrong values about coaching, I guess."

Keady grabbed his coat, called Pat and started to leave to eat dinner. "Let's go, honey," he said. He turned back to the coaches. "The players need anything?"

They didn't.

"Well, we did the best we could," Stallings said. "And we'll play again next year."

The players dealt with the disappointment in different ways. Scheffler laid across his bed, naked, and stared at some B movie from the 1960s, lost in his thoughts. His season had ended in frustration, but he had shown remarkable improvement. He had hit 70 percent of his field goals, a school record. He had earned the respect of his teammates. And he had two years still to go.

Lewis, who had managed 19 points against a defense designed to key on him, was met by his mother in the hallway outside his room. She told him to keep his head up, that plenty of good things still were awaiting him. It was 2:30 a.m. before he peeled off his uniform, for the last time. Then he sat up, alone, watching "The Untouchables" on television. At 5 a.m., he finally climbed in bed.

Kip Jones, Stephens and Mitchell got hold of a few beers and stayed up most of the night talking and laughing quietly with some of the cheerleaders, trying to forget. At 5 a.m., just for a joke, Stephens borrowed one of the female cheerleaders' uniforms and posed for a picture.

After a few hours' sleep, however, the emotional cloud cover was starting to lift for everyone. While the luggage was loaded onto the bus that would take them to the airport, the team members and the rest of the traveling party stood outside and mingled. Keady was cheerful, visiting with Scheffler's parents and others. Stephens and Mitchell joked with McCants about the premier role he would have with the team next season. Stephens held up an imaginary microphone to his mouth and played the part of public address announcer.

"Ladies and gentlemen, starting at senior, from Chicago, Illinois, Melvin McCants!" he announced.

"Big Mel's going to have four guys guarding him next year," he added, turning to Mitchell.

"Teams will be bringing managers off the bench to guard him," Mitchell said, and they all burst out laughing.

Three hours later they were back in West Lafayette, where still another reception awaited them. About 200 fans, braving cold, windy weather, began cheering as the plane touched down and continued as the players passed through them on the way to their cars. There were more autographs, more thank yous, and some goodbyes. The season was over.

20

•

Aftermath

If anyone had slept through the weekend and then shown up at Mackey on Monday, they would have assumed the team was still alive in the tournament. It was business as usual, for players and coaches alike.

Sunday, a few of the players had gone to the campus recreation center and played in some pickup games. They had allowed themselves only a one-day break, proof of Keady's belief that the team wasn't burned out. Monday afternoon, Lewis and Mitchell put on their practice gear and headed for the weight room. They ran into Arnold, who had continued to work out on his own to stay in shape for his amateur competition.

Arnold approached Mitchell and shrugged. The two exchanged a knowing glance. Who could say, perhaps Arnold's presence would have been worth three points in Pontiac.

"I'm sorry, man," Arnold said.

"That's all right," Mitchell said. "Don't worry about it."

Then Stephens walked in, carrying a new toy: an NBA basketball, which is slightly different than the collegiate version.

"Hey, check out the new rock!" Mitchell said, laughing.

For the seniors, a new era had dawned. The NBA would be conducting a camp for prospective draftees in Portsmouth, Virginia beginning April 7, and all three were going. It amounted to an audition for the pro scouts, and it would be a crucial factor in determining their draft position. After that, they would play in a series of 14 barnstorming games across the state with other Big Ten players, for which they would be paid $500 a game. They were told it would have been $700 if Purdue had reached the Final Four, and $900 if it had won the national title. Already, basketball had shifted from a game to a business opportunity.

Lewis and Mitchell in particular would cash in. A local booster was printing, for free, a poster from a picture *Sports Illustrated* had taken, but never used. They would sell it at the barnstorming games for five dollars each, pure profit. And they were agreeing to appear at as many speaking engagements, autograph sessions and camp appearances as they could handle, for fees ranging as high as $500. They would receive the money in deferred payments, however, so they wouldn't lose their scholarships.

Keady, meanwhile, had rebounded sharply from the post-game self-doubt. He shook off the loss quickly, much more easily, in fact, than the one to Florida the previous season. He hadn't been able to bring himself to watch the video of the Florida game until June, after the team returned from its trip abroad. This time, he watched the video replay after returning home Saturday. He even watched Kansas beat Kansas State on television Sunday afternoon for the Final Four berth he had hoped to fill with his team, and didn't agonize too much over Kansas State's more human-like performance in that game.

Already, his thoughts were on the upcoming season—a season without Lewis, Mitchell and Stephens, but with six new, promising players in Oliver and the five recruits.

The recruits also showed promise. Austin wound up leading the state in scoring with a 33.3 average, was voted Indiana's Mr. Basketball as Keady had predicted and qualified academically. Stewart led his team to the state championship of the private school division in Wisconsin, and was also named Mr. Basketball. Clyburn led his team to the semifinals of Michigan's state tournament, and was voted first team all-state. Riley was voted Player of the Year in his conference, was first-team all-state, and was the valedictorian of his class. White made some JUCO all-American teams, and his team won California's state tournament.

From top to bottom, it was probably Keady's best recruiting class. He now coached a program with both a past and a future to brag about.

"If we keep going, we'll have a team someday that goes further than what you think it will," Keady told the assistant coaches when they met in his office Monday. "Just keep getting players. Next year we won't be considered a factor anyway."

"And yet if somebody comes through that we don't expect to come through, like happens every year...if that can be the right person, we can be pretty good next year," Stallings said.

"Oh, yeah. I have faith we'll be pretty good, because we're going to play hard," Keady said. "We're going to have a helluva time scoring, but I think we're going to have a pretty good defensive team by tournament time."

There were many questions still to be answered about the next Purdue team. Would Scheffler, who was more comfortable playing off the bench, but had played so well late in the season, have to start? Could Kip Jones shoot well enough to play small forward? If not, who would fill that spot? Berning? Oliver? Tony Jones seemed a lock at point guard, but who would start with him in the backcourt? Reid? A freshman?

"It's weird going into a year when you don't know what to expect," Stallings said.

"It's going to be fun though, coach," Keady said, smiling. "Boy, October 15th's going to be a booger."

Keady met with the players for the final time as a group later that afternoon. There were 41 more balls to sign, but the primary purpose was to vote on two awards, Most Valuable Player and Mr. Hustle. Stephens and Lewis wound up sharing MVP honors. And Barrett, the freshman who had endured such a rude introduction to college basketball back the first two days of practice in October, but had gone on to set a standard for practice enthusiasm despite getting just 43 minutes of playing time all season, won the hustle award. He voted for Tony Jones, but he received eight of his teammates' 12 votes to win by a landslide. Stephens later recalled being so enthusiastic about his choice that he wrote Barrett's name in bold letters on his ballot.

Keady congratulated the players once again for their success, and told them it had been the most enjoyable season of his career. Then he wrote three words on the board: Live, Listen and Learn.

"Man, we lived through another one," he said. "We didn't win it all, but we got close; scared the hell out of some people. And we got a lot of people that think we got a great program now, and in my eight years here it's never been that way before. We won seven out of eight national television games, so a lot of people have to be knowing you're a national power now.

"You listened—we've got some underclassmen that need to listen better—and you learned. That's what we're here for, guys, this is a learning institution. But we've gone full cycle. Next year we're going back to this."

He wrote three more words on the board: Dedication, Discipline and Defense. They had been the theme for Keady's first season, eight years earlier. Now, he was ready to start anew. He told each of the returning scholarship players to come back in June, either for summer school or to work, so that they could lift weights and scrimmage together. He had never insisted on that before, but he was now. It was a time to bear down even more, not relax.

"Guys, you did a tremendous job this year, but there's still an empty feeling there," he said. "That's OK. That's what drives people. I may be 65 years old before I win the national championship, but I'm going to do it someday. I just wanted it to be this team, because you're special to me. But that's not the way it went. But we had a great season, and they can't take that away from us.

"You seniors, we want to wish you the best. You guys are like three sons to me. Twenty years from now, if I need help or you need help, we'll still feel like we can help each other. John Brugos, you made a great amount of progress. Marvin Rea, you were a great guy to be around. Eric Ewer and Dave Barrett, I'm just as proud of you as the seniors, even though I love them like sons. All of you were important to me."

Keady then addressed the rumor that had been circulating about the opening at Texas since the day before the Memphis State game. It had been stirring up a stiffer breeze the past few days, and some of the underclassmen had expressed private concerns about losing their coach.

"I'm not going to Texas," Keady told them. "If they say we'll give you half a million dollar home and a million dollar contract and a million dollars when you retire, then I'd be nuts not to go there. But you know they're not going to do that in Texas. You can quit worrying about that. I'm going to be back to get after your ass next year."

The players laughed. But the rumor wasn't a laughing matter for Keady when he flew to Kansas City for the finals later in the week.

There, the rumor grew from a brushfire to a five-alarm blaze, ultimately producing enough heat to drive Keady and his wife back to their hotel room. On Thursday, a story hit the newswires that Keady was the top choice for the opening. On Friday, word leaked out that he had met with Texas' athletic director DeLoss Dodds, a college football teammate from Kansas State. The Cable News Network went so far as to report that afternoon that two coaches would take new jobs that day, North Carolina State's Jim Valvano to UCLA and Gene Keady to Texas; the network even began speculating on whom Keady's successor might be.

Keady's phone had been ringing all week, but by Saturday—the day of the Final Four semifinal games—the media interest was raging out of control. One wire service story had quoted an anonymous coach in Kansas City as saying, "If they make him the right offer, he's gone."

Fueled by all the speculation and rumors, a small army of reporters was waiting for Keady at the arena, ready to pounce. Bill Benner, a sportswriter with the Indianapolis Star, called Keady from the arena and told him of the reception committee, offering to take a statement to them. Keady and his wife decided to watch the first game on television and slip into the second one to avoid the crunch.

Back in West Lafayette, the phones in Keady's office were jangling a sour melody for Lorraine, who had to answer a flurry of inquiries about the rumors. Some were from alumni threatening to cut off their financial support if Keady left. The local fans were growing increasingly nervous, having read the increasingly ominous headlines in the Lafayette paper: "Purdue intends to keep Keady as coach." "Keady hasn't ruled out Texas." "Report: Texas talks to Keady."

Weber, in Kansas City with the rest of the assistant coaches, woke up one morning to find a pile of message slips had been shoved under his door, all of them regarding the rumor. He, too, called Lorraine to ask what was going on.

For a frightening moment later that day, Weber thought he had found out. Reiter called him in his hotel room from the swimming pool with a desperate tone in his voice. "Bruce, you've got to get down here!" he said.

Weber hurried down to find all the assistants sitting by the pool, with dread etched on their faces.

"Bruce, you better sit down," Stallings said.

"Why?" Weber asked.

"How do you look in burnt orange?" Stallings asked, referring to Texas' school color.

"What?" Weber said.

Reiter looked at him and announced with dramatic finality: "It's done."

Weber sat down, in disbelief.

"I can't believe it!" he said.

The assistants let him consider the consequences in silence: Moving his family to Austin. Starting over with a new program. And recruiting. God, how could he establish a recruiting base in the heart of football country? He got up to return to his room, to ponder his fate alone.

Finally, Reiter spoke up.

"Bruce, what day is this?" he asked.

"Friday," Weber answered.

Then a man sitting at the next table, who had been let in on the prank, turned to his young daughter.

"Honey, what day is this?" he asked.

"It's April Fool's Day!" the girl shouted.

Everyone burst out laughing—including, after a split second of realization, Weber.

Keady had talked with Dodds, but they spent more time reminiscing about their college days than discussing the opening. Keady had publicly left his options open, saying he would have to listen to any offers, but knew, as he had told the players, that Texas was unlikely to do much better than his financial package at Purdue, which included an annual base salary of $90,750 and added income which extended the bottom line to more than $200,000.

Keady also knew, all along, that another university would announce an opening—one he was more intrigued by—in the days ahead. New Mexico had decided to fire Gary Colson, who had directed 20-win seasons the previous two seasons. Keady had nearly accepted a football scholarship from New Mexico out of junior college, and he had passed through Albuquerque several times on family vacations as a kid. He liked the city, the climate, and the returning talent. And, Thrash lived there. Keady had tried to woo Thrash to Purdue as an assistant coach when openings had arisen over the years. This might be a chance for them to hook up.

Keady's name became linked with that opening the first week of May, shortly before he left for a vacation in Las Vegas. And although Keady continued to give the same noncommittal responses to reporters' questions, this rumor had more substance. He talked with New Mexico's athletic director, John Koenig. There was mention of a house to go along with a solid financial package. Keady almost visited the campus, but finally backed out.

He had too many concerns. He didn't think the offer had been presented professionally. He figured the chances for success were better at Purdue. He didn't want to back out on his players and recruits. And, most of all, he liked the job he had just fine.

Another round of rumors had been laid to rest. For awhile, at least.

By July, the normal cycle of personal victories and disappointments had resumed, offering a great deal of new hope and a few new problems.

Mitchell and Lewis both sacrificed much of their studies to take advantage of their basketball/business opportunities, but still received their degrees in May. Mitchell went on the become a second-round draft choice of the NBA's Denver Nuggets. Lewis was passed over in the draft, but accepted an offer to try out for the San Antonio Spurs. His new coach would be Larry Brown, who had tried to sign him at Kansas four years earlier.

Stephens enrolled in summer school to begin work on the final six hours of credit he needed to graduate. He was drafted the highest of the three, by the Philadelphia 76ers in the second round.

Arnold, who had played well in amateur competition, talked with Keady about returning to the team the following season. He had flunked six of his seven courses during the second semester because of all the class time he missed while traveling to tournaments, and he would still need to pick up 15 more credits in the summer to be eligible in the fall. After discussing it with Keady, he decided to try his luck with professional basketball.

The underclassmen on scholarship all returned to campus the first week of June to enroll in summer school or work, while continuing to lift weights and scrimmage. McCants and Kip Jones were the seniors now, and would have to adjust to roles of leadership. Tony Jones slid into the starting point guard's position, and wore it like an old shoe. He, too, would have to take command. Brugos returned, still free-spirited, but in shape and more devoted than ever. Berning and Reid, who would face likely turning points in their careers, with the opportunity for considerable playing time ahead of them but threats from newcomers on their heels, also were working hard. And so, of course, was Scheffler, who returned somewhat grudgingly. He had hoped to spend his summer in Michigan, taking bicycle trips, walking in the woods and visiting with friends.

Each of the incoming recruits joined them for varying lengths of time, and showed vast potential. Austin, however, added to the controversy already surrounding him and punctured the optimism that had been building around him, on July 2, when he was arrested for drunken driving. He was later sentenced to a two-day jail sentence, and his status for the team was uncertain as August approached.

Rea, the walk-on who had had a striking impact on the fans and team for someone who played just 18 minutes the entire season, left for Milwaukee for a summer management internship. But Keady awarded him with the last scholarship for the following season.

Ewer, a 12-minute veteran of college basketball who had missed much of his potential playing time with a severe leg bruise late in the season, was offered the chance to return as a walk-on if an opening was available. Keady also asked if he would like to come back as a graduate assistant coach in three years. As of the end of the semester he was planning to call it quits and become a fulltime student. He left with no regrets and one appropriate souvenir of his season: a pus-stained piece of the gauze used to wrap the leg injury that kept him out for nearly a month.

Barrett, meanwhile, faced an impending decision. Before long, he probably would have to choose between basketball and baseball. He had worked his way into the starting lineup on Purdue's baseball team by the end of the season, and was showing great potential. That season, too, had gotten off to a rocky start, however. In one of his first practices, he fouled off a pitch and the ball hit his coach, Dave Alexander, in the mouth.

But at least it was someone else's mouth this time. Hope sprang eternal.